Contents

List of Figures

vii

List of Tables

List of Contributors

David Backwith
Anglia Polytechnic University

Peter Beresford
Loughborough University

Jonathan Bradshaw
Social Policy Research Unit

Glen Bramley
Edinburgh College of Art/Heriot-Watt University

Roger Burrows
University of York

Daniel Dorling
University of Bristol

Martin Evans
London School of Economics

David Gordon
University of Bristol

David Green
Loughborough University

Ian Gregory
Queen Mary & Westfield College

Jennifer Harris
University of Central Lancashire

Linda Harvey
Anglia Polytechnic University

Ruth Lister
Loughborough University

Sue Middleton
Loughborough University

Michael Noble
University of Oxford

Lou Opit
University of Kent at Canterbury

Jan Pahl
University of Kent at Canterbury

Ian Paylor
University of Central Lancashire

David Rhodes
University of York

Roy Sainsbury
Social Policy Research Unit

George Smith
University of Oxford

Humphrey Southall
Queen Mary & Westfield College

Liz Tadd
Department of Social Security

Peter Townsend
University of Bristol

John Washington
University of Central Lancashire

Kirsty Woodward
Loughborough University

Preface

SIR PETER BARCLAY, CHAIRMAN
JOSEPH ROWNTREE FOUNDATION

As chairman of Joseph Rowntree Foundation, I welcome the publication of these volumes containing the proceedings of the conference sponsored by the Foundation.

The Foundation was delighted to support this event for a number of reasons:

- First and foremost, it marks the Centenary of Seebohm Rowntree's first study of poverty in York. It is indisputable that that survey constituted a large milestone in social research in this country.

  It was Beatrice Webb who called it a *'sort of Modern Doomsday Book'* (1980). Seebohm says in his report that *'it was a contribution to the knowledge of facts in relation to poverty that any enquiry was undertaken'* (1903) and it was its factual, evidential base which gave it such impact and authority - with material gathered through unemotional objective, detailed and conscientious research. In doing so, he was making a major reference in establishing the British empirical social research tradition.

- Secondly, the Foundation, being always primarily concerned with translating research into social change, recognises and celebrates the extraordinary social policy influence which was exerted by the survey on the thinking of Liberal party policy makers in the early years of this century, which led to reform, from which, eventually, emerged the Welfare State as we knew it in the years following the last War.

  His work and his ideas also had a great influence on his father Joseph and in 1904 were partly responsible for Joseph's decision to establish his three trusts.

  If you read about the debates which followed the publication of the survey, in Asa Briggs' (1961) fascinating and comprehensive study of

Seebohm's life, they have an uncomfortably modern ring. The Charity Organisation Society had, throughout the previous century, maintained that poverty was caused by the moral turpitude of the poor (shades of *'benefit dependency?'*) - in answer to which Seebohm was able to show that poverty was a real phenomenon with clear structural causes. He called for a minimum wage and warned his opponents, as Asa Briggs recounts, *'not to pit their uninformed feelings about poverty against his facts'*. If they saw people who by his standards were in primary poverty appearing to live well (as we see sometimes in TV documentaries today), let them not, said Seebohm confuse *'things that are seen with consequences of poverty which are not seen'* - (in our time, isolation, bad health, bad living and social exclusion in general).

Finally, the Foundation welcomes this publication because it provides a unique opportunity to review the theory method and policy relevance of poverty research. As a consequence, I hope that after 20 years in which such research has been largely ignored - in fact, in recent years only the brave even dared to mention the word *'poverty'* at all - I hope we can bring high quality research in this area back into the centre of both social research effort and informed policy debate and that we shall look back on these conference proceedings as a significant turning point.

References

Briggs, A.S. (1961), *Social Thought and Social Action: A Study of the Work of Seebohm Rowntree, 1871-1954*, Longmans.

Cole, M. (ed.) (1956), *Beatrice Webb's Diaries 1924-1932*, Longmans, London.

Rowntree, B.S. (1901), *Poverty: A Study of Town Life*, Macmillan, London.

Acknowledgements

The editors would like to acknowledge the generous financial support provided by the Joseph Rowntree Foundation to the conference to mark the centenary of Seebohm Rowntree's *Poverty: A Study of Town Life* held at the University of York in March 1998.

We would like to offer heartfelt thanks to all the contributors to this volume, not only for their excellent papers but also for their patience during the seemingly inevitable delays that accompany the preparation of an edited book.

The help and guidance of our colleagues at Ashgate Publishing has been invaluable. Our thanks to them.

And, finally, our support team at the University of York have carried out their contributions to the production of the book with their usual enthusiasm and efficiency without which we would be lost. Thank you Sally Pulleyn, Lucy Bradshaw and Nico Bradshaw.

Jonathan Bradshaw
Roy Sainsbury

University of York, March 2000

1 Editors' Introduction

JONATHAN BRADSHAW and ROY SAINSBURY

The conference to mark the centenary of Seebohm Rowntree's first study of poverty in York has resulted in three volumes of proceedings. The first volume *Getting the measure of poverty: the early legacy of Seebohm Rowntree* (Bradshaw and Sainsbury, 2000) is largely devoted to papers covering the pre Second World War era. This volume *Researching Poverty* and the third volume *Experiencing Poverty* (Bradshaw and Sainsbury, 2000) represent a picture of the state of poverty research in the late 1990s, after a period of 20 years when Britain had a government not particularly concerned with poverty and not much interested in funding research into it.

It is clear from the papers in these volumes that poverty research is nevertheless alive and well. Thanks to the individual commitment of scholars, the generosity of trusts, and particularly the Joseph Rowntree Foundation who funded many of the projects on which the chapters in these volumes are based, poverty studies have continued to flourish with some significant advances both in concepts and method. In a session at the end of the conference we invited a panel to apply their minds to thinking about the future of poverty research but we think that the papers in these volumes represent an effective review of the present of poverty research.

It is absolutely appropriate that this volume should open with a paper by **Peter Townsend**. If Seebohm Rowntree could be described as the father of poverty research in the pre war era. Townsend is by far the dominant figure in the post war era. It was his work mainly which led to a move away from pre-war notions of poverty as lack of physical necessities or minimum subsistence towards an understanding of poverty as relative deprivation (Townsend, 1962). It was his pioneering study with Brian Abel Smith *The Poor and the Poorest* which was more or less responsible for the 'rediscovery of poverty' (Abel Smith and Townsend, 1965). He was the first to operationalise the concept of relative poverty in empirical research using deprivation indicators in his mammoth *Poverty in the United Kingdom* (Townsend, 1979). He has consistently sought to link poverty in industrialised nations with the poverty of the Third World (for example see his essay in the *Concept of Poverty*

1

(Townsend, 1970) and his collection of essays *The International Analysis of Poverty* (Townsend, 1993). He has also been the leading figure in debates about health inequalities (Townsend, Davidson and Whitehead, 1982) and in research on the subject (Townsend, Phillimore and Beattie, 1988). All this is in addition to his two great classic studies *The Family Life of Old People* (Townsend, 1957) and *The Last Refuge* (Townsend, 1962). Some of this work he refers to in his essay in this volume on post war poverty research in which he reflects on the interconnected themes of concepts; operational definitions; explanation and policies. In particular he stresses the scientists' obligation to have regard to policy something he has always done - in the Fabian Society, the Labour Party, the Child Poverty Action Group and the Disability Alliance. In his chapter he reasserts that poverty can be scientifically determined as a line or threshold and also argues for the internationalisation of poverty research, not least because the causes of poverty are to be found outside national boundaries in the policies of international agencies and trans-national corporations. He ends with a challenging comment '... the body of work on poverty towards the end of the 20th century lacks scientific focus. This is because the subject is too strongly appropriated by political and economic, not to say global ideology.'

In the next chapter **David Gordon** takes up Townsend's argument by showing that there can be objective scientific measures of poverty and in doing so explores the notions of 'Absolute' and 'Overall' poverty and some other ways that poverty and social exclusion can be operationalised. **Sue Middleton** outlines how it is possible to bring together consensual measures of poverty with budget standards techniques to establish agreed poverty lines by using carefully selected focus groups to discuss, negotiate and agree minimum essential needs.

One of the most encouraging modern developments in poverty research has been in the use of administrative data - especially data on benefit receipt to analyse the spatial distribution of poverty at the University of Oxford. **Smith and Noble's** chapter presents some of this recent work based on housing benefit records and demonstrates some of the advantages and disadvantages of administrative data and how it can be used to answer important questions. Another welcome new source of data for poverty researchers and one as yet under exploited is the Family Resources Survey which has a much larger sample than the Family Expenditure Survey which has been used most commonly to analyse income poverty since the 1950s. **Liz Tadd** who is responsible for the Family Resources Survey at DSS shows in her chapter how the survey can be used to explore incomes by ethnicity, gender, age and region.

There follow four chapters devoted to the spatial analysis of poverty - but of a very different kinds. **Ian Gregory, Humphrey Southall and Daniel Dorling** explore the distribution of poverty at four periods over the century to explore the north-south divide, urban rural differences, inter-urban patterns and whether relative poverty has become less extreme. **Glen Bramley and Martin Evans** report some results of their major study for DETR on the distribution of public expenditure and highlight in particular how the distributional pattern relates to the relative poverty or affluence of neighbourhoods. **Roger Burrows and David Rhodes** draw on an analysis of the Survey of English Housing to establish the sources of variation in residents perception of the areas in which they live. By applying this to 1991 census data they develop a spatial patterning of households in England who are dissatisfied with the area in which they live and then relate this to indices of area disadvantage. **Linda Harvey and David Backwith's** chapter is a detailed analysis of Haverhill where a young population suffers high levels of unemployment and ill-health, poverty, family breakdown and high mortality due to female suicide - all due to the post-war relocation of families there from London.

Jan Pahl and Lou Opit, who pioneered the study of the distribution of money within the household, turns her attention to the impact of the electronic economy (credit cards, debit cards, telephone and computer banking) on the intra household distribution and on the financial exclusion of unemployed people and older people.

John Washington, Ian Paylor and Jennifer Harris examine the shift from the use of the word poverty to the use of social exclusion in the context of the European Union's three poverty programmes and the implications of this for social work practice in Europe.

Finally, **Ruth Lister and Peter Beresford** draw on a study in which they spoke to groups of people with extensive experience of poverty to argue that there needs to be more emphasise in poverty research in what people who are poor think about poverty and what they think should be done about it.

References

Abel Smith, B. and Townsend, P. (1965), *The Poor and the Poorest*, Bell, London.
Bradshaw, J. and Sainsbury, R. (2000), *Getting the Measure of Poverty: The Early Legacy of Seebohm Rowntree*, Ashgate, Aldershot.
Bradshaw, J. and Sainsbury, R. (2000), *Experiencing Poverty*, Ashgate, Aldershot.
Townsend, P. (1962), *The Last Refuge*, Routledge and Kegan Paul, London.

Townsend, P. (1957), *The Family Life of Old People*, Routledge and Kegan Paul, London.

Townsend, P. (1962), 'The Meaning of Poverty', *BJ Sociology*, September.

Townsend, P. (1979), *Poverty in the United Kingdom*, Penguin Books and Allen Lane, London.

Townsend, P. (ed) (1970), *The Concept of Poverty*, Heinemann, London.

Townsend, P. (1993), *The International Analysis of Poverty*, Harvester Wheatsheaf, Hemel Hemstead.

Townsend, P., Davidson, N. and Whitehead (eds) (1993), *Inequalities in Health: The Black Report and the Health Divide*, Penguin Books.

Townsend, P., Phillimore, P. and Beattie, A. (1988), *Health and Deprivation: Inequality and the North*, Croom Helm, London.

2 Post-1945 Poverty Research and Things to Come

PETER TOWNSEND

Britain has a long tradition of concerned investigation of poverty. There have been low points and high points in that history - in scientific accomplishment, government acknowledgement of the problem and action to increase or reduce it. Each of these is a huge, inviting and properly controversial, theme.

The subject drew me like a magnet. I was a child in the depression years of the 1930s. I was the only child in a lone parent family. My grandmother spoke of dead babies having to be placed in makeshift wooden coffins by poor families in the back streets of Middlesbrough, where we lived in my early years. My mother was a soprano whose fees depended on the unpredictable invitations from theatrical agents for single evening shows, interspersed with more regular work in summer concert parties on seaside piers. When I was four we moved from Yorkshire to Pimlico in London and from one cheap room or flat to the next. My version of rags to riches as a boy was from eating tripe and onions warmed up for a second and third day when I came back at lunch-time from school in London, to revelling in Italian ice-cream several times each August day under the Central pier at Blackpool. For three months each year, when my mother sang in concert-parties on seaside piers, I was taken from school and spent my days on the sands with my grandmother. Another, deeply imprinted, pair of contrasting images are of cricket on a pitch across a city street, with wickets chalked on the house walls, and the glorious boundless expanse of cricket on the Blackpool sands. I did not register how often my grandmother sought to protect me from the worst effects of those switchback living standards.

History is in part personal history. The two are inseparable - however tiny the individual is in the shape of things. Experience can lead to research, but that research then becomes experience. The interchangeability of the two is highly charged and can become influential. The connectedness took me a long time to understand. One familiar current example is post-modernism, in which the idea is embedded. History works with the present and dismembers the certainty of contemporary fashions of thought. At the same time the potentialities of

5

designing the future become as exhilaratingly unhindered as they become constrained.

A second example of this connectedness for me is the Black Report on Inequalities in Health (Black, 1980; Townsend, Whitehead and Davidson, 1992; and see also a number of studies bearing out the original analysis during the 1990s, including Benzeval, Judge and Solomon, 1992; McCarron, Davey-Smith and Wormersley, 1994; Phillimore, Beattie and Townsend, 1994; Botting, 1995; Harding, 1995 and Davey-Smith and Brunner, 1997). In the late 1970s I had the luck to be involved in its preparation. I found myself drawing on the unconscious as well as conscious lessons of previous research and personal life. The structure of the Black Report came to be seen as critical. In presenting the results of a review of inequalities in health four key themes were linked but had to be distinguished - and so they were in successive chapters of the report: the construction and reconstruction of: 1) concepts; 2) operational definitions, including measurement, 3) explanation, and 4) policies.

Science and Policy

These four are of equal importance. Advances in one depend on advances in the others. I do not believe it is possible to deal with one of these in a publication without either discussing the others or at least anticipating in style and content what are the implications for the others in what is written. Any one of the four can be the starting point. None of the four can be regarded as analytically distinct from the others. However hard some people try not to put into words the implications for the others they are there - in the language and conventions chosen, the theories which may be unspoken, and in the ambiguities left unresolved in the presentation of results. If this idea is fully accepted then research papers will become different vehicles from the conventional models of the current era. Perhaps most significantly, policies which involve planning, programming, costing and action cannot be relegated to the fourth division of research.

Scientists too often accept a false dichotomy between what is properly scientific and what political. In particular, policies get confused with what is political. Science is thereby restricted in scope. Self-designated realists among both scientists and politicians behave as if the division of labour agreed between them is as immutable as it is convenient. Consciously, but more often unconsciously, scientists accept all or a very large part of what is ordained by those exercising power. In the long run people's professional outlook and practice is conditioned by the structural context within which they have learned their trade. In the short run they are sensitive to what is expected of them and what practices are most approved and rewarded.

The assumption is that science consists of concepts, measurement and explanation - or theory - but not policy analysis or policy construction. The role of policy is the ugly duckling of the four and is separated from the analysis. The results of work on the first three elements, it is supposed, have to be prepared and presented to a generalised body of 'policy makers', inviting action. The 'purity' of science is achieved, it is supposed, by disentangling and jettisoning the fourth element. Policy is not part of pure but only of applied science.

There are fundamental objections to this characterisation. At the most preliminary level we can find political constraints and prohibitions to do with concepts as well as measurement and explanatory analysis. It is less than ten years since a Secretary of State argued that 'poverty' was an irrelevant **concept** for 20th century British society (Moore, 1989). The absurdity of **measuring** unemployment in terms of claimants - when the category of claimant is subject to the edicts of the state - is only now being counterbalanced officially by data produced from the Labour Force Survey - but that survey seriously underestimates the problem (Thomas, 1998; Levitas, 1996, and ONS, 1998). And the burden of **cause** is still misrepresented as primarily individual rather than as primarily structural or collective. The technical aspects of conceptualisation, measurement and cause are not immune from political influence.

Science is 'contaminated' in different ways. There are statutory procedures and organisational matters decided by, say, governments and transnational corporations that shape professional practice and objectives. There are research programmes depending on grants serving the pre-dispositions and expectations of those making the grants rather than the independent views of the scientists themselves. These are examples of what properly can be described as 'political' influence. Science is externally conditioned and even manipulated to produce results that are acceptable to governments. This applies especially to statistical artefacts (Levitas and Guy, 1996; Dorling and Simpson, 1998). In turn the results come to be treated as 'realistic' by governments in what they imply for change and, for example, public spending. Such pressures are not necessarily reprehensible or avoidable. But they have to be understood so that they can be countered or balanced by more independent evidence. Thus, government departments can be pressed to issue their data in more rounded, or revealing, forms. Sharp attention can be called to gaps and inconsistencies in such reports as they are issued (for illustrations from answers to parliamentary questions and statistical data from other sources see Corston, 1994; Nissel 1995, Levitas and Guy 1996, and a series of papers on the Households Below Average Income Surveys from the Bristol Statistical Monitoring Unit, for example Townsend and Gordon, 1992).

The problem of adopting a scientific approach to the problem of poverty is therefore one of generally establishing an independent as well as universalistic (or cross-national) approach in one's work, but also specifically of moving 'policy' into the very heart of the analysis. The exploration of policy is not an exploration of effect, or only what, alternatively, *might* be done in the future. It is also an exploration of policy as cause. Policies shape events - and are not just shaped by them. Inequalities in health, social exclusion and poverty are clearly matters of such immense importance that they demand interrelated efforts to disentangle the three great themes of conceptualisation, measurement and cause. But any success in handling these three is ultimately dependent also in treating the fourth interrelated theme of 'policy' as of equivalent importance. It is policies - in the shape of strategies, programmes of action and the unintended and intended effects of the activities and ideologies of major institutions of government, church and business which have been predominant in causing them in the first place. This message will be disconcerting to some and objectionable to others, but will have to be learned.

Priority Concern with Poverty

In Britain there has been exceptional interest in poverty as a concept and as a problem throughout the history of its rise as an advanced industrial country. This could be illustrated from the worlds of politics, professional history, the church and the media, and not just the social sciences. There have been the conflicts of **class**, typified by the prominence in the Parliamentary debates of the 18th and 19th centuries about the Poor Law and the workhouse, the struggle for working class rights, and the Tolpuddle Martyrs, and in the 1990s of the poll tax. There has been the journalism of Henry Mayhew, George Orwell, James Cameron, John Pilger, ITV's World in Action or Channel 4's Dispatches. There are the images of Picture Post, Low and Steve Bell.

The pioneer scientific investigators of the early 19th century were provoked by the exploitation of working people and the raw desperation of their conditions of life induced by the early stages of the industrial revolution. Whether precipitated by the novelty of the industrial revolution or in response to its harsher effects there were statisticians and public health exponents who established high standards of routine enquiry. These contributed to the dawn of the welfare state in the late 19th century. They contributed to the philanthropic concern of those like Charles Booth and Seebohm Rowntree in the last years of the century. There were principled efforts to establish the facts. There were successive surveys of poverty in the UK in the years prior to 1939 - and there is no doubt that these deeply influenced the design of social security in the war years.

From a thousand different perspectives the idea of poverty, and indeed the fact of poverty, took root in national consciousness. Repeatedly since then the idea and the fact have been refreshed from the deep well of learning, topped up by a continuing flow of new information and commentary. It is an ever-present concern, yes, a national guilt, and from some points of view a thoroughly undesirable and even undeserved member of the British family of ideas. There are folk-memories which are disparaged or dismissed. But there are observations too from 1998 - of hunger, homelessness and hopelessness - which are not so easily dismissed.

What happened in the post-war years was at first very uneven, or piece-meal. Doubts began to surface about groups in the population who seemed to have missed taking the welfare-state wonder drug. They had not all escaped poverty, even in the restricted sense intended by Beveridge. Moreover, when some of those who at the time were backroom social scientists for new Labour, like Brian Abel-Smith, Richard Titmuss, Dorothy Wedderburn and myself, began to examine the available material about the distribution of income, put together empirical reports on certain population groups, and undertake field enquiries ourselves, it was clear that there had been a large element of national self-deception (see Townsend, 1979, for an account of the post-war studies).

The hopes that the Welfare State had been delivered for the poor were premature - or had obscured harsh realities. There were then, as now, powerful political forces ill-disposed to accept those realities. Britain never went as far or as fast as did some other European countries. Through the years this has been a theme of cross-national reports, including, for example, the OECD. On the other hand the economy was operating at near full capacity in the early post-war years, and the combination of enlarged public ownership, more professional public service, relatively full employment, relatively progressive taxation, and more universal, if minimalist, social security, restricted the scale of poverty and kept it shallow.

The social scientists of poverty tended at the time to be critical of achievements, but perhaps over-optimistic about the potentialities for greater success in influencing government to act in conformity with the analysis. But during the 1980s and 1990s the indicators of poverty and of social division have revealed a worse situation than did the corresponding indicators in the 1950s and 1960s. The rates of unemployment, premature retirement, insecure wages, excessive salaries and bonuses for top earners, discrimination by gender and race as well as by disability and age, diminished status for unpaid work, and undervaluation of public service and homelessness have increased or have remained stubbornly high for two decades. Despite the criticisms and exhortations of the time, those earlier decades, of the 1950s and 1960s, are beginning to take on the aura of being Britain's 'Golden Age'.

The band of social scientists who kept the subject alive included many from whom I personally learned a lot. Some, like Tony Atkinson, have published a great deal and shown dispassionate tenacity as well as sharp, original insights. A fine mathematician and economist, Tony Atkinson has helped humanise the econometric and monetarist tendency in UK economics and steer economists back to appreciating that poverty is a fundamental, if not the fundamental, issue to be resolved by the discipline (see, for example, Atkinson 1984, 1987,1990a; 1990b; 1991; 1993, 1995 and 1998). There are others like Meghnad Desai (Desai, 1985; Desai and Shah, 1985; 1988), Robin Murray, and Brian Abel-Smith who set the highest standards of comprehensive analysis, who have a similar capacity to penetrate. Among sociologists who have contributed distinctively since the war to the British tradition have been Peter Worsley, Barbara Wootton (especially 1959 and 1962), Gary Runciman (for example, Runciman, 1966), John Rex (for example, Rex and Moore, 1967), John Scott (for example, Scott, 1994).

I hope to testify elsewhere about strength in depth. I have worked closely with friends and colleagues who are currently making original contributions to the subject. They include Carol and Alan Walker, Dorothy and Adrian Sinfield, Jonathan Bradshaw, Dennis Marsden, Hilary Land, David Donnison, Ruth Lister, John Veit-Wilson, Graham Room, John Hills, David Piachaud, Fiona Williams, Caroline Glendinning, Jane Millar, Vic George, Fran Bennett, Carey Oppenheim, Joanna Mack, Stewart Lansley, Alan Marsh, Peter Taylor-Gooby, Sarah Payne, David Gordon, Bob Holman, and Susanne MacGregor. In the references below I have listed some of their work. Britain is rich in the number of social scientists writing on the subject at the present time.

Two things should not go unnoticed. One is that women more than men fail to get the recognition their work deserves. I have mentioned Barbara Wootton, who did gain public recognition at the end of her life but whose achievements are still under-estimated (see especially Wootton, 1945, in which she was the first and most effective critic of Hayek; and her major contribution to the social sciences, 1959). Hilary Rose has documented the grudging acknowledgement of the scientific achievements of women in the list of Nobel prize-winners (Rose, 1996). Joan Brown has written copiously and impressively on the connection between policy and poverty (see for example, Brown, 1984; 1990). Teresa Hayter achieved an early breakthrough in our understanding of the complex links between international agencies and world poverty (Hayter, 1981). There are a large number of other examples.

In overseas poverty research there are household names, like the Galbraiths and the Myrdals, but there are also unacknowledged stars like Gordon Fisher, who burrowed away in his spare time in a Department of State for more than 30 years with skill and unassailable integrity (Fisher 1992; 1997; 1998).

The Poverty Threshold

Any account of the course of post-war research on poverty will have implications for future programmes of research. I want to highlight two themes. One is that the criteria for the poverty threshold have become, and will become, increasingly demanding, and scientific. The other is that research has become, and will become, increasingly international.

In 1918 Seebohm Rowntree published his book *The Human Needs of Labour*. It was rewritten and republished in 1937. As in York in 1898 Rowntree set out to devise a 'measuring rod, to enable us to assess the wage necessary to physical efficiency' (Rowntree, 1937, p.10). He drew a distinction between the principles which should guide the method of fixing 'minimum wages and those which should determine wages above the minimum', the former being based on 'the human needs of the worker' and the latter on 'the market value of the services rendered' (Ibid, p.111). His account begged a lot of awkward questions. The objective which he bequeathed generated furious debate but was fundamentally correct - that the poverty line on which a minimum wage could and should be based had to be established independently of the distribution of wages.

In the 1950s and early 1960s analysts showed that the line recalculated by Beveridge was lower than that defined by Rowntree, and that when eventually implemented in national insurance scale rates was lower still. They also showed that the criteria offered for the cost of meeting physical subsistence included circular or arbitrary reasoning. Although Rowntree looked to measures by the British Medical Association of dietary sufficiency in calculating food needs, he chose the average amounts spent by the poorest families in formulating what were the necessary costs of fuel, clothing and shelter to make up the poverty line. Once this approach became better-known, and especially once the hazards of putting a price on dietary needs began to be spelt out, there were explosive reactions. The definition of a poverty line was said to be arbitrary, or political, and that operationalising the concept took second place to the ranking of households and individuals in order of income to find who were, relatively, the poorest. This allowed economists in particular to be cavalier about independent criteria. For them it didn't matter exactly where the line was drawn. What mattered was in distinguishing how many might be assigned to the bottom ranks so that the benefits of adopting alternative models of taxation or economic growth could be demonstrated.

There are two problems for this school of thought. One is in suggesting that there cannot be a scientifically determined line or threshold of resources necessary to satisfy a set of defined living conditions and activities which membership of society denotes.

This is untenable. It disparagingly relegates poverty to a derivative instead of primary concept. There are analogies of thresholds established on independent criteria throughout science. There are levels of pollution, radiation, infestation, iron deficiency and many more. By routine statistical techniques - monitoring, RCT, correlation, linear discriminant analysis, appropriate thresholds can be established. And indeed there is strong empirical support subjectively and objectively for a similar 'threshold' of poverty, which is not addressed seriously by governments (for example, Townsend and Gordon, 1982, 1997; Desai, 1986; Desai and Shah, 1985 and 1988; Hutton, 1989, 1991; Fisher, 1998; Vaughan, 1993, 1996).

But it seems that the precise scientific identification of a poverty threshold poses more political problems than does the identification of most other thresholds. The delineation of such a threshold is believed to call for drastic structural action of a sweeping national or even international kind to reduce the demonstrably large numbers of people found to have standards of living below the threshold, which is difficult for many politicians, and for those playing a leading role in key political institutions, to accept. Compared with the scientific definition of most other kinds of threshold - as a guide for social development - there seems to be considerable resistance to doing the same for 'poverty'.

World Bank's Denial of a Threshold

The resistance is not crudely political. It takes quite complex, elaborate and sophisticated technical and professional forms, nowadays mounted with awesome authority. One example is a 501 page report issued by the Governing Board of the National Research Council of the US Academy of Sciences (see in particular the argument that a poverty threshold is more a matter of expert judgment than a matter for science, Citro and Michael, 1995, Chapter 2, especially pp.97-100).

Another example is provided in various reports issued by or on behalf of the World Bank. Thus in a 479-page compilation of the methodologies of household surveys world-wide, in particular those associated with the Bank's Living Standards Measurement series of country-specific studies, one major economist was so convinced of the 'conceptual and practical difficulties over a choice of the poverty line' that he suggested it does not much matter where exactly the line is drawn, and retreated to a view expressed previously by economists, that 'for policy evaluation, the social welfare function is all that is required to measure welfare, including an appropriate treatment of poverty' (Deaton, 1997, p.144).

This author expressed scepticism about a threshold, or line.

> Many writers have expressed grave doubts about the idea that there is some discontinuity in the distribution of welfare, with poverty on one side and lack of it on the other, and certainly there is no empirical indicator - income, consumption, calories, or the consumption of individual commodities - where there is any perceptible break in the distribution or in behaviour that would provide an empirical basis for the construction of a poverty line.
> (Ibid, p.141)

I believe his major book faithfully represents the World Bank's position on poverty. Nevertheless, Deaton did not review, or cite, the contrary evidence.

This must be a starting point for future research into the question of establishing an international poverty line, or much-improved cross-national attempts to track trends in poverty and explain them. In principle, national studies have to be conceived and carried out within an international framework. And this will only begin to work if the huge output of the international agencies, and particularly the World Bank, is called into serious critical review.

In determining a threshold, the key variables are certainly hard to measure, and good research is needed to refine and amend them. In the present case we are dealing with two key variables, level of deprivation and level of resources or overall income, whose interaction is affecting the third - poverty. There are of course sub-components of these variables, and contextual theory and social structure, including policy determinants, which play their part in scientific discovery and advance. What is particularly needed is not more 'indicators' research - that has been profuse despite the extraordinarily slender amount of comparative information available, such as limited census data, for different countries - but exhaustive survey research in depth to provide a better basis for agreeing and using short-cut indicators, plus sharp investigation of the measured contribution made to trends in poverty by each of the existing policies being applied by government.

Aligning Income with Material and Social Deprivation

Let me turn to the second problem for the 'poverty is arbitrary' school of thought. Income is given a role that it cannot perform. It is too blithely assumed that income is easier to measure than poverty, and that the level of cash income in particular gives a good approximation of standard of living. The truth is that a measure of household cash income can be difficult to produce and in many instances does not provide a reliable indicator of standard of living. Instead, a measure of overall income, or overall resources including goods in kind, free and subsidised services and the use value of the assets owned, is needed. That is quite complex, and is yet a necessary part of the scientific remit. Working with rough and ready approximations can be distorting and misleading. They are self-evidently crude or over-simplified. Public confidence in those engaging in such a trade is apt to falter.

In writing the final passages of *Poverty in the United Kingdom* I found I had left insufficient time to digest the full implications of our decision to measure income in the widest sense. Almost as an afterthought one of its most significant findings was shovelled into Appendix 13. When net income worth plus the value of employer welfare benefits in kind was substituted for net disposable income the correlation with indicators of deprivation was more highly significant. I have regretted not developing earlier the full gamut of methods unveiled in that Appendix (see pp.1173-76).

In the body of that report (mainly in Chapter 5) we showed that the measure of income could be enlarged on the basis of survey investigation to include imputed income from assets, free and subsidised goods and services from employers, public social services and private sources. Some see this as a mere refinement to the methods of income measurement already established in official surveys like the Family Expenditure Survey. Thus, our measure of 'income net worth' produced a higher statistical correlation with a large number of indicators of deprivation than did 'net disposable cash income'. When the value of employer welfare benefits in kind was added (a measure which was better in coverage than the restricted additional measure conventionally used in the FES) the correlation was even stronger. But while this is a result which deserves to be better known, and tested in future research to find whether it can be routinely reproduced, the methodology has virtues which have not been fully understood. This 'comprehensive' approach does more than measure capacity to fulfil different levels of living. Let me explain.

A principled investigation of income in this overall sense demonstrates the structural position of households and individuals in society and has to take account of the multiple relations in which they are involved. Differences between rich and poor in their living standards are not, as a consequence, minimised or obscured. Conventional measures and discussions of inequalities of income greatly underestimate the extent of the differences in living standards that exist. Some of the latter-day approaches to operational definition and measurement of income are also so rough and ready that they conceal more than they reveal. I believe that the problem of spurious measurement of living standards through restricted and often extremely crude measures of gross and disposable income is becoming more serious in today's so-called flexible labour market. Over-simplified measurement is becoming increasingly unrepresentative of the actual resources individuals and families have at their disposal and also of the dispersion of resources between rich and poor. By insisting on a more comprehensive methodology in constructing accounts of the national distribution of living standards we can also lay a better basis for regional and area comparisons, and cross-national comparisons.

One of the orthodox technical objections to making comparisons between industrial and developing countries is that self-generated income from the land in the form of production for household consumption and exchange is important for the latter but not for the former. However, international work obliges us to improvise and then confirm international statistical and scientific standards. To argue that income in kind is irrelevant to living standards in the UK is no excuse. On the contrary, it matters substantially to some in the population, and routine valuation will pave the way not just for reliable comparison but allow western scientists to be less insular and 'Third World phobic'.

In summary, the concept of income, like the concept of poverty, can be widened or narrowed. Either way there will be problems in analysis, because the conditions which conceptualisation seeks to clarify are complex. I believe a restricted approach is more likely to lead to substantive problems. In this case I believe there is much to be gained from treating cash income as a sub-component of the larger idea of 'resources' or at least distinguishing between 'overall disposable income' and, say, 'disposable income'. National and regional comparisons are thereby facilitated. More importantly, types and severity of material and social deprivation can be more exactly related to level or amount of resources to identify the threshold below which particular harm is caused.

In *The Concept of Poverty* (1970) the idea of the threshold was broached. We said we were experimenting with a 'deprivation' index, based on 'a list of activities and customs which are common for a majority of the population of the UK. ... At a depressed level of resources families and individuals may be excluded from participation in common social activities and enjoyments. ...The deprivation will not be correlated uniformly with total resources at the lower levels [of income] and there will be a 'threshold' of resources below which deprivation will be marked' (p.29).

In *Poverty in the United Kingdom* (1979, Chapter 6) I stated that at lower levels of income, deprivation increased disproportionately in relation to falling income. This was true for different types of households. There were, however, measurement problems. And the numbers of certain types of households in the national sample were also small. I hoped these problems might be resolved in follow-up research. In the late 1980s, partly prompted by studies by Desai (1986) and Desai and Shah (1985 and 1988) and Hutton (1989 and 1991) David Gordon and I (Townsend and Gordon, 1989) reported a poverty survey of Greater London and provided stronger evidence for the existence of a threshold, undertaking cluster analysis on the basis of Ward's method of dissimilarity, and also building up Average Linkage clusters on the basis of similarity. We found that hierarchical algorithms generally produced more reliable cluster solutions. The dendograms were very clearly distinguished and allowed thresholds of income to be defined for different types of household.

The overall research task was therefore seen as two-fold. Household resources have to be measured comprehensively and fine-tuned and ranked if 'income' is to be understood and used for comparative international purposes to derive vital scientific knowledge. That seems to me to have become a bigger priority at the end of the 1990s than it was at the end of the 1960s. And correspondingly, multiple and severe material and social deprivation also have to be investigated comprehensively. All aspects of material and social life have to be examined. Critics have sometimes pounced on the summary index of relative deprivation used in the early study of 1967-68 (see the discussion in Townsend, 1993a, Chapter 5) and mocked one of the 12 ingredients - not having a special meal like a Sunday roast at least weekly. But the summary of 12 was in fact drawn from 68 indicators constructed to reflect different elements of material and social life. And what was also forgotten was that the investigation of individual and collective household behaviour was intended to be comprehensive, and certainly to cover all the major aspects of material and social life. That was not put into effect as well as it might be today. But in principle the results were open to refutation and amendment. A broad set of deprivation criteria for the establishment of a poverty line was drawn up and put into practice. Future research workers will want to build upon, and improve, the early formulation.

The Internationalisation of Poverty Research

The point of departure for my final theme is my edited book *The Concept of Poverty* (1970). This was based on an international conference in 1967 financed by the then Joseph Rowntree Memorial Trust as a trail-blazer for the national poverty study which the Trust had agreed in 1964 to finance. There were papers representing poverty in other European countries, but also developing countries, and papers taking forward specialised work on nutrition and the unemployed, and the advantages and disadvantages of measuring poverty by means of the distribution of expenditure or the distribution of income.

The internationalisation of poverty research has pursued a chequered course since the 1939-45 war. It has produced entirely new demands on the research community, and developments at the end of the 20th century deserve attention. In the early years the empirical approaches of Rowntree but also of the official social survey in the UK, leading into the launch of the Family Expenditure Survey in 1957, prompted comparable initiatives in parts of the former British Empire, especially in India and South Africa. The 1970s and 1980s saw a retrenchment from that development and the simultaneous growth of Europeanisation and US-dominated international agency work.

Europeanisation of research into poverty promised much more than has so far been delivered. High hopes were invested in the first anti-poverty programme (1975-80). I still remember my embarrassment in responding to a note in a principal report in 1980 that all the national reports would be sent to individuals who requested them. The postman staggered into my office with two large sacks. When reports were piled one upon another I found I had a paper pillar four feet deep.

In the first and the second (1986-89) European anti-poverty programmes the research was wide-ranging, the aspirations significant. But the European Community decided not to pursue the clear implications of the work. Even the definition of poverty originally devised with the social sciences carried implications for action which members of the Commission were not inclined to pursue. Social science had over-reached government capacity and inclination. The third programme (1990-94) was a pale shadow of the first and second programmes - setting out a list of worthy but small-scale, mainly local, projects around the continent. After a struggle in the mid-1990s the fourth programme was aborted (see Room, 1995).

There is therefore a huge problem in concerting European strategy and policies to eradicate poverty both internally and externally. Social scientists have not been permitted to play a sufficiently creative and independent role in the management by the Commission of European social policy. The indirect effect of this has been to increase the influence of the international agencies operating from the United States, especially the IMF and the World Bank, and of the United States itself in setting the policy agenda on poverty. As a consequence critical new themes in the investigation of poverty, like the growing power of the Trans-national Corporations, and the growing influence of global economic policies that are introducing large-scale privatisation – in the transitional economies and the Third World as well as the industrialised

West, cuts in public expenditure on social services, and the withdrawal of social insurance, are neglected.

The direct effect of the EC's limited vision has been to hold back the emergence of more effective development as well as anti-poverty programmes in the world. Despite a considerable range of original and important work going on in individual countries around Europe, on the investigation of poverty, on methods of preserving and improving social protection, or social security, on introducing practical and relevant new employment programmes and on finding what kind of balance can be struck, and needs to be struck, between the private and public sectors to prevent social instability and disintegration, the Commission neither publicises nor tries to pull together the key findings from this work.

Of course, the pressures to control European Union approaches to the investigation or non-investigation of poverty are considerable and come from different quarters. Much depends, for example, on events concerned with the democratic deficit, monetary union, and the enlargement of the European Union. Thus, the emerging terms whereby the UK fulfils its membership of Europe will transform the nature of poverty research in this country but will also have a knock-on effect elsewhere.

The home-grown empirical traditions and perspectives of Europe - including those of people in Eastern European countries like Poland and Hungary are productive and, with collaboration, could be more widely known. In some member countries of the European Union there is vigorous and original work which is not publicised internationally. A lot of that work is theoretical in the structural sense, technically varied and original, sometimes very policy-conscious, and empirically grounded in a comprehensive as well as individual sense. These qualities are not so pronounced in the equivalent literatures of the United States and the leading international agencies.

Research scientists in Europe need to capitalise on these strengths to serve a larger population. In the UK there are many examples of work in progress on poverty - the British Household Panel Survey, the Suntory Toyota's International Centre on the Welfare State Programme at the London School of Economics, the Child Poverty Action Group, the New Economics Foundation, Oxfam. Such work needs to be emulated at European level. There is a temptation - because of the official suspension of the anti-poverty programme - to re-organise research around, for example, social exclusion and social quality. But there is a problem of sustaining a genuine scientific momentum, and not just of entering into the swing of latter-day diversionary and complementary tactics.

Absolute and Overall Poverty

My argument is therefore that scientific anti-poverty strategy has to be Europeanised and globalised. One current illustration is a new initiative in Europe. More than 100 leading European social scientists signed a statement to carry forward the 1995 United Nations commitment to apply two levels of poverty, absolute and overall, in national studies of their extent (see Townsend, Gordon and Bradshaw, 1997). This commitment, one of the key features of the agreement signed by 117 heads of state, offers a breakthrough in establishing a measure that can be compared across countries. European scientists are actively producing varied but overlapping results of research into poverty - even if their work is not properly reflected in the programmes and administration of the European Commission. Many of these scientists agree that what they have in common, or what they find in common, needs to be broadcast widely, at the same time as the more individual or specialised features of their work are made available for scrutiny. Recent history suggests there is almost as much political resistance to adopting international measures of poverty as international policies to reduce poverty. The European group is actively developing a programme to put more pressure on the EC and national governments to undertake poverty research and to distil and circularise the lessons of that research. The Economic and Research Council has agreed to finance a two-year programme of international seminars to report progress.

If European research can be organised effectively there will be wider international gains. The arguments for an international poverty line, or for a lower-level and higher-level poverty line, are becoming irresistible.

Despite the growing sophistication of their work, the international agencies, and especially the World Bank, seem to be resisting this conclusion. The operational definitions of poverty have been inappropriate as well as diverse. The volume of World Bank papers on poverty in different countries has grown enormously, but the delineation of poverty has been trite. For the least developed countries the measure is $1 a day; for Latin America it is $2, and for the transitional economies of Eastern Europe and the former Soviet Union it is $4. No systematic empirical research on these arbitrary choices is being carried out to find how far, through matching common elements, more reliable comparative measures can be introduced. In its LSMS and country-specific studies the World Bank tries to give the impression of fulfilling this task, but signally fails to deliver reliable cross-national results. Its expert advisers (for example, Deaton, 1997) do not appear to have explored the problem, either in conceptual or detailed empirical terms. Crude estimates of poverty are based on little more than conjecture for many countries. The measure applied in the advanced industrial countries often turns on surveys carried out more than 10 years previously and reflects variable national standards or measures related to average household income.

Full documentation of the recent and current work of the international agencies will have to be presented elsewhere. What is at issue? Living standards are not compared rigorously across countries. Neither are available resources, needs and forms of material and social deprivation. Against the evidence, countries and regions are still being interpreted and compared as self-contained islands, with independent problems carrying implications of independent solutions to be found by each national government. Research workers at the World Bank are being encouraged to behave like King Canute, defiantly resisting the encroaching global tide. Ignored are the growing multi-national causes of national and local impoverishment. Ignored too is the growing overlap between First and Third World countries in living standards, taking say the poorest 20 per cent and richest 20 per cent in each country (for example Townsend, 1993, p.8). There is the growing structural inequality *within* most countries (Smeeding, O'Higgins and Rainwater, 1989; Osberg, 1991; Cornia, 1993, 1994a, 1994b; Committee on Ways and Means, 1992-1997; DSS, 1990-1997; Vogel, 1997), and the growing structural inequality *between* richest and poorest countries (UNDP, 1997, 1998).

The evidence suggests that the world's poverty problem will be one of wealth and poverty becoming more and more polarised within every country rather than one of poverty being diminished automatically if economic growth can be given sufficient priority. The evidence also suggests that as the structural causes of poverty move steadily from locality and nation state to global and multi-national institutions, including TNC's, international anti-poverty strategy will have to be given priority over national programmes of action. That will transform thinking about the nature of social policy, and not only about anti-poverty programmes and related research.

The prospective continuing polarisation of wealth and income will provoke other social problems. There are two which have been relatively neglected by the exponents of poverty research and which will have to be given more attention. One is **instability**. Markets are becoming more volatile, and can crash. Corporations have incentives to close plants and transfer jobs on a huge scale around the world. In the last two decades there have been extreme examples of the **collapse** of living standards, especially in the former Soviet Union, Africa and the Middle East. The extent of that collapse has rarely been monitored exactly. Information about sudden impoverishment is hard to come by, and the discussion of poverty tends to be confined to the relatively stable parts of the world. This can too easily mislead analysis and the construction of priority policies. There are war-torn countries and others exhibiting extreme features of ethnic animosity, nationalist fervour and religious bigotry. There are also countries where there is evidence of swiftly damaging effects of liberalisation and structural adjustment. These extremes are rarely examined in describing the growth and decline of poverty. Comparative analysis of the phenomenon is usually restricted to countries with relatively stable recent economic and social conditions.

The second neglected problem is the deepening **hierarchy of power**. This might be illustrated variously. In the United States and the United Kingdom the 'underclass' has emerged as a means of fashioning explanation of poverty. Logically such a characterisation should correspond with the emergence of a counter-balancing 'overclass'. With the growth of transnational conglomerates class stratification in nation-states and globally has become elongated. Unemployment has become steadily more substantial - even in Europe. The hierarchy of power is much deeper, and the percentage of the world's income available to the poorest 20 per cent of world population has shrunk since 1960 from 2.5 per cent to 1.1 per cent. The latest UNDP Human Development Report (UNDP, 1998, p.30) calls attention to the fact that the wealth of the world's 32 richest people exceeds the total GDP of South Asia.

The development affects institutions and not only individuals well-placed in the conglomerates. The growth, and policies, of the TNC's deserve far more scrutiny. When nation states and transnational corporations are ranked according to the annual value of resources produced (GDP or value of transnational sales) there are only 21 nation states with annual production values of more than the biggest transnational companies (Donald, 1997). There is a clutch of seven transnationals each with sales larger in value than the GDP of Indonesia, Norway, Denmark and Saudi Arabia. Another 30 TNC's have sales greater than the GDP of Ireland, Pakistan and New Zealand. These companies usually operate in 50 or more countries. Labour mobility is increasing and geographical inequalities in the values of transactions and trade generally are widening. Economic and social relations are being globalised very rapidly and the analysis of developing inequalities and poverty has to be brought up to date.

World-wide privatisation serves to concentrate such global power (Townsend, 1997). It has been, and remains, a key feature of economic policy, whether in Africa, through structural adjustment policies, Eastern Europe, through liberalisation programmes and 'safety-net' substitutes for universal state services, or Western Europe and other industrialised OECD countries, through welfare 'reform'. The process is not just from state to local or national company, but from state to transnational conglomerate. For example, the privatisation of pensions in Chile has resulted in four American-owned transnationals controlling more than two-thirds of the assets of Chilean pension funds.

The World Bank is publishing a stream of reports designed to encourage further privatisation and to justify, *post hoc*, the policies that have been pursued in Latin America, Africa and Eastern Europe (see for example, Campbell-White and Batia, 1998; Lieberman and Kirkness, 1998; Psacharapoulos *et al.*, 1997). Documentation of success, and the counter-arguments for collectively provided welfare, modern public services and public ownership, are not addressed, whether comparatively or nationally (see for example, Townsend, 1997; Williamson, 1997; Lancet, 1994).

In unravelling the causes of local poverty, attention now has to be given to the decisions and policies of TNC's, international agencies, and regional trading associations of states and of TNC's that are broadly affiliated in a hierarchy of powerful institutions (examples of what can be done being provided by Korten, 1996; Lang and Hines, 1994; Oxfam, 1995). The extent of local poverty may depend on decisions to close plants and companies in one country and open or reinvigorate them in another - hence increasing unemployment in the former. It may depend on the lowering of wages and the social costs of labour to maintain competitiveness with overseas companies and labour forces. Or it may depend on privatising public services, pensions and welfare benefits only to find ownership and management slipping into hands overseas whereby there is less access, but greater cost, for the local community.

There is therefore a large programme of investigatory research for the social scientist. In developing appropriate definitions and measures of poverty, and in pursuing the predominantly structural causes of the problem, **instability** and the quickly-evolving **hierarchy of power** are inescapable modern themes.

Conclusion

Before Charles Booth reported the results of his survey of poverty in London and Seebohm Rowntree did the same for York around the end of the 19th century a strong British tradition of concerned investigation was already established. Government as well as individual studies of poverty and of the Poor Law had been considerable in number. In the early decades of the 20th century numerous area studies were carried out. Since 1939 more specialised studies, and national as well as area studies have multiplied.

During the last half-century the extent of knowledge about poverty has undoubtedly grown. However, that knowledge has become subject to serious distortion. There is better understanding of the groups who live in poverty and their experiences and conditions. The interconnections of material deprivation through food, fuel, housing, environment, work and health have been revealed. And the relevance of the post-war institutions of the welfare state are everywhere examined and re-examined. But the body of work on poverty towards the end of the 20th century lacks scientific focus. This is because the subject is too strongly appropriated by political, and economic, not to say global, ideology.

This chapter therefore amounts to being a plea for the development of a more scrupulously independent, international and scientific research perspective - even if that means coming into conflict with powerful interests. Serving that objective depends, of course, on making an assessment of past developments and future prospects. The most reputable investigations (examples of which are listed above) call attention to the **large scale** of the problem, and the **structural** rather than the individual or narrowly cultural causes. Together these investigations demonstrate that major changes need to be made in current policies, that the wholesale reconstruction of some key institutions has to be set in motion, and that the distribution of income and wealth has to be re-cast. Not least is the cumulative evidence for more generous social security benefits to be introduced in the UK. All this is demonstrably affordable and acceptable to the population. On good authority it seems also to be economically viable and sustainable.

There are powerful forces prepared not merely to quarrel with the results of such investigations, but to quarrel with, and hence distort, definition, measurement and attribution of cause. Some seek to take over the entire subject. Through financial sponsorship and grant-aided mechanisms, and setting up research and statistical institutions, departments of state, international agencies and large corporations hugely influence the work of the scientific community. I have given examples of how that distortion arises.

Trying to follow a more calculated and positive scientific approach to the problem of poverty carries a number of implications, some of which I have attempted to describe. One is to put policy analysis at the heart of the investigation of poverty, with equal status to that of (1) conceptualisation, (2) operational definition and measurement, and (3) explanation or theory. The exploration of policy is not just an exploration of what might be added in the future to deal with the extent of poverty exposed by empirical and statistical research, but an exploration of how past and current policies have themselves contributed to worsening and not only relieving the problem. Policies have to be treated as potential causes of the problem under investigation. They must become an automatic part of the remit.

A second conclusion is that scientific consensus on the identification of a poverty threshold or line has to be, and can be, sought, and that a consensus can be built on the 1995 UN Copenhagen agreement about the desirability of defining and measuring 'absolute' and 'overall' poverty in every country, as a basis for drawing up national plans for the eradication of poverty - also agreed by the 117 Heads of State signing the declaration and programme of action. The advantages would be considerable. More thought will have to be given to spelling out the criteria for absolute and overall poverty so that the commonalities of human need can be better distinguished from those which are country- or culture-specific. This would represent a huge improvement in cross-country comparison, and therefore establish authoritative measurement of cross-national poverty and hence authoritative backing for the selection of priorities in policy.

It would help research workers and public to surmount the barriers of old-fashioned sovereignty. Increasingly the causes of local poverty are to be found outside national boundaries - in the policies and action of international agencies, Trans-National Corporations, and economic and regional associations of states. Unfortunately these too are sources of the distortion of the understanding of poverty and have to be examined in great detail. They compose the governing elements of a new hierarchy of international power, which is itself a neglected theme in poverty research. I have illustrated above from the huge input of reports of the World Bank, and have argued that its approach both to the definition of a poverty line and the construction of anti-poverty strategies is inappropriate and even devious, and shows little sign of dealing with a growing world problem.

I have drawn on the idea of the 'scientific community'. I realise that term begs many questions, but it allows me both to testify to historical gain and yet to insist that in contemplating future research into poverty we have to decide our most useful point of departure. In the UK, as this book shows, there is a large number of social scientists interested in, indeed committed to, the eradication of poverty. The problem they are dealing with is increasingly international and global, and not only local. To register the extent of the present morass in national and international affairs, and how to find a way out of it, will be to call on greater collaborative effort and resolve to maintain scientific independence.

References

Abel-Smith, B. (1978), *Poverty, Development and Health Policy*, World Health Organisation, Geneva.

Atkinson, A.B. (1984), 'How Should We Measure Poverty: Some Conceptual Issues'. Paper for Symposium on the Measurement of Poverty, Berlin.

Atkinson, A.B. (1987), 'Income Distribution and Differences in Needs', in G.R. Feiwel (ed), *Arrow and the Foundations of the Theory of Economic Policy*, New York University Press, New York.

Atkinson, A.B. (1990a), *A National Minimum? A History of Ambiguity in the Determination of Benefit Scales in Britain*, Suntory-Toyota International Centre for Economics and Related Disciplines, WSP/47, London School of Economics, London.

Atkinson, A.B. (1990b), *Comparing Poverty Rates Internationally: Lessons from Recent Studies in OECD Countries*, Suntory-Toyota International Centre for Economics and Related Disciplines, WSP/53, London School of Economics, London.

Atkinson, A.B. (1991), *Poverty, Statistics, and Progress in Europe*, Suntory-Toyota International Centre for Economics and Related Disciplines, WSP/60, London School of Economics, London.

Atkinson, A.B. (1993), *Beveridge, the National Minimum and its Future in a European Context*, Suntory-Toyota International Centre for Economics and Related Disciplines, WSP/85, London School of Economics, London.

Atkinson, A.B. (1995), *Incomes and the Welfare State: Essays on Britain and Europe*, Cambridge University Press, Cambridge.

Atkinson, A.B. (1998), *Poverty in Europe*, Blackwell, Oxford.

Bennett, F. (1997), *Child Support: Issues for the Future*, CPAG, London.

Benzeval, M., Judge, K. and Solomon, M. (1992), *The Health Status of Londoners: A Comparative Perspective*, King's Fund, London.

Berthoud, R. and Kempson, E. (1992), *Credit and Debt: The PSI Report*, Policy Studies Institute, London.

Beveridge (1943), *The Pillars of Social Security*, Allen and Unwin, London.

Black Report (1980), *Inequalities in Health*, Report of a Research Working Group, DHSS, London.

Booth, C. (1892-1903), *Life and Labour of the People in London*.

Botting, B. (ed) (1995), *The Health of Our Children: Decennial Supplement, The Registrar General's Supplement for England and Wales*, OPCS Series DS No. 11, HMSO, London.

Bradbury, B. (1989), 'Family Size Equivalence Scales and Survey Evaluations of Income and Well-Being', *Journal of Social Policy*, vol. 18, no. 3, pp.383-408

Bradshaw, J. (1990), *Child Poverty and Deprivation in the UK, Special Sub-series: Child Poverty in Industrialised Countries*, UNICEF International Child Development Centre, Innocenti Occasional Papers No. 8, UNICEF, Florence, Italy.

Bradshaw, J. (1993a), *Household Budgets and Living Standards*, Joseph Rowntree Foundation, York.

Bradshaw, J. (1993b), *Budget Standards for the United Kingdom*, Avebury/Ashgate Publishing Ltd., Aldershot.

Bradshaw, J. (1996), *Budget Standards for the United Kingdom*, Avebury, Aldershot.

Bradshaw, J., Gordon, D., Levitas, R., Middleton, S., Pantazis, C., Payne, S. and Townsend, P. (1998), *Perceptions of Poverty and Social Exclusion 1998*, Report on Preparatory Research, University of Bristol.

Bradshaw, J. and Holmes, H. (1989), *Living on the Edge*, Tyneside Poverty Action Group, London.

British Household Panel Survey, University of Essex, ESRC Research Centre on Micro-social Change.

Brown, J. (1984), *Children in Social Security: Studies in the Social Security System*, No. 3, Policy Studies Institute, London.

Brown, J. (1990), *Social Security in Retirement*, Joseph Rowntree Foundation, York.

Burrows, R. and Rhodes, D. (1998), *Unpopular Places? Area Disadvantage and the Geography of Misery in England*, University of York, Centre for Housing Policy, York.

Campbell-White, O. and Bhatia, A. (1998), *Privatisation in Africa*, Series on Directions in Development, The World Bank, Washington D.C.

Canadian Council on Social Development (1984), *Not Enough: The Meaning and Measurement of Poverty in Canada*, CCSD, Ottawa.

Carvalho, S. and White, H. (1997), *Combining the Quantitative and Qualitative Approaches to Poverty Measurement and Analysis: The Practice and the Potential*, World Bank Technical Paper No. 366, The World Bank, Washington D.C.

Chow, N.W.S (1981), *Poverty in an Affluent City: A Report on a Survey of Low Income Families*, Department of Social Work, Chinese University of Hong Kong.

Chu, K-Y. and Gupta, S. (eds) (1998), *Social Safety Nets: Issues and Recent Experiences*, International Monetary Fund, Washington D.C.

Citro, C.F. and Michael, R.T (1995), *Measuring Poverty: A New Approach*, Panel on Poverty, National Research Council, National Academy Press, Washington D.C.

Clarke, S. with Holmes, J. (1997), *Poverty in Transition: A Report Prepared for the Department for International Development*, University of Warwick (publication forthcoming).

Cohen, R., Coxhall, J., Craig, G. and Sangster, A.S. (1992), *Hardship in Britain: Being Poor in the 1990s*, Child Poverty Action Group, London.

Commission of the European Communities (1981), *Final Report from the Commission to the Council on the First Programme of Pilot Schemes and Studies to Combat Poverty*, CEC, Brussels.

Commission of the European Communities (1991), *Final Report on the Second European Poverty Programme 1985-1989*, Luxembourg, Office for the Official Publications of the European Communities.

Committee on Ways and Means (1992-1997), *1992 Green Book*, US Government Printing Office, Washington.

Cornia, G. A. (1993), *Public Policy and Social Conditions; Central and Eastern Europe in Transition*, Regional Monitoring Report Number 1, UNICEF, Florence.

Cornia, G.A. (1994a), 'Poverty, Food Consumption, and Nutrition During the Transition to the Market Economy in Eastern Europe', *American Economic Association Papers and Proceedings*, May, pp. 297-303.

Cornia, G. A. (1994b), *Crisis in Mortality, Health and Nutrition, Central and Eastern Europe in Transition; public policy and social conditions*, Regional Monitoring Report Number 2, UNICEF, Florence.

Corston, J. (1994), 'Written Answers to Parliamentary Questions about Low Income (collected set)', *Hansard*, 26 October 1994, cols. 689-703.

Craig, G. and Glendinning, C. (1990), *The Impact of Social Security Changes: The Views of Families Living in Disadvantaged Areas; 2. The Views of Families Using Barnado Pre-School Services; and 3. The Views of Young People*, Barnado's Research and Development Section, Ilford, Essex.

Davey-Smith, G. and Brunner, E. (1997), 'Socio-Economic Differentials in Health: The Role of Nutrition', *Proceedings of the Nutrition Society*, 56, pp. 79-90.

Deaton, A. (1997), *The Analysis of Household Surveys: A Microeconometric Approach to Development Policy*, Published for the World Bank, Baltimore and London, The Johns Hopkins University Press.

DeRose, L., Messer, E. and Millman, S. (1998), *Who's Hungry? And How Do We Know?: Food Shortage, Poverty and Deprivation, Tokyo*, UN Universities Press, New York and Paris.

Desai, M. and Shah, A. (1985), *An Econometric Approach to the Measurement of Poverty*, Suntory-Toyota International Centre for Economics and Related Disciplines, WSP/2, London School of Economics, London.

Desai, M. (1985), 'Drawing the Line: On Defining the Poverty Threshold', in P. Golding (ed), *Excluding the Poor*, Child Poverty Action Group, London.

Desai, M. and Shah, A. (1988), 'An Economic Approach to the Measurement of Poverty', *Oxford Economic Papers*, vol. 40, pp. 505-22.

DHSS (1988), *Low Income Statistics, Report of a Technical Review*, Department of Health and Social Security, London.

Donald, A. (1997), 'Developing International Law', *Global Security*, Spring.

Donnison, D. (1998), *Politics for a Just Society*, Macmillan, London.

Dorling, D and Simpson, S. (eds) (1998), *Statistics and Society: The Arithmetic of Politics*, Arnold, London.

DSS (1988), *The Measurement of Living Standards for Households Below Average Income*, Reply by the Government to the Fourth Report from the Select Committee on Social Services, Cm 523, HMSO, London.

DSS (1990a), *Households Below Average Income: A Statistical Analysis 1981-87*, Government Statistical Service, July, London.

DSS (1990b), *The Measurement of Living Standards for Households Below Average Income*, Cm 1162, HMSO, London.

DSS (1991), *Households Below Average Income: Stocktaking Report of a Working Group*, Department of Social Security, London.

DSS (1994), *Households Below Average Income: A Statistical Analysis 1979-1991/92*, HMSO, London.

DSS (1995a), *Households Below Average Income: A Statistical Analysis 1979-1992/93*, HMSO, London.

DSS (1995b), *Low Income Statistics: Low Income Families 1989-1992*, Cm 2871, HMSO, London.

DSS (1997), *Households Below Average Income: A Statistical Analysis 1979-1994-5*, The Stationery Office, London.

De Vos, K. and Hagenaars, A. (1988), 'A Comparison Between the Poverty Concepts of Sen and Townsend', Erasmus University, Rotterdam.

Eurostat (1991), *Poverty in Figures: Europe in the Early 1980s*, Luxembourg.

Eurostat (1994), *Poverty Statistics in the Late 1980s: Research Based on Micro-Data*, Office for Official Publications of the European Communities, Luxembourg.

Family Expenditure Survey, Central Statistical Office, HMSO, London.

Figueiredo, J. B. and Shaheed, Z. (1995), *Reducing Poverty through Labour Market Policies*, International Institute for Labour Studies, Geneva.

Fisher, G.M. (1992), 'The Development and History of the Poverty Thresholds', *Social Security Bulletin*, vol. 55, no. 4.

Fisher, G.M. (1997), 'Poverty Lines and Measures of Income Inadequacy in the United States Since 1870: Collecting and Using a Little-Known Body of Historical Material', Paper presented to the Social Science History Association, Washington D.C., 17 October.

Fisher, G.M. (1998), 'Setting American Standards of Poverty: A Look Back', *Focus* (Newsletter of the Institute for Research on Poverty), vol. 19, no. 2.

Franklin, N.N. (1967), 'The Concept and Measurement of "Minimum Living Standards"', *International Labour Review*.

Frayman, H. (1991), *Breadline Britain - 1990s, The Findings of the Television Series*, LWT and the Joseph Rowntree Foundation, London.

Gaudier, M. (1995), *Poverty, Inequality, Exclusion: New Approach to Theory and Practice*, International Institute for Labour Studies, Geneva.

Glendinning, C. (1992), *Women and Poverty in Britain: The 1990s*, Harvester Wheatsheaf, Hemel Hempstead.

Gordon, A. (1992), *Economics and Social Policy: An Introduction*, Martin Robertson.

Gordon, D. and Pantazis, C. (1994), *Breadline Britain in the 1990s: A Report to the Joseph Rowntree Foundation*, Joseph Rowntree Foundation, York.

Grayson, L., Hobson, M. and Smith, B. (1992), *INLOGOV Informs on 'Poverty'*, University of Birmingham, Birmingham.

Hallerod, B. (1993), 'Poverty in Sweden: A New Approach to the Direct Measurement of Consensual Poverty', Department of Sociology, University of Umea, and Social Policy Research Centre, University of New South Wales.

Harding, G. (1995), 'Social Class Differences in the Mortality of Men: Recent Evidence from the OPCS Longitudinal Study', *Population Trends*, vol. 80, pp. 31-7.

Hayek F.A.V. (1945), *The Road to Serfdom*, Longman.

Hayter, T. (1981), *The Creation of World Poverty*, The Pluto Press, London.

Hewitt de Alcantara, C. (1994), *Structural Adjustment in a Changing World*, UNRISD, Geneva.

Hewlett, S.A. (1993), *Child Neglect in Rich Nations*, UNICEF, Florence, Italy, and New York.

Hills, J. (1995), *Inquiry into Income and Wealth, Vol. 2*, Joseph Rowntree Foundation, York.

Hills, J. (ed) (1996), *New Inequalities: The Changing Distribution of Income and Wealth in the UK*, Cambridge University Press, Cambridge.

Holman, R. (ed) (1970), *Socially deprived families in Britain*, NCSS.

Holman, R. (1978), *Poverty: Explanations of Social Deprivation*, Martin Robertson, London.

Households Below Average Income, Department for Social Security, HMSO, London.

Huther, J., Roberts, S. and Shah, A. (1997), *Public Expenditure Reform Under Adjustment Lending: Lessons from the World Bank Experience*, World Bank Discussion Paper No. 382, The World Bank, Washington D.C.

Hutton, S. (1989), 'Testing Townsend: Exploring Living Standards Using Secondary Data Analysis', in S. Baldwin, C. Godfrey, and C. Propper (eds), *The Quality of Life*, Routledge and Kegan Paul, London.

Hutton, S. (1991), 'Measuring Living Standards Using Existing National Data Sets', *Journal of Social Policy*, vol. 20, no. 2.

International Institute for Labour Studies (1993), *The Framework of ILO Action Against Poverty*, IILS, Geneva.

International Monetary Fund (1995), *Social Dimensions of the IMF's Policy Dialogue, World Summit for Social Development*, International Monetary Fund, Washington D.C.

Jazairy, I., Alamgir, M. and Panuccio, T. (1992), *The State of World Rural Poverty, Rome and New York*, IFAD (International Fund for Agricultural Development), New York University Press.

Kirdar, U. and Silk, L. (1995), *People: From Impoverishment to Empowerment*, special edition for the World Summit for Social Development, New York

Ksiezopolski, M. (1993), 'Social Policy in Poland in the Period of Political and Economic Transition: Challenges and Dilemmas', *Journal of European Social Policy*, special issue on Central and Eastern Europe, vol. 3.

Korten, D. C. (1996), *When Corporations Rule the World*, Earthscan, London.

Lancet (1994), 'Structural Adjustment Too Painful?', *The Lancet* (editorial), vol. 344, no. 8934, pp. 1377-8.

Land, H. and Lewis, J. (1997), *The Emergence of Lone Motherhood as a Problem in Late Twentieth Century Britain*, LSE Publication, London.

Lang, T. and Hines, C. (1994), *The New Protectionism: Protecting the Future Against Free Trade*, Earthscan Publications, London.

Lee, P. and Townsend, P. (1993), 'Trends in Deprivation in the London Labour Market: A Study of Low Incomes and Unemployment in London Between 1985 and 1992', A Report for the International Institute for Labour Studies, Geneva.

Levitas, R. (1996), 'Fiddling While Britain Burns? The Measurement of Unemployment', in R. Levitas.and W. Guy (eds), *Interpreting Official Statistics*, Routledge, London and New York.

Levitas, R. and Guy, W. (eds) (1996), *Interpreting Official Statistics*, Routledge, London and New York.

Lieberman, I.W. and Kirkness, C.D. (eds) (1998), *Privatisation and Emerging Equity Markets*, The World Bank and Flemings Investment Bank, Washington D.C.

Lister, R. (1991), 'Concepts of Poverty', *Social Studies Review*, May, pp. 192-5.

MacGregor, S. (1981), *The Politics of Poverty,* Longman, London.

Mack, J. and Lansley, S. (1985), *Poor Britain*, George Allen, London.

Marsh, A. and McKay, S. (1993), *Families, Work and Benefits*, Policy Studies Institute, London.

Marsden, D. (1982), *Workless: An Exploration of the Social Contract Between Society and the Worker,* revised edition, Croom Helm, London.

McCarron, P.G., Davey-Smith, G. and Wormersley, J.J. (1994), 'Deprivation and Mortality: Increasing Differentials in Glasgow, 1979-1992', *British Medical Journal*, vol. 309, pp. 1481-2.

Meereboer, M.T.W. (ed) (1994), *Social (In)Security and Poverty as Global Issues*, Conference in preparation of the UN world summit on social development, Copenhagen, Maastricht, 4 and 5 March 1994, The Hague, Development Cooperation Information Department of the Ministry of Foreign Affairs.

Moore, J. (1989), *The End of the Line for Poverty*, Conservative Political Centre, London.

Narayan, D. (1997), *Voices of the Poor: Poverty and Social Capital in Tanzania*, The World Bank, Washington D.C.

Newman, B.A. and Thompson, R.J. (1989), 'Economic Growth and Social Development: A Longitudinal Analysis of Causal Priority', *World Development*, pp. 461-71.

Nissel, M. (1995), 'Social Trends and Social Change', *Journal of the Royal Statistical Society*.

Nolan, B. and Whelan, C.T. (1996), *Resources, Deprivation and Poverty*, Clarendon Press, Oxford.

Oldfield, N. and Yu, A.C.S (1993), *The Cost of a Child: Living Standards for the 1990s*, Child Poverty Action Group, London.

Oldfield, N. (1992), *Using Budget Standards to Estimate the Cost of Children*, Working Paper No. 15, Family Budget Unit, University of York.

ONS (1998), *How Exactly is Unemployment Measured?* Third edition, Office of National Statistics, London.

Oppenheim, C. (1990a), 'Count Me Out: Losing the Poor in the Numbers Game', *Poverty, Journal of the Child Poverty Action Group*, no. 76, Summer, pp. 11-14.

Oppenheim, C. (1990b), *Holes in the Safety Net*, Child Poverty Action Group, London.

Oppenheim, C. (1993), *Poverty: The Facts*, revised and updated edition, Child Poverty Action Group, London.

Oppenheim, C. and Harker, L. (1996), *Poverty: The Facts*, revised and updated 3rd edition, Child Poverty Action Group, London.

Osberg, L. (ed) (1991), *Economic Inequality and Poverty: International Perspectives*, Sharpe, New York and London.

Oxfam (1995), *Poverty Report*, Oxfam, Oxford.

Oyen, E., Miller, S.M. and Samad, S.A., (eds) (1996), *Poverty: A Global Review: Handbook on International Poverty Research*, Oslo, Scandinavian University Press.

Payer, C. (1982), *The World Bank: A Critical Analysis*, Monthly Review Press, New York.

Payer, C. (1991), *Lent and Lost: Foreign Credit and Third World Development*, Zed Books, London and New Jersey.

Payne, S. (1991), *Women, Health and Poverty: An Introduction*, Harvester, Hemel Hempstead.

Piachaud, D. (1979), *The Cost of a Child*, Child Poverty Action Group, London.

Piachaud, D. (1984), *Round About Fifty Hours a Week: The Time Costs of Children*, Child Poverty Action Group, London.

Phillimore, P., Beattie, A. and Townsend, P. (1994), 'Widening Inequality of Health in Northern England, 1981-1991', *British Medical Journal*, vol. 308, pp.1125-8.

Psacharapoulos, G., Morley, S., Fiszbein, A., Lee, H. and Wood, B. (1997), *Poverty and Income Distribution in Latin America: The Story of the 1980s*, The World Bank Technical Paper No. 351, The World Bank, Washington D.C.

Ravallion, M. (1993), *Poverty Comparisons: A Guide to Concepts and Methods*, LSMS Working Paper No. 88, The World Bank, Washington D.C.

Ravallion, M. (1994), *Poverty Comparisons*, Chur Harwood.

Ravallion, M. (1987), *Markets and Families*, Open University Press.

Ravallion, M. (1998), *Poverty Lines in Theory and Practice*, LSMS Working Paper No. 133, World Bank, Washington D.C.

Renwick, T.J. and Bergmann, B. (1993), 'A Budget-Based Definition of Poverty', *Journal of Human Resources*, vol.12, no.1, pp. 1-24.

Rex, J. and Moore, R. (1967), *Race, Community and Conflict: A Study of Sparkbrook*, OUP, London.

Rodgers, G. (1995), *New Approaches to Poverty Analysis and Policy- II: The Poverty Agenda and the ILO: Issues for research and action*, International Institute for Labour Studies, Geneva.

Rodgers, G. and van der Hoeven, R. (1995), *New Approaches to Poverty Analysis and Policy - III: The Poverty Agenda: Trends and Policy Options*, International Institute for Labour Studies, Geneva.

Room, G. (ed) (1995), *Beyond the Threshold: The Measurement and Analysis of Social Exclusion*, The Policy Press, Bristol.

Rose, D. and Sullivan, O. (1996), *Introducing Data Analysis for Social Scientists*, Open University Press.

Rose, H. (1994), *Love, Power and Knowledge: Towards a Feminist Transformation of the Sciences*, Polity Press, Cambridge.

Rowntree, S. (1937), *The Human Needs of Labour* (New Edition), Longmans, London.

Ruggles, P. (1990), *Drawing the Line: Alternative Measures and their Implications for Public Policy*, The Urban Institute Press, Washington D.C.

Runciman, W.G. (1966), *Relative Deprivation and Social Structure*, Routledge and Kegan Paul, London.

Scott, J. (1994), *Poverty and Wealth: Citizenship, Deprivation and Privilege*, Longmans, London and New York.

Sinfield *et al.* (1991), *Excluding Youth: Poverty Among Young People Living Away From Home: First Report*, University of Edinburgh, Centre for Social Welfare Research.

Smeeding, T.S., O'Higgins, M., Rainwater, L. and Atkinson, A.B. (1989), *Poverty, Inequality and Income Distribution in Comparative Perspective*, Simon and Schuster, London.

Social Security Committee (1991), *Low Income Statistics: Households Below Average Income Tables 1988, First Report, Session 1990-91*, House of Commons 401, HMSO, London.

Social Services Committee (1988), *Families on Low Income: Low Income Statistics, Fourth Report, Session 1987-88*, House of Commons 565, HMSO, London.

Social Services Committee (1989), *Minimum Income, Memoranda laid before the Committee, Session 1988-89*, House of Commons 579, HMSO, London.

Sparks, C. (ed) (1995), *Factfile '95*, NCH Action for Children, Rochester.

Subbarao K., *et al.* (1997), *Safety Net Programs and Poverty Reduction, Lessons from Cross-Country Experience*, The World Bank, Washington D.C.

Taylor-Gooby, P. (ed) (1999), *The End of the Welfare State?: Responses to State Retrenchment*, Routledge, London.

Thomas, R. (1998), 'The Politics of Unemployment and Employment Statistics', in D. Dorling and S. Simpson (eds), *Statistics and Society*, Arnold, London.

Titmuss, R. (1950) *Problems of Social Policy*, HMSO, London.

Townsend, P. (ed) (1970), *The Concept of Poverty*, Heinemann, London.

Townsend, P. (1979), *Poverty in the United Kingdom*, Allen Lane and Penguin, London and University of California Press, Berkeley.

Townsend, P. (1987), 'Deprivation', *Journal of Social Policy*, vol. 16, no. 2, pp. 125-46.

Townsend, P. *et al.* (1989), *Health and Deprivation: Inequality and the North*, Routledge, London.

Townsend, P. (1991a), *The Poor are Poorer: A Statistical Report on Changes in the Living Standards of Rich and Poor in the United Kingdom, 1979-1989*, No. 1, Bristol Statistical Monitoring Unit, University of Bristol, Department of Social Policy.

Townsend, P. (1991b), *Meaningful Statistics on Poverty 1991*, No. 2, Bristol Statistical Monitoring Unit, University of Bristol, Department of Social Policy.

Townsend, P. (1993a), *The International Analysis of Poverty*, Harvester Wheatsheaf, Milton Keynes.

Townsend, P. (1993b), 'The Repressive Nature and Extent of Poverty in the UK: Predisposing Cause of Crime', Symposium on the Link Between Poverty and Crime, Proceedings of the 11th Annual Conference of the Howard League on 'Poverty and Crime', 8th-10th September, 1993. Summary in *Criminal Justice*, the magazine of the Howard League, 11, 4 (October).

Townsend, P. (1994b), 'Possible Solutions for Poverty Alleviation', in T. Meereboer (ed), *Social (In)Security and Poverty as Global Issues, Poverty and Development: Analysis and Policy No. 10*, Ministry of Foreign Affairs, Development Cooperation Information Department, The Hague.

Townsend, P. (1995a), 'The Need for a New International Poverty Line', in K. Funken and P. Cooper (eds), *Old and New Poverty: The Challenge for Reform*, for the Friedrich Ebert Foundation, Rivers Oram Press, London.

Townsend, P. (1995b), 'Poverty in Eastern Europe: The Latest Manifestation of Global Polarisation', in G. Rodgers and R. van der Hoeven (eds), *New Approaches to Poverty Analysis and Policy III: The Poverty Agenda: Trends and Policy Options*, International Institute for Labour Studies, Geneva.

Townsend, P. (1997), 'Privatisation: The Search for the Right Balance Between the Public and the Private Sectors', 1997 Copenhagen Seminar, Royal Danish Ministry of Foreign Affairs, Copenhagen.

Townsend, P. (1998a), 'Ending World Poverty in the 21st Century', *Radical Statistics*, vol. 68, pp. 5-14.

Townsend, P. (1998b), *Will Poverty Get Worse Under Labour?*, New Waverley Papers, University of Edinburgh, Department of Social Work, Edinburgh, EH8 9LL.

Townsend, P. and Gordon, D. (1989), 'What is Enough?', in *House of Commons Social Services Committee, Minimum Income*, House of Commons 579, HMSO, London.

Townsend, P. and Gordon, D. (1992), *Unfinished Statistical Business on Low Incomes? A Review of New Proposals by the Department of Social Security for the Production of Public Information on Poverty*, No.3 in a series of reports from the Statistical Monitoring Unit, University of Bristol.

Townsend, P., Whitehead, M. and Davidson, N. (eds) (1992), *Inequalities in Health: The Black Report and the Health Divide*, Penguin, Harmondsworth.

Townsend, P. with Donkor, K. (1996), 'Global Restructuring and Social Policy: An Alternative Strategy: Establishing an International Welfare State', International seminar on *Economic Restructuring and Social Policy*, sponsored by UNRISD and UNDP, United Nations, New York, 1995, Policy Press, Bristol.

Townsend, P., Gordon, D., Bradshaw, J. and Gosschalk, B. (1997), *Absolute and Overall Poverty in Britain in 1997: What the Population Themselves Say*, Report of the Second MORI Survey, Bristol Statistical Monitoring Unit, Bristol.

United Nations (1995), The Copenhagen Declaration and Programme for Action: The World Summit for Social Development 6-12 March 1995, United Nations Department of Publications, New York.

UN (1996), 'Special Issue on the Social Summit', *Social Policy and Social Progress*, a review published by the United Nations, vol. 1, no. 1, UN Department of Publications, New York.

UNDP (1993), *Human Development Report 1993*, Oxford University Press, New York and Oxford.

UNDP (1995), *Human Development Report 1994*, Oxford University Press, New York and Oxford.

UNDP (1996), *Poverty Eradication: A Policy Framework for Country Strategies, a policy paper*, UNDP, New York.

UNDP (1997), *Human Development Report 1997*, Oxford University Press, New York and Oxford.

UNDP (1998), *Human Development Report 1998*, Oxford University Press, New York and Oxford.

UNRISD (1995a), *States of Disarray: the social effects of globalisation*, an UNRISD Report for the World Summit for Social Development, UNRISD, Geneva.

UNRISD (1995b), *Adjustment, Globalisation and Social Development*, Report of the UNRISD/UNDP International Seminar on Economic Restructuring and Social Policy, New York, January 1995, UNRISD, Geneva.

Vaughan, D.R. (1993), 'Exploring the Use of the Public's Views to Set Income Poverty Thresholds and Adjust Them Over Time', *Social Security Bulletin*, vol. 56, no. 2.

Vaughan, D.R. (1996), 'Self-Assessments of Income Needs and Financial Circumstances: Two Decades of Seeking a Place in Federal Household Surveys', Paper presented to the Government Statistics Section of the American Statistical Association, August 5 1996, Chicago, Illinois.

Veit-Wilson, J.H. (1987), 'Consensual Approaches to Poverty Lines and Social Security', *Journal of Social Policy*, vol. 16, no. 2, pp. 183-211.

Veit-Wilson, J.H. (1989), 'Memorandum', in *House of Commons Social Services Committee, Minimum Income*, House of Commons 579, HMSO, London.

Veit-Wilson, J. (1998), *Setting Adequacy Standards: How Governments Define Minimum Incomes*, Policy Press, Bristol.

Vic, G. (1985), *Ideology and Social Welfare*, Routledge, London.

Vogel, J. (1997), *Living Conditions and Inequality in The European Union 1997*, Statistics Sweden, University of Umea, Eurostat.

Ward (1998) *Perceptions of Poverty*, IDS Press.

Walker, A. and C. (1997), *Britain Divided: The Growth of Social Exclusion in the 1980s and 1990s*, CPAG, London.

Walker, R. (1987), 'Consensual Approaches to the Definition of Poverty: Towards an Alternative Methodology', *Journal of Social Policy*, vol. 16, no. 2, pp. 213-26.

Wedderburn, D. (1975), *Poverty, Inequality and Class Structure*, Cambridge.

Whiteford, P. (1981), 'The Concept of Poverty', *Social Security Journal*, published for the Australian Department of Social Security, December.

Whiteford, P. (1983), 'A Family's Needs: Equivalence Scales and Social Security', *Social Security Journal*, Melbourne.

Whiteford, P. (1985), *A Family's Needs: Equivalence Scales, Poverty and Social Security*, Research Paper No. 27, Development Division, Department of Social Security, Canberra

Williams, F. (1989), *Social Policy: A Critical Introduction: Issues of Race, Gender and Class*, Polity Press.

Williamson, J.B. (1997), 'A Critique of the Case for Privatising Social Security', *The Gerontologist*, vol. 17, no. 5, pp. 561-71.

Wolfson, M.C. and Evans, J.M. (1989), 'Statistics Canada's Low Income Cut-Offs: Methodological Concerns and Possibilities', Research Paper Series, Statistics Canada, Analytical Studies Branch.

Wootton, B. (1959), *Social Science and Social Pathology*, Allen and Unwin, London.

Wootton, B. (1962), *The Social Foundations of Wages Policy*, New Edition, Unwin University Books, London.

World Bank (1990), *World Development Report 1990: Poverty*, The World Bank, Washington D.C.

World Bank (1993a), *Implementing the World Bank's Strategy to Reduce Poverty: Progress and Challenges*, The World Bank, Washington D.C.

World Bank (1993b), *World Development Report 1993: Investing in Health*, Oxford University Press for the World Bank, Washington D.C. Appendix: Glossary of principal definitions.

World Bank (1994), *The World Bank and the Poorest Countries: Support for Development in the 1990s*, The World Bank, Washington D.C.

World Bank (1995a), *Advancing Social Development: A World Bank Contribution to the Social Summit*, The World Bank, Washington D.C.

World Bank (1995b), *Investing in People: The World Bank in Action*, The World Bank, Washington D.C.

World Bank (1996), *Poverty Reduction and the World Bank: Progress and Challenges in the 1990s*, The World Bank, Washington D.C.

World Bank (1997), *Poverty Reduction and the World Bank: Progress in Fiscal 1996 and 1997*, The World Bank, Washington D.C.

World Bank (1997), *The State in a Changing World: World Development Report 1997*, The World Bank, Washington D.C.

Worsley, P. (1987), *The New Introducing Sociology, 3rd Edition*, Penguin.

3 The Scientific Measurement of Poverty: Recent Theoretical Advances

DAVID GORDON

Introduction

This paper is based on the theoretical discussions on the measurement of poverty that have arisen as part of a new Joseph Rowntree Foundation project to update the *Breadline Britain* methodology of Mack and Lansley (1985) to include new concepts of 'social exclusion' and 'absolute' and 'overall' poverty. This methodological research is being undertaken collaboratively by research teams at the Universities of Bristol, Loughborough and York and at MORI. Many of the ideas in this paper are those of my co-researchers not my own. However, I take full responsibility for any errors in this paper.

In addition this paper will draw on the work and ideas of a wide range of European researchers; but particularly that of Ruud Muffels in the Netherlands (Muffels, 1993), Bjorn Halleröd in Sweden (Halleröd, 1995, 1998), Brian Nolan, Tim Callan and Christopher Whelan in Ireland (Callan and Nolan, 1991, Nolan and Whelan, 1996a, 1996b), and Jonathan Bradshaw, Peter Townsend and John Veit-Wilson in Britain (Bradshaw, 1993, 1996; Townsend, 1993, 1996; Veit-Wilson, 1998). In Europe much of this research has been funded by the European Union's Poverty 2 and 3 programmes (Ramprakash, 1996; Vogel, 1997). While much of the recent British work on poverty has been funded by the Rowntree Foundation (Hills, 1995, 1998; Kempson, 1996; Middleton *et al.*, 1996; Gordon and Pantazis, 1997; Lee and Murie, 1997; Dobson and Middleton, 1998).

What is Poverty?

Poverty is a widely used and understood concept but its definition is highly contested. The term 'poverty' can be considered to have a cluster of different overlapping meanings depending on what subject area or discourse is being examined (Gordon and Spicker, 1998). For example, poverty like evolution or health, is both a scientific and a moral concept. Many of the problems of measuring poverty arise because the moral and scientific concepts are often confused. In scientific terms, a person or household in Britain is 'poor' when they have both a low standard of living and a low income. They are not poor if they have a low income and a reasonable standard of living or if they have a low standard of living but a high income. Both low income and low standard of living can only be accurately measured relative to the norms of the person's or household's society.

A low standard of living is often measured by using a deprivation index (high deprivation equals a low standard of living) or by consumption expenditure (low consumption expenditure equals a low standard of living). Of these two methods, deprivation indices are more accurate since consumption expenditure is often only measured over a brief period and is obviously not independent of available income.

Figure 3.1 below illustrates this concept.

Figure 3.1   Definition of poverty

The 'objective' poverty line/threshold is shown in Figure 3.1, it can be defined as the point that maximises the differences **between** the two groups ('poor' and 'not poor') and minimises the differences **within** the two groups ('poor' and 'not poor'). Unfortunately, this can best be done using multivariate statistics (which makes it hard to explain) since there are no accurate equivalisation scales (Whiteford, 1985; Bradbury, 1989). Therefore, dummy variables for each different household type have to be put into the model (Townsend and Gordon, 1989). Usually some variant of the General Linear Model is used, such as, Discriminant analysis, MANOVA or Logistic Regression depending on the nature of the data.

This 'scientific' concept of poverty can be made universally applicable by using the broader concept of resources instead of just monetary income. It can then be applied in developing countries where barter and 'income in kind' can be as important as cash income. Poverty can then be defined as the point at which resources are so seriously below those commanded by the average individual or family that the poor are, in effect, excluded from ordinary living patterns, customs and activities. As resources for any individual or family are diminished, there is a point at which there occurs a sudden withdrawal from participation in the customs and activities sanctioned by the culture. The point at which withdrawal escalates disproportionately to falling resources can be defined as the poverty line or threshold (Townsend, 1979; Townsend and Gordon, 1989).

Income and Resources

The term 'resources' is often used in poverty studies but it is seldom discussed in detail. It is often assumed to be synonymous with 'usual' income in industrialised nations like Britain. However, the concept of resources is broader than just 'current' or 'usual' cash income. Income in many poverty studies is often used to refer only to the main component of monetary income for most households - i.e. wages and salaries or business income. Others use the term widely to include all receipts including lump sum receipts and receipts that draw on the household's capital.

Classically, income has been defined as the sum of consumption and change in net worth (wealth) in a period. This is known as the *Haig-Simons approach* (see Simons, 1938 in Atkinson and Stiglitz, 1980, p.260). Unfortunately, this approach fails to distinguish between the day-to-day 'living well' and the broader 'getting rich' aspects of individual or household finances (in technical terms, it fails to distinguish between current and capital receipts).

Recently, (January 1997) the Australian Bureau of Statistics (ABS) tried to get an international agreement on definitions of income, consumption, saving and wealth. The ABS (1995) has proposed the following definition:

> income comprises those receipts accruing (in cash and in-kind) that are of a regular and recurring nature, and are received by the household or its members at annual or more frequent intervals. It includes regular receipts from employment own business and from the lending of assets. It also includes transfer income from government, private institutions and other households. Income also includes the value of services provided from within the household via the use of an owner-occupied dwelling, other consumer durables owned by the household and unpaid household work. Income excludes capital receipts that are considered to be an addition to stocks, and receipts derived from the running down of assets or from the incurrence of a liability. It also excludes intra-household transfers.

Townsend (1979, 1993) has argued that broad definitions of income should be used, particularly if international comparisons are to be made. It is crucial, when comparing individual or household incomes of people in different countries, that account is taken of the value of government services in, for example, the fields of health, education and transport (Evandrou *et al.*, 1992). Unfortunately, attempts in Britain to measure income and wealth using broad definitions of these concepts have often ended in failure (Knight, 1980).

The concept of resources can be considered to encompass elements of human capital and therefore can be even wider than even a broad concept of income. A households resources can be considered to include both financial resources and the human resources of time, abilities and energy of each household member (Andreβ, 1998). However, in practice most poverty surveys in industrialised nations only analyses poverty in terms of 'usual' income and occasionally 'standard of living'. The rest of this paper will discuss poverty as defined in these terms.

The History and Criticisms of the Scientific Measurement of Poverty

The modern origin of scientific attempts to measure poverty can be traced to Peter Townsend's (1979) pioneering study of *Poverty in the UK*. Townsend devised 60 indicators of deprivation based on a detailed study of people's style of living and resources conducted in 2000 households between 1968-1969. These 60 indicators could be summed to create a single composite deprivation index score for each household. By plotting deprivation score against the log of income as a percentage of the Supplementary Benefit rates that existed then (Figure 2.2), Townsend determined, by eye, that a poverty threshold might exist at around 150 per cent of the Supplementary Benefit standard. This result has since been confirmed by weighted regression analysis and canonical correlation analysis that placed the threshold at 160 per cent of the Supplementary Benefit standard (Desai, 1986; Desai and Shah, 1988).

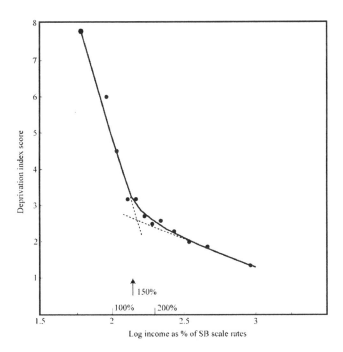

Figure 3.2   Modal deprivation by logarithm of income as a percentage of supplementary benefit scale rates (Townsend, 1979)

However, serious and detailed criticisms have been made by Professor Piachaud (1981, 1987) who argued that poverty couldn't be 'objectively' measured since:

- The deprivation indicators used by Townsend (1979) did not allow for the identification of the effects of personal choice from those of constraint (i.e. those who could not afford an item and those who did not want an item).
- The goal of objective, scientific measurement of poverty was not attainable.
- The poverty threshold does not exist. He postulated that there may not be a marked change in deprivation below a certain level, only a continuum.

Piachaud's first criticism, relating to the separation of choice from constraint, was overcome by the 1983 and 1990 *Breadline Britain* studies which identified both those households/people who '*don't have but don't want*' and those who '*don't have and can't afford*' an item. However, it must be noted that the results of Townsend's (1979) study were relatively robust (Desai, 1986). The 'rich' rarely choose to live like the 'poor' and the choices the 'poor' can make are generally constrained.

Piachaud's second criticism is, of course, key. If the objective, scientific measurement of poverty is unattainable, then 'poverty' surveys such as the *Breadline Britain* studies are of only limited academic value. In addition, poverty could never be conquered since it could never be adequately measured and the requisite steps taken to alleviate it. Fortunately, I believe that Piachaud is wrong. The scientific measurement of poverty is both possible and attainable.

The Problem of 'Experts'

The reasoning behind many claims that poverty cannot be measured 'objectively' is that, in order to measure deprivation, a selection of questions must first be drawn up by 'experts'. There is no 'objective' way of selecting these questions. They are just the experts' opinion of what is important. Even if a subset of these questions is also selected as important by the general population (the methodology of the *Breadline Britain* surveys), this selection can be made only on the basis of the larger group of questions the experts first chose. There may be better questions for measuring poverty that were not chosen and, if they had, a different result might have been obtained.

There are two separate issues here that will be dealt with in turn:

• Can the answers to a selection of deprivation questions, chosen by experts, ever form the basis of the scientific, objective measurement of poverty?

• If a different set of questions were asked, would the results be the same, i.e. is the measurement of poverty reliable?

Scientific Measurement

All scientific observations/measurements are theory-dependent. None can be independently objective. All measurement, whether it be the height of a person, the charge on an electron or the level of poverty, is dependent on the theory. There can be no objectively true value to these measurements that are independent of the theories that are used to measure them. As Albert Einstien famously stated, the theory tells you what you can observe (see Chalmers, 1978; The Economist, 1981; Shapere, 1982; Medwar, 1984; for discussion).

For a measurement of poverty to be 'scientific', the theory it is based upon must also be 'scientific'. The theory must not only be logically internally consistent but also fulfil a number of strict criteria.

1. The theory must be falsifiable, e.g. it must be capable of being shown to be untrue. The existence of a Loving God and Freudian psychology are unfalsifiable theories and therefore unscientific.
2. The theory must be testable.
3. The theory must have predictive value.
4. The results of the theory must be reproducible. Other people using the same methods will reach the same results.

These criteria are known to philosophers as the Falsificationist View of science and are attributable to the work of Karl Popper (1968, 1972). They contain the idea of a logical asymmetry that a theory can never be proved only falsified. This work has been extended by Imre Lakatos (1974), who claimed that scientific research programmes must also:

5.   Possess a degree of coherence that involves the mapping out of a definite programme for future research.
6.   Lead to the discovery of novel phenomena, at least occasionally.

Modern sociology often fulfils the second of Lakatos' requirements but rarely the first. For the measurement of poverty to be scientifically 'objective', the theory on which the measurement is based must fulfil the criteria of Popper and Lakatos. Both the relative and the consensual theories of poverty can make this claim (Gordon and Pantazis, 1997). For example, with respect to the relative deprivation theory of poverty as formulated by Townsend (1979), it can be shown that:

1.   The relative theory of poverty can be falsified. If a survey finds that there are no people/households whose resources are so low that they are excluded from the ordinary living patterns, customs and activities of their culture, then no poverty exists. For example, Kibbutz societies would have no poverty and several Scandinavian countries have little poverty.
2.   Surveys, such as the *Booth Centenary Survey*, have provided tests of the relative poverty theory.
3.   Numerous predictions are made by the relative poverty theory. For example, the 'poor' will experience a disproportionate 'fear of crime' (relative to their experience of crime) because of the greater consequences of crime for the 'poor' (Gordon and Pantazis, 1997).
4.   Several deprivation surveys have produced similar results, both in Britain and in other countries. Therefore, conclusions based on the relative poverty theory are reproducible.
5.   Since Townsend's (1979) initial work, extensive research on relative poverty has been carried out by many researchers in several countries. This research has extended and developed the concepts and findings of the relative poverty model. (For example, see the studies referenced Townsend and Gordon, 1989 and Grayson *et al.*, 1992.)
6.   A number of novel phenomena, predicted by the relative poverty theory, have been confirmed. The identification of poverty/deprivation as a major cause of ill health of equal or greater consequence to genetic, pathogenic and behavioural factors, has led to:
    i)   the recognition of the effects of stress on health, particularly cardiovascular disease (Blaxter, 1990);

ii)   the identification of some of the mechanisms by which poor housing conditions cause disease (Strachan, 1988); and

iii) the use of deprivation indicators in conjunction with workload factors as the best method for health resource allocation (Carstairs, 1981; Jarman, 1983).

Much of the recent research on the links between poverty and ill health in Britain has been stimulated by two influential reports (Davey-Smith *et al.*, 1990); '*The Black Report*' and '*The Health Divided*' (Townsend and Davidson, 1988; Whitehead, 1988). In both these reports the relative theory of poverty was central to the analysis.

Both the relative and consensual theories of poverty allow scientific measurements of poverty to be made.

Reliability

All measurement is subject to error which can take the form of either random variations or systematic bias (Stanley, 1971, lists many causes of bias). Random errors of measurement can never be completely eliminated. However, if the error is only small relative to size of the phenomena being studied, then the measurement will be reliable. Reliable measurements are repeatable, they have a high degree of precision.

The theory of measurement error has been developed mainly by psychologists and educationalists and its origins can be traced to the work of Spearman (1904). The most widely used model is the Domain-Sampling Model, although many of the key equations can be derived from other models based on different assumptions (see Nunnally, 1981, Chapters 5-9, for detailed discussion). The Domain-Sampling Model assumes that there is an infinite number of questions (or, at least, a large number of questions) that could be asked about deprivation. If you had an infinite amount of time, patience and research grant, you could ask every person/household all of these questions and then you would know everything about their level of deprivation, i.e. you would know their 'true' deprivation score. The 32 questions used in the *Breadline Britain in the 1990's* study can be considered to be a subset of this larger group (domain) of all possible questions about deprivation (Gordon and Pantazis, 1997).

Some questions will obviously be better at measuring deprivation than others, however, all of the questions that measure deprivation will have some common core. If they do not, they are not measuring deprivation by definition. Therefore, all the questions that measure deprivation should be intercorrelated such that the sum (or average) of all the correlations of one question, with all the others, will be the same for all questions (Nunnally, 1981). If this assumption is correct, then by measuring the average intercorrelation between the answers to the set of deprivation questions, it is possible to calculate both:

1.   an estimate of the correlation between the set of questions and the 'true' scores that would be obtained if the infinite set of all possible deprivation questions had been asked; and
2.   the average correlation between the set of questions asked (the deprivation index) and all other possible sets of deprivation questions (deprivation indices) of equal length (equal number of questions).

Both these correlations can be derived from Cronbach's Coefficient Alpha which, when transformed for use with dichotomous questions, is known as KR-20, short for Kurder-Richardson Formula 20 (Cronbach, 1951, 1976; Cronbach *et al.*, 1971; Kurder, 1970).

Cronbach's Coefficient Alpha is 0.8754 for the 32 questions used in the *Breadline Britain in the 1990s* study. This is the average correlation between these 32 questions and all the other possible sets of 32 questions that could be used to measure deprivation. The estimated correlation between the 32 Breadline Britain questions and the 'true' scores, from the infinite possible number of deprivation questions, is the square root of Coefficient Alpha, i.e. 0.9356.

Nunnally (1981) has argued that:

in the early stages of research ... one saves time and energy by working with instruments that have modest reliability, for which purpose reliabilities of 0.70 or higher will suffice ... for basic research, it can be argued that increasing reliabilities much beyond 0.80 is often wasteful of time and funds, at that level correlations are attenuated very little by measurement error.

Therefore, the Alpha Coefficient score of 0.87 for the Breadline Britain questions indicates that they have a high degree of reliability and also that effectively similar results would have been obtained if any other reliable set of 32 deprivation questions had been asked instead (Gordon and Pantazis, 1997).

Coefficient alpha can also be used to test the reliability of individual questions, Table 3.1 shows how the Alpha Coefficient would change if any single question was deleted from the deprivation index. There are only three questions (highlighted in bold) which would yield an increase in Alpha if they were removed.

The Poverty Threshold/Line

Piachaud's final major criticism of the 'relative' theory of poverty relates to the problem of identifying the poverty threshold/line; he considered that a continuum of life styles may exist. Piachaud (1981) comments that:

> The combination of two factors - that there is a diversity in styles of living, and that poverty is relative: mean that you would not, in fact, expect to find any threshold between the 'poor' and the rest of society.

Townsend (1979) originally identified the poverty line/threshold at 150 per cent of the Supplementary Benefit standard by observing the position of the break of slope on a graph of deprivation index plotted against the logarithm of income as a percentage of the Supplementary Benefit Scale that then existed (see Figure 3.2).

Regression analysis of Townsend's data showed that, statistically, the best position for the poverty line/threshold was at 160 per cent of the Supplementary Benefit standard (Desai, 1986; Desai and Shah, 1988). Piachaud (1987) argued that the poverty line/threshold was a statistical artefact resulting from the transformation of the income data (the reciprocal of income equivalised by the Supplementary Benefit scale was used). Piachaud objected to the reciprocal transformation (1 Income) rather than to the equivalisation procedure used (the 1968 Supplementary Benefit scale). Even though, the 1968 Supplementary Benefit scale was based largely on political rather than scientific criteria.

Table 3.1   Reliability analysis on the deprivation questions from Breadline Britain in the 1990s that more than 50 per cent of the population thinks are necessary and people should be able to afford

		Corrected item - total correlation	Alpha if item deleted
1	A damp-free home	.3672	.8726
2	**An inside toilet (not shared with another)**	**.0824**	**.8761**
3	Heating to warm living areas of the home if it's cold	.4031	.8720
4	Beds for everyone in the household	.2422	.8749
5	**Bath not shared with another household**	**.0512**	**.8763**
6	Enough money to keep your home in a decent state of repair	.5735	.8673
7	Fridge	.2100	.8752
8	A warm waterproof coat	.5072	.8696
9	Two meals a day (for adults)	.2648	.8746
10	Insurance of contents of dwelling	.5816	.8669
11	Fresh fruit and vegetables every day	.4853	.8698
12	Carpets in living rooms and bedrooms in the home	.2701	.8743
13	Meat or fish or vegetarian equivalent every other day	.3662	.8726
14	Celebrations on special occasions such as Christmas	.4306	.8713
15	Two pairs of all-weather shoes	.5600	.8680
16	Washing machine	.2578	.8746
17	Presents for friends or family once a year	.5227	.8689
18	Regular savings of £10 a month for 'rainy days'	.5002	.8723
19	A hobby or leisure activities	.4703	.8701

Table 3.1 (continued)

		Corrected item - total correlation	Alpha if item deleted
20	New, not second-hand clothes	.4582	.8706
21	A roast joint or its vegetarian equivalent once a week	.4566	.8705
22	**Television**	**.1478**	**.8757**
23	Telephone	.3746	.8729
24	An annual week's holiday away, not with relatives	.5717	.8681
25	A 'best outfit' for special occasions	.5460	.8680
Extra questions for families with children			
1	Three meals a day for children	.2875	.8745
2	Toys for children, e.g. dolls or models	.3200	.8740
3	Separate bedrooms for every child over ten of different sexes	.2540	.8747
4	Out of school activities, e.g. sports, orchestra, scouts	.4718	.8703
5	Leisure equipment for children, e.g. sports equipment or a bicycle	.4263	.8715
6	An outing for children once a week	.5012	.8694
7	Children's friend round for tea/snack once a fortnight	.4799	.8703

Coefficient Alpha for the 32 Questions = 0.8754

The criticism that the poverty threshold observed by Townsend (1979) was a statistical artefact that resulted from the procedures used to equivalise income is impossible to entirely refute. However, many different researchers using different poverty datasets and methods of equivalisation have detected poverty thresholds in British data. For example, recently, Halleröd, Bradshaw and Holmes (1997) independently analysed the *1990 Breadline Britain Survey* using the Proportional Deprivation (PDI) and Major Necessities (MNI) methods to weight the deprivation indices and various standard procedures to equivalise income[1] (see Figure 3.3 below). They concluded that:

> Both MNI and PDI scores increase as income falls and there is a clear threshold at about £150 per week where decreasing income leads to accelerated deprivation.

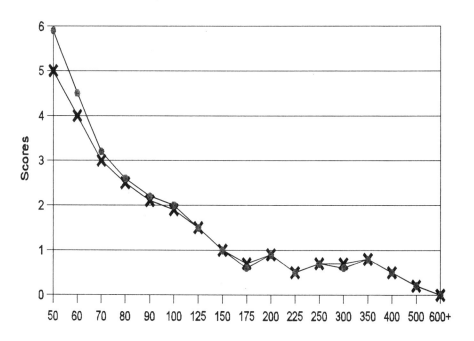

Figure 3.3 Relationship between equivalent household income and MNI and PDI showing a clear Poverty Threshold at £150 per week (Halleröd, Bradshaw and Holmes, 1997)

Halleröd (1995, 1998) has undertaken a comparative analysis of poverty in Britain and Sweden using the *1990 Breadline Britain Survey* and the *1992 Swedish Standard of Living Survey.* He found a clear poverty threshold in the British data but not in the Swedish data. It appears that the poverty threshold that has been found in Britain may be result from the interaction between the dynamics of poverty in Britain and the welfare state. In other industrialised countries with different dynamics of poverty and different welfare states a poverty threshold may not exist or may be less easy to detect. Piachaud (1981) may have been correct in doubting the existence of a poverty threshold in general but not about doubting the existence of a poverty threshold in Britain.

The Dynamics of Poverty in Britain

The question then remains why is such a clear poverty threshold found in British poverty surveys over the past 30 years. The answer lies in the way people become 'poor' in Britain and the way the welfare state and benefits system operates.

People/households in British poverty surveys with a high income and a high standard of living are not poor whereas those with a low income and a low standard of living are poor. However, two other groups of people/households that are 'not poor' can also be identified in a cross-sectional (one point in time) survey, such as *Breadline Britain Survey*:

1. *People/households with a low income but a high standard of living.* This group is not currently poor but if their income remains low they will become poor - they are currently sinking into poverty. This situation often arises when income falls rapidly (e.g. due to job loss) but people manage to maintain their life style, for at least a few months, by drawing on their savings.
2. *People/households with a high income but a low standard of living.* This group is currently 'not poor' and if their income remains high their standard of living will rise - they have risen out of poverty. This group is in the opposite situation to the previous group. This situation can arise when the income of someone who is poor suddenly increases (e.g. due to getting a job), however, it takes time before they are able to buy the things that they need to increase their standard of living. Income can both rise and fall faster than standard of living.

These two groups have been found in both British poverty surveys and Irish studies (Callan *et al.*, 1993, Nolan and Whelan, 1996a, 1996b). A cross-sectional 'poverty' survey can provide some limited but useful information on the dynamics of poverty since it is possible not only to identify the 'poor' and the 'not poor' but also those sinking into poverty (i.e. people/households with a low income but a high standard of living) and those escaping from poverty (i.e. people/households with a high income but a low standard of living).

Poverty is, by definition, an extremely unpleasant situation to live in so it is not surprising that people go to considerable lengths to avoid it and try very hard to escape from poverty once they have sunk into it. Therefore, a cross-sectional poverty survey ought to find that the group of households sinking into poverty was larger than the group escaping from poverty since, when income falls people will try to delay the descent into poverty, but if the income of a poor person increases she will quickly try to improve her standard of living.

Figure 3.4 illustrates this concept.

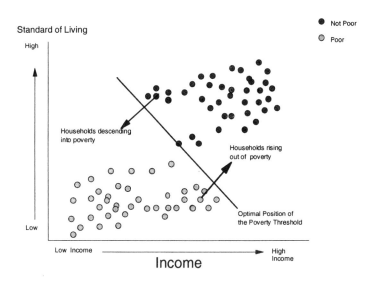

Figure 3.4   The dynamics of poverty

Between time 0 and 1 the household has both a high standard of living (dotted line) and a high income (solid line): it is 'not poor'. At time 1 there is a rapid reduction in income (e.g. due to job loss, the end of seasonal contract income, divorce or separation, etc.), however, the household's standard of living does not fall immediately. It is not until time 2 that the household's standard of living has also fallen below the 'poverty' threshold. Therefore, between time 1 and time 2, the household is 'not poor' but is sinking into poverty (i.e. it has a low income but a relatively high standard of living). Between time 2 and time 3 the household is living in poverty, they have both a low income and a low standard of living. At time 3 income begins to rise rapidly, although not as fast as it previously fell. This is because rapid income increases usually result from gaining employment but there is often a lag between starting work and getting paid. Standard of living also begins to rise after a brief period as the household spends its way out of poverty. However, this lag means that there is a short period when the household has a high income but a relatively low standard of living. By time 5 the household again has a high income and a high standard of living.

On the basis of this discussion, it is possible to update Figure 3.1 to give a more realistic picture of movements into and out of poverty. Figure 3.5 overleaf illustrates this.

In Figure 3.5, the sizes of the groups moving into and out of poverty have been exaggerated for clarity. However, it is clear that movements into and out of poverty tend to occur close to the X and Y-axes and there is little movement across the poverty threshold at the centre of the graph. Households in Britain typically become poor when their income falls precipitously followed by a gradual decline in their standard of living. Households rarely slide into poverty because their income and standard of living declines gradually together. Similarly, moves out of poverty tend to follow a rise in income followed by a rise in standard of living. It would be rarer for both income and standard of living to rise gradually together.

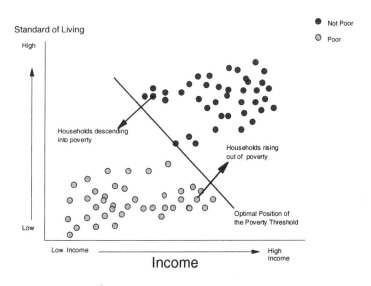

Figure 3.5   Movements into and out of poverty

Therefore, Piachaud's (1981) argument that there 'may not be a marked change in deprivation below a certain level, only a continuum of living styles' can probably be rejected on both theoretical and empirical grounds in Britain. People become 'poor' after their income has dropped catastrophically. However, they usually successfully manage to maintain a reasonable standard of living for a period after this drop in income. Similarly people stop being poor usual after a substantial rise in income (e.g. after finding a job, new partner, etc.). The major causes of poverty in Britain, job loss, family break-up, retirement, severe ill health, etc are all typified by rapid declines in income. Relatively few people in Britain suffer from a simultaneous decline or rise in both their standard of living and income which leads to a gradual decent into or rise out of poverty. Some pensioners who are supplementing their pension by drawing on a declining amount of capital may experience a simultaneous decline in both income and standard of living. However, this situation is comparatively rare compared with the other causes of poverty in Britain.

The benefits system in Britain also operates in a manner that accentuates the existence of poverty threshold/line. There is a large literature that identifies the numerous 'poverty traps' in the British benefits system, which result in 90 per cent or even over 100 per cent marginal 'tax' rates for people whose income rise slightly above the Income Support standard. Steep tapers in Housing Benefit and the withdraw of other 'passported' benefits results in there being a relatively large number of people with incomes on or just below the Income Support standard but relatively few people whose incomes are just above this level e.g. there are a lot of people/households whose income is 100 per cent of the 'benefit standard' but relatively few people/households with incomes of 105 per cent or 110 per cent of the 'benefit standard'.

People typically escape from the benefits system when they gain a new job which often pays substantially more than State Benefits. Therefore there is a gap between the incomes of those living on benefits and those in work. This gap has widened over the 1980s and 1990s in Britain due to the removal of the link between State Benefits and average earnings. This and the inadequacy of State Benefits has accentuated the poverty threshold/line in Britain.

Conclusion

The early attempts by Townsend (1979) to provide a scientific basis for measuring poverty were criticised by Piachaud (1981) on three grounds:

- The deprivation indicators used did not allow for the identification of the effects of personal choice from those of constraint.
- The goal of objective, scientific measurement of poverty was not attainable.
- The poverty threshold did not exist, only a continuum of living styles.

Over the past 18 years considerable progress has been made in the methodology of poverty research in both Britain and Europe and all of Piachaud's criticisms have been examined and answered.

The 'scientific' measurement of poverty is both achievable and desirable. Scientific definitions of poverty are of great importance. We can only eradicate poverty quickly if we can accurately measure the effectiveness of anti-poverty policies and this requires scientific measurement of poverty. To paraphrase the old 'Marxist' adage 'the purpose of poverty research is not just to understand the world, but to change it'.

Note

1   For example, the McClements and OECD scales.

References

Andreβ, H.J. (ed) (1998), *Empirical Poverty Research in a Comparative Perspective*, Ashgate, Aldershot.

Atkinson, A.B. and Stiglitz, J.E. (1980), *Lectures on Public Economics*, McGraw-Hill, London, xvi, 619.

Australian Bureau of Statistics (1995), *A Provisional Framework for Household Income, Consumption, Saving and Wealth*, Australian Government Publishing Service, Canberra.

Blaxter, M. (1990), *Health and Lifestyle*, Tavistock, London.

Booth, A. (1995), *British Economic Development Since 1945*, Manchester University Press.

Bradbury, B. (1989), 'Family Size Equivalence Scales and Survey Evaluations of Income and Well-Being', *Journal of Social Policy*, vol. 18, no. 3, pp.383-408.

Bradshaw, J. (ed) (1993), *Budget Standards for the United Kingdom*, Avebury, Aldershot.

Bradshaw, J. (1996), 'Family Policy and Family Poverty', *Policy Studies*, vol. 17, no. 2, pp.93-106.

Callan, T. and Nolan, B. (1991), 'Concepts of Poverty and the Poverty Line', *Journal of Economic Surveys*, vol. 5, no. 3, pp. 243-61.

Callan, T., Nolan, B. and Whelan, C.T. (1993), 'Resources, Deprivation and the Measurement of Poverty', *Journal of Social Policy*, vol. 22, no. 2, pp.141-72.

Carstairs, V. (1981), 'Multiple Deprivation and Health State', *Community Medicine*, vol. 3, pp.4-13.

Chalmers, A.F. (1978), *What is this thing called Science?*, The Open University Press, Milton Keynes.

Cronbach, L.J. (1951), 'Coefficient Alpha and the Internal Structure of Tests', *Psychometrika*, vol. 16, pp.297-334.

Cronbach, L.J. (1976), *Research on Classrooms and Schools: Formulation of Questions, Design and Analysis*, Stanford University Evaluation Consortium, Stanford.

Cronbach, L.J., Gleser, G.C., Nanda, H. and Rajaratnam, N. (1971), *The Dependability of Behavioural Measurements*, Wiley, New York.

Davey-Smith, G., Bartley, M. and Blane, D. (1990), 'The Black Report on Socio-economic Inequalities in Health 10 Years On', *British Medical Journal*, vol. 301, no. 1, pp.373-77.

Desai, M. (1986), 'Drawing the Line: On Defining the Poverty Threshold', in Golding, P. (ed), *Excluding the Poor*, Child Poverty Action Group, London.

Desai, M. and Shah, A. (1988), 'An Economic Approach to the Measurement of Poverty', *Oxford Economic Papers*, vol. 40, pp.505-22.

Dobson, B. and Middleton, S. (1998*), Paying to Care: The Cost of Childhood Disability*, York Publishing Services, York.

The Economist (1981), 'The Nature of Knowledge', *Economist*, December 26, pp.99-105.

Evandrou, M. Falkingham, J. Hills, J. and Le Grand, J. (1992), *The Distribution of Welfare Benefits in Kind*, Welfare State Programme Discussion Paper WSP/68, London School of Economics, London.

Gordon, D. and Pantazis, C. (eds) (1997), *Breadline Britain in the 1990's*. Ashgate, Aldershot.

Gordon, D. and Spicker, P. (eds) (1998), *CROP International Glossary of Poverty*, Zed Books, New York.

Grayson, L., Hobson, M. and Smith, B. (1992), *INLOGOV Informs on Poverty* vol. 3, issue 1, Institute of Local Government Studies, University of Birmingham, Birmingham.

Halleröd, B. (1995), 'The Truly Poor: Indirect and Direct Measurement of Consensual Poverty in Sweden', *Journal of European Social Policy*, vol. 5, no. 2, pp.111-29.

Halleröd, B. (1998), 'Poor Swedes, Poor Britons: A Comparative Analysis of Relative Deprivation', in Andreβ, H.J. (ed), *Empirical Poverty Research in a comparative Perspective*, Ashgate, Aldershot.

Halleröd B., Bradshaw, J. and Holmes, H. (1997), 'Adapting the Consensual Definition of Poverty', in Gordon, D. and Pantazis, C. (eds), *Breadline Britain in the 1990s*, Ashgate, Aldershot.

Hills, J. (ed) (1995), *Joseph Rowntree Inquiry into Income and Wealth*, 2 Vols., Joseph Rowntree Foundation, York.

Hills, J. (1998), *Income and Wealth: The Latest Evidence*, Joseph Rowntree Foundation, York.

Jarman, B. (1983) 'Identification of Underprivileged Areas', *British Medical Journal,* vol. 286, pp.1705-09.

Kempson, E. (1996*), Life on a Low Income*, York Publishing Services, York.

Knight, I. (1980), 'The Feasibility of Conducting a National Wealth Survey in Great Britain', *New Methodology Series NM6*, OPCS, London.

Kurder, F. (1970), 'Some Principles of Interest Measurement', *Educational and Psychological Measurement*, vol. 30, pp.205-26.

Lakatos, I. (1974), 'Falsification and the Methodology of Scientific Research Programmes', in Lakatos, I. and Musgrave, A.E. (eds), *Criticism and the Growth of Knowledge*, pp.91-196, Cambridge University Press, London.

Lee, P. and Murie, A. (1997), *Poverty, Housing Tenure and Social Exclusion*, Policy Press, Bristol.

Mack, J. and Lansley, S. (1985), *Poor Britain*, Allen and Unwin, London.

McClements L.D. (1978), *Economics and Social Security*, Heinemann, London.

Middleton, S., Ashworth, K. and Braithwaite, I. (1996*), Small Fortunes: Spending on Children, Childhood Poverty and Parental Sacrifice, Joseph Rowntree Foundation, York.

Medwar, P. (1984), *The Limits of Science*, Oxford University Press, Oxford.

Muffels, R. (1993), 'Deprivation Standard and Style of Living Indices', in Bergman, J. and Cantillon, B. (eds), *The European Face of Social Security*, Avebury, Aldershot.

Nolan, B. and Whelan, C.T. (1996a), *Resources, Deprivation and Poverty*, Clarendon Press, Oxford.

Nolan, B. and Whelan, C.T. (1996b), 'Measuring Poverty Using Income and Deprivation Indicators: Alternative Approaches', *Journal of European Social Policy*, vol. 6, no. 3, pp.225-40.

Nunnally, J.C. (1981), *Psychometric Theory*, Tate McGraw-Hill Publishing Company Ltd, New Delhi.

Piachaud, D. (1981), 'Peter Townsend and the Holy Grail', *New Society*, vol. 10, September.

Piachaud, D. (1987), 'Problems in the Definition and Measurement of Poverty', *Journal of Social Policy*, vol. 16, no. 2, pp.125-46.

Popper, K.R. (1968), *The Logic of Scientific Discovery*, Hutchinson, London.

Popper, K.R. (1972), *Objective Knowledge*, Oxford University Press, Oxford.

Ramprakash, D. (1996), *Social Trends*, Central Statistical Office, HMSO.

Shapere, D. (1982), 'The Concept of Observation in Science and Philosophy', *Philosophy of Science*, vol. 49, pp.485-525.

Spearman, C. (1904), 'General Intelligence Objectively Determined and Measured', *American Journal of Psychology*, vol. 15, pp.201-93.

Stanley, J.C. (1971), 'Reliability', in Thorndike, R.L. (ed), *Educational Measurement*, American Council on Education, Washington DC.

Strachan, D.P. (1988), 'Damp Housing and Childhood Asthma: Validation of Reporting Symptoms', *British Medical Journal*, vol. 297, pp.1223-26.

Townsend, P. (1979), *Poverty in the United Kingdom*, Allen Lane and Penguin Books, Harmondsworth, Middlesex and Berkeley, University of California Press.

Townsend, P. (1993), *The International Analysis of Poverty*, Harvester Wheatsheaf, Milton Keynes.

Townsend, P. (1996), *A Poor Future: Can we Counter Growing Poverty in Britain and Across the World*, Lemos and Crane, London.

Townsend, P. and Davidson, N. (1988), *Inequalities in Health: The Black Report*, 2nd edn., Penguin Books, London.

Townsend, P. and Gordon, D. (1989), What is enough? New evidence on poverty in Greater London allowing the definition of a minimum benefit. *Memorandum of evidence to the House of Commons Social Services Select Committee on Minimum Income 579*: 45-73, HMSO, London.

Veit-Wilson, J. (1998), *Setting Adequate Standards: How Governments Define Minimum Incomes*, Policy Press, Bristol.

Vogel, J. (1997), *Living Conditions and Inequality in the European Union 1997*, Eurostat Working Papers: Population and Social Conditions E/1997-3, Eurostat, Luxembourg.

Whitehead, M. (1988), *Inequalities in Health: The Health Divide*, 2nd edn., Penguin Books, London.

Whiteford, P. (1985), *A Family's Needs: Equivalence Scales, Poverty and Social Security*, Research Paper No. 27, Development Division, Australian Department of Social Security, Canberra.

4 Agreeing Poverty Lines: The Development of Consensual Budget Standards Methodology

SUE MIDDLETON

Introduction

> Most experts now consider that there is no objective way of reaching a definition of poverty just by basing it on physical needs, observing the world, or by asking the population for their views.
> (Roll, 1992)

In the last 12 months 'poverty' has re-entered the political lexicon after almost 20 years of, at worst, denial of its existence and, at best, insistence that it affects only a tiny proportion of the British population. Poverty is now back on the political agenda. Yet it seems that an agreed definition of what poverty is and how it is best measured is no nearer.

Methods for establishing poverty lines and measuring poverty variously define people as poor if they:

- have much lower than average incomes (income measures);
- spend much less than average (expenditure measures);
- are dependent for their income on benefits (benefit measures);
- believe themselves to be poor (self-assessed measures);
- have a standard of living lower than a pre-determined minimum (budget standards measures);
- lack certain goods and services which are believed by the majority of the population to be essential (consensual measures).

Each method has its advantages and disadvantages and it is not my intention to rehearse in this paper the long-running academic and political debates about the best method of setting 'poverty lines' (see Roll, 1992). Such debates have been ongoing in the United Kingdom since at least the latter years of the nineteenth century, when Seebohm Rowntree undertook his seminal work on poverty in York (Rowntree, 1902). The focus here is on the last three of the poverty measures: budget standards, self-assessed and consensual measures.

Rowntree used a method for defining minimum standards which developed into 'budget standards' methodology and which is now widely used throughout the world. Essentially budget standards are established by committees of experts who draw up a list of goods and services necessary for a particular household type to achieve a pre-determined standard of living. This list is then costed and the resulting figure is the 'budget standard'. The problem with this method is that it relies, in the final analysis, on the decisions of experts about what is 'necessary', which may not reflect how people spend their money or, indeed, the priorities of real families (Middleton *et al.*, 1994).

Budget standards were largely neglected in the United Kingdom for many years (although the methodology has been much used throughout Europe to set minimum living standards). Within the last ten years interest in budget standards has been revived, almost entirely as a result of the work of the Family Budget Unit (FBU), based at the University of York. The FBU used budget standards methodology to produce a range of budgets for different household types (Bradshaw, 1993). They improved on the methodology to some extent by drawing on the findings of surveys of household consumption in order to take into account items which most families have, and by consulting small groups of lay people. However, expert committees were still the driving force behind their budget standards. Consensual measures, more commonly referred to in recent years as 'democratic' measures, have at their crux the belief that if society is to accept a definition of poverty, and the consequent financial cost of trying to keep people out of poverty, then there needs to be agreement or 'consensus' in society about what constitutes a 'minimum'. People are asked, usually through surveys, about minimum income levels or ownership of particular goods and services which they believe are essential for people to have in 'today's society' Gordon and Pantazis, 1997). The minimum standard, or 'poverty line' produced by these methods is a list of goods and services which more than 50 per cent of the population believe to be essential. Poverty is then measured by the enforced lack of these necessities, that is the percentage of people who go without a pre-determined number of these 'socially perceived necessities' because they cannot afford them. These measures developed from the early work of Townsend (Townsend, 1979) and others on the concept of relative poverty and have been widely used in the UK and Europe. For example, the European Community Household Panel survey includes a number of such measures in an attempt to measure deprivation from a comparative perspective. Their strength lies in the consultative process with representative samples of the population about what people need in order to avoid poverty. They allow us to move away from expert judgements towards a more democratic understanding of the meaning of poverty.

However, there are a number of problems with these methods but the central difficulty lies in the very fact that they are survey based and, therefore, generate *'consensus by coincidence'* (Walker, 1987). As Walker pointed out, in an article in the Journal of Social Policy, consensus means more than a selection of individuals giving instant responses to a pre-determined survey question about what is essential.

> the danger is that the 'people' will mouth back what they think the 'experts' want to hear, or, perhaps more correctly, what they think the experts 'ought to hear'... the survey methodology will not have tapped the interactive process through which informed consensus is forged.
> (Walker, 1987)

Consensus is reached through a process of discussion, negotiation and eventual agreement, not by a selection of individuals giving 'top of the head' responses to a survey question.

Self-assessed measures have some similarity with consensual or democratic measures in that they rely on people making a judgement about what constitutes income inadequacy, or poverty for people, families or households in their circumstances. These measures usually take the form of asking survey respondents to estimate a level of income which they believe to be necessary to keep a family or household like theirs out of poverty (see for example, Hagenaars and de Vos, 1988). Poverty is then measured either by comparing this figure with reported income or by asking respondents to describe the extent to which their family or household income exceeds or falls short of this figure. The strength of these measures is that they ask people to consider the meaning of poverty in relation to their own family circumstances.

The difficulty lies in understanding how people approach the task of responding to such questions. How do they define poverty and what do they take into account in setting the level of income? They may simply think of their own family's income and reduce it or increase it by some amount. They might give a figure which relates to the currently obtaining benefit levels for a family like theirs. However, it could be argued that the respondent is really being asked to undertake an extremely complex task in the very short space of time which can be allowed in a survey situation. First, the respondent should decide what goods, services and activities are essential for her/his family to avoid poverty. Next s/he has to work out the cost of this mental list to the family. Finally, s/he has to decide what would be the lowest cost for which the list could be purchased. Recent research by the author suggests that, in fact, many people pluck a figure out of the air. Others are extremely uncertain about what is being asked of them - should they, for example, include the cost of their current accommodation or guess at the minimum cost of the cheapest possible form of housing in their area necessary to keep their family out of poverty? (Middleton, 1998).

To summarise, therefore, budget standards, socially perceived necessities and self-assessed measures for setting poverty lines and measuring poverty all have great strengths but serious weaknesses. Some years ago the Centre for Research in Social Policy began to consider how a methodology might be developed which played to the strengths of these measures, whilst avoiding the pitfalls of 'expert' judgements, 'plucking a figure out of the air' and 'consensus by coincidence'. Our starting point was Walker's suggestion that,

> the consensual definition of a monetary poverty line would be derived from the deliberations of a series of group discussions.
> (Walker, 1987)

The Methodology

A method has been developed which uses a variant of focus group methodology to define poverty lines.[1] People living in the household circumstances for which it is aimed to construct a minimum essential budget standard, (pensioners, lone parents, single males and so on). are brought together to act as their own budget standards committees. Each group is carefully sampled to include people from differing social backgrounds and economic circumstances. Similar methods developed in New Zealand have included in groups only people in deprived economic circumstances (Sawrey and Waldegrave, undated). In our view mixed groups are essential. The aim of the research is to achieve a consensus and this cannot be done by isolating people in differing socio-economic circumstances from each other. Furthermore, asking deprived people to set poverty lines is simply asking them to define their own poverty.

Each group begins by discussing and agreeing a definition of 'essential minimum'. The definition usually adopted by groups is adapted from the United Nations definition of an adequate lifestyle,

> things which are necessary for a person's physical, mental, spiritual, moral and social well-being.

It will be noted that this definition does not mention the financial resources available to households, and groups are also encouraged to avoid considerations of cost as far as possible. There are a number of reasons for this, the most important of which is that as soon as people begin to discuss incomes and costs issues of spending patterns arise. This gives rise to judgements about whether some groups of the population are more 'deserving' than others. Since the aim of the research is to produce budget standards which apply to **all** people in similar household types, such discussions need to be avoided.

Figure 4.1 describes the process of the methodology as it was developed for our first piece of research to establish agreed poverty lines for children. Group discussions take place in three phases. The first phase, or **orientation phase**, explores the language concepts and priorities which people use in thinking about spending and consumption. This phase was particularly important to subsequent research undertaken to establish agreed poverty lines for children with disabilities. The orientation groups of parents having children with severe disabilities developed pen pictures of notional children with different combinations of disabilities which parents felt would differentiate between spending patterns.

Prior to the second phase participants are asked to complete consumption diaries and inventories of clothing, furniture and other household items. This provides a necessary context for negotiation of the budget standards, encouraging participants to begin to think about the things which they own and consume. In other words, it helps to ensure that an informed consensus is reached - participants are negotiating lists of necessities on the basis of a knowledge of their own standards of living.

In the **task groups**, which form the second phase of the research, each budget area is considered in turn; clothing, activities, furniture and so on.. Participants are first asked to allocate each item which they own or consume to one of three categories 'Essential', 'Desirable' or 'Luxury'. They are then asked to produce an agreed list of items which they feel to be an essential minimum for someone in their circumstances, or in the case of children, for a child living in Britain today. This is achieved by working as a group through the lists in their diaries and inventories and deciding among themselves which items are essential. The groups are also asked to agree:

- the number of each items which are necessary;
- the proportion of new to second hand which is acceptable;
- durability or replacement rates;
- where items should be bought.

A different approach is necessary for some budget components. The agreed essential minimum list for food, for example, is arrived at by groups first compiling an agreed minimum diet for one day and then considering the need for variation in that diet. Groups discuss whether anything should be allowed for entertaining friends and relatives or eating outside the home. An amount of money is also agreed to maintain stores of dry goods and groceries. Minimum amounts of money are also allocated for budget components such as activities and holidays where individual choice must inevitably play a part.

The facilitator intervenes as little as possible in the discussions and negotiations. Her role is to record decisions reached on a flip chart; to move the negotiations along - particularly if discussions become deadlocked; to remind the group when necessary of the definition of essential minimum to which they are working; and to ensure that all aspects of the budget are covered. On completion of each budget component the group is asked to consider their list in its entirety and say whether they feel they have been too restrictive or too generous in their judgements.

Once all the task groups have been completed the lists are amalgamated and costed at shops recommended by participants. Any judgements made by researchers in costing lists are noted. Food is costed by constructing menus for one week, on the basis of the decisions reached in the task groups, and turning these menus into a shopping list for food. Transcripts of the discussions in the task groups are examined to identify outstanding issues which need to be resolved in the final phase of the groups. Uncosted lists of items agreed by the task groups are drawn up.

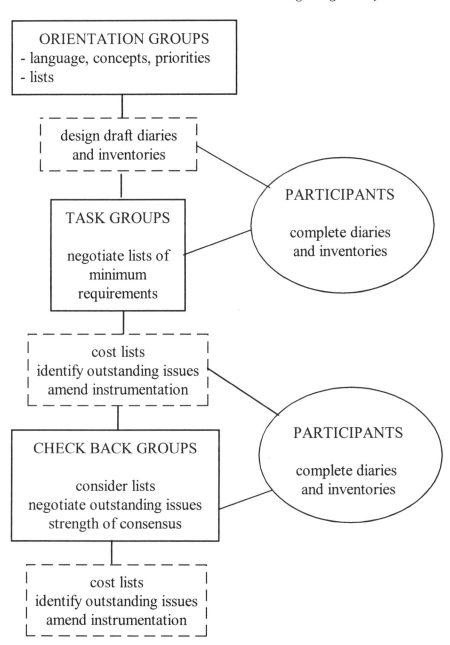

Figure 4.1 Research process

The final phase of groups, or **check-back** phase, is in some ways the most important. As well as resolving outstanding issues, the strength of the consensus which has been reached needs to be tested. When participants arrive at the group they are given the uncosted list of items compiled in the task groups. The purpose of the meeting is explained to them as in the task groups and they are asked to go through the list ticking those items which they think are essential and crossing those items which are not. The group then works through the lists together, discussing items in each budget area and reaching a final consensus. Outstanding issues are resolved. Throughout a second researcher makes amendments to the costing produced by the task groups.

The strength of the consensus is tested in two stages. First, once agreement has been reached on each budget component, participants are told how much it would cost to provide the agreed list of items. They are asked whether they think the amount is too high or too low and, in the light of this, whether they wish to remove items from or add to the list. This is repeated for the overall costed budget. Secondly, the budgets are set in a national policy context. The facilitator asks the group to imagine that she is the Chancellor of the Exchequer and that they have come to her with their budget to be told that, unfortunately, the country cannot afford to ensure that every person in their circumstances has all the items on the lists. They are asked how they would respond. Would they be prepared to reduce the budget or not and, if so, how?

On completion of the check back phase the budget lists are recosted and amended in the light of decisions reached and the final budget standards are compiled.

Since the original consensual minimum budget standards for children were produced in 1994, budget standards have also been developed for children with severe disabilities (Dobson and Middleton, 1998). As part of their contribution to the International Year for the Eradication of Poverty, the States of Jersey commissioned a pilot project to begin to establish minimum household budgetary requirements for people living in Jersey. There is concern that significant levels of 'hidden' poverty exist in Jersey but that there is no method of identifying its extent or severity. To date, poverty lines have been agreed for single female pensioners and lone parents living in Jersey and the next stage is to produce agreed poverty line for remaining household types (Middleton, 1997). This is unproblematic for those households comprising a single adult: single males and females of working age and single male pensioners. The challenge is to refine and adapt the methodology to enable minimum budget standards to be agreed for households with more than one adult, for example, couples of working age with no children. In other words, a method is needed which will allow groups of **individual** adults to arrive at agreed budgets for **all** adults in a household.

A number of issues arise:

- how to measure and allow for economies of scale involved in having more than one individual in a household;
- how to take into account the potentially differing lifestyles of families with and without children;
- the need to agree budgets for 'public goods', that is commodities which are shared by all members of the household, such as washing machines, furniture and so on.
- how to avoid a situation where budgets are constructed by one individual in a household reflecting on and agreeing the needs of other adults.

These issues will be resolved in the following manner. During the task group phase gender specific groups of people living in households with more than one adult will be recruited. Each group will draw up essential lists for an individual of their gender and then consider the additional needs of a second adult of the opposite sex. The check back groups will contain a mixture of men and women to negotiate and agree the final budget lists for two adult households. The budgets for individual adults (and children) in particular household types can then be added together, taking into account the economies of scale defined by the groups. This has the added advantage of allowing budgets for public goods to be considered by both male and female members of similar households.

Agreed Poverty Lines

In the remainder of this paper some of the agreed poverty lines which have been developed to date are described and compared with benefit levels and other budget standards. Some of the priorities of the groups in drawing up their minimum budget standards are also described.

Children

Table 4.1 compares the agreed poverty line for children with amounts allowed in Income Support calculations for children, including an element to take account of the family premium.[2] It is assumed that the child is living in a two parent, two child household.

Table 4.1   Minimum budget standards and income support

	Parent's essential minimum budget	Income support plus family premium	Percentage difference[a]
Under two years	£26.49 (G) £26.33 (B)	£20.68[b]	- 28 (G) - 27 (B)
Two to five years	£30.73 (G) £32.25 (B)	£20.68[b]	- 49 (G) - 56 (B)
Six to ten years	£28.12 (G) £27.67 (B)	£20.68[b]	- 36 (G) - 34 (B)
Eleven to sixteen years	£31.04 (G) £31.09 (B)	£28.03[c]	- 11 (G) - 11 (B)

[a] Percentage difference between income support plus family premium and parent's essential minimum budget.
[b] Child aged under 11 years
[c] Child aged 11 - 15 years

The Income Support rate in 1994/5 would need to have been increased by between 11 per cent and 56 per cent to meet the agreed poverty line. Children in the two to five year age group fare particularly badly, whilst the shortfall is smallest for 11-16 year olds. These findings suggest that Income Support allowances for all children are insufficient to meet what parents consider to be necessary to keep children out of poverty. Further, the age relativities in benefit calculations do not reflect the patterns of relative need identified by parents. This finding has been confirmed by other research undertaken by the author on actual spending patterns on children (Middleton *et al.,* 1997). It seems that whilst the needs of children do, in general, increase with age they do so by nowhere near as much as is implied by increases in Income Support allowances. The result is that younger children are particularly disadvantaged in benefit calculations.

Direct comparisons of the agreed poverty line for children with the Family Budget Unit's low cost budget for children are difficult since they include different elements, reflecting the differing priorities of mothers and experts (Oldfield and Yu, 1993). However, on average the FBU's low cost budget was approximately 25 per cent lower than the agreed poverty line. Most of this difference can be explained by the different approach which mothers took to drawing up the budget standard, in particular their emphasis on 'participation'. The extent to which mothers stressed the right of every child to fully participate in the life of the community in which they live was striking. They reiterated again and again the need for every child to be able to 'fit in', not to be 'singled out' from their peers.

> Eleanor   with your first, it's got to have everything in't it? If it'd got to have a bright red nose you'd punch it.

Three further priorities were identified in the way in which mothers negotiated the minimum budgets for children. First, there was a view that society should prioritise the needs of its children above everything else in order to ensure the future health of society.

> Sally   ... they've got to look at it as an investment in the future. He (the Chancellor) would invest in, I don't know, British Telecom ... but they won't invest in the children's future. And I think the children's future is more important than a telephone.

Second, there was the flip side view of what might happen to children who weren't allowed this essential minimum. Mothers were concerned that continual deprivation can have serious negative effects on children, perhaps even leading to crime.

Jan   I mean, it sounds exaggerated, but you don't know, if you tell them they can't do anything because you can't afford it, are they going to turn to other means to get the money so they can do it? ... I mean you don't know what road you're pushing them down, you know, crime and ...

Third, mothers contrasted what they saw as the very limited amounts which they had allowed in the lists with what their own children had, as in this conversation between three mothers of 6-10 year old children.

Ann   I mean you've not given them the things you'd like to give them, you're only giving them the bare essentials.

Sandy   How would you feel if your children had to manage on that?

Laura   Gutted.

Finally, they contrasted what they saw as the privileged material position of the Chancellor as a parent with their own situation.

Jane   I bet your children went to all these things.

Alison   Bet they had private schooling as well.

Jane   More!

This is not to say that mothers were unaware of the dangers of giving children too much, of spooling them. Their budgets did not make allowance for designer label clothes, videos or even computers, despite a recognition of the increasing educational pressure for children to have access to computers at home. Mothers genuinely felt that their lists represented an absolute basic minimum and the consensus which they reached was extremely strong.

Single Female Pensioners and Lone Parents

The agreed poverty lines for single female pensioners and lone parents are shown in Figure 4.2 and are compared, respectively, with the basic retirement pension in Jersey and the maximum benefit which a lone parent with two children, aged eight years and 12 years, might receive. A couple of points about the benefits system in Jersey need to be explained. First, the state retirement pension is higher than on the mainland. Second, there is no unified system of means-tested benefits on Jersey to which people, such as lone parents, automatically become entitled when their incomes fall below certain levels. People who find themselves without an (adequate) income have to apply to their local Parish for assistance. Whilst there are recommended levels of support, the granting of benefit, the amount and the length of time for which it is paid is discretionary. Therefore, the amounts of Parish Welfare for lone parents included in Figure 4.2 are based on the assumption that the lone parent receives the maximum recommended benefit from her Parish.

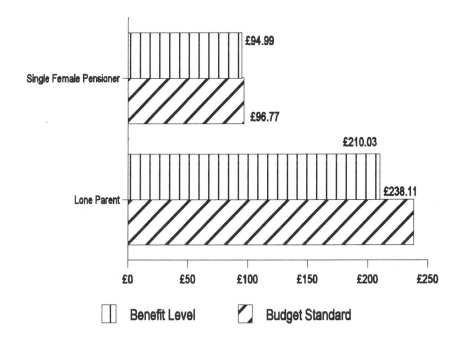

Figure 4.2   Minimum budget standards and benefit levels in Jersey

Old Age Pensions would need to be increased by just two per cent to ensure that the minimum standard of living for single female pensioners could be achieved. The lone parent family would need their benefits increased by 13 per cent to achieve a minimum standard of living.

Pensioners and lone parents had somewhat different priorities in drawing up the minimum essential budgets. For the pensioners items included were all essential to allow a lifestyle on Jersey which would combine survival with a little dignity and self-respect.

> Barbara   It's what every pensioner should be entitled to (Yes, yes) to live a life with a bit of dignity.

For many of the pensioners the final costed budget was very close to what they lived on themselves, and they did not consider their lifestyle to be extravagant by any means.

> Doris   We've not exactly been over-generous.

> Freda   And I mean these are only basics really.

> May   I don't think we've been over-generous. We've just taken a general ... just a middle. A minimum she would need money-wise.

When asked to consider whether they would reduce their lists if the Treasurer to the States said that the budget could not be afforded, a number of themes emerged. First, the pensioners felt strongly that there is a lot of misallocation of resources by the States which, if rectified, could be used to assist pensioners. Wage increases for States personnel and 'wasteful' schemes were particularly singled out for criticism.

> Freda   You should save something on the higher-ups payments. All these big knobs who get these tremendous wages. I mean look at the top civil servants who just got a big whack and all the ordinary workers are being kept to a very low minimum. In other words the most get more and the least get less.

> Barbara   Cut down on the waste of money on things people don't want.

> May   They spend money on a load of rubbish. All the money they're spending on the waterfront. Nobody wants all that.

Second, the pensioners felt that they had a right to a decent standard of living because of their past contributions to the Island, both generally and specifically.

Barbara   Well I think all old age pensioners in Jersey should be well looked after because its what they've put into the Island to make the Island what it is today. It's not newcomers into the Island that's made the island. It's the very old people, my parents before me, my generation. The next generation, what are they going to do, what are they going to put into the Island?

Freda   We've all worked and we've all paid our insurance and our taxes so we're entitled to it.

Finally, the group believed that to make pensioners manage on less was an affront to their dignity and deprived them of a standard of living to which everyone has a right.

May   I mean you've got a right to a living, not just to exist haven't you? You've got a right to a bit of luxury.

Doris   You want a bit of dignity as well, don't you?
             (Yes, yes).

May   You just don't want to exist you want to live, don't you?

Freda   You don't want to have to crawl for every penny.

The main difference between the pensioners and lone parent groups was that the pensioners felt that their budgets reflected what they themselves managed on. The lone parents, in contrast, lived on a lot less than the budget they had agreed but felt strongly that they should not have to do so.

Denise   We all live on a lot less but we all think we should have that as a minimum.

Overall, they were finding it harder to survive financially than the single female pensioners. Many were dependent on their own parents to survive.

Belinda   If I didn't have my parents I'd be struggling.

Denise   I think a lot of single parents in Jersey have to rely on their parents.

Others   Absolutely.

The over-riding concern of the lone parents was to meet the needs of their children which, to some extent, meant meeting their own needs. As a result their priorities bore more relationship with the priorities of mothers in setting the earlier minimum budgets for children than with the pensioners. Their children always came first but, even so, they were concerned about the effects of their frugal lifestyle on the children. They felt that they had not been over-generous and that their budgets realistically reflected the high cost of living on Jersey. The lone parents felt that Jersey should make better provision for them, if only because their children 'are the future'. Help with childcare costs, if nothing else, would make a great deal of difference and would also make sense in policy terms.

Denise   Childcare is the biggy - that's what we'd appreciate. They want women to work because they don't want an influx of people into the Island so they ought to help with childcare.

Conclusion

A number of methodological and policy conclusions have emerged to date from these negotiations of agreed poverty lines. First, it is perfectly possible for groups of people from differing socio-economic circumstances to reach an informed consensus on a poverty line for people in their household circumstances. The methodology could have vast potential in other social policy areas, such as negotiation and consensus formation on options for possible future reforms of the social security system. Its advantage lies in the emphasis on **informed** consensus. Participants are encouraged to think about and reflect on their own living standards before the group begins. They are constructing poverty lines for people in similar household circumstances to themselves. In other words, this is **not** 'government by focus group', designed to identify which policy options, benefit levels, or poor people are viewed as most deserving by particular groups of the electorate. Participants in such groups are frequently being asked to consider and reflect on matters about which prior to the group they have thought rarely, know little and, often, care less.

Second, the agreed poverty lines are not 'wish lists' representing what everyone should be able to have in an ideal world. They are the absolute minimum which people believe to be necessary for a dignified and participatory lifestyle in the communities which they live. Therefore, they avoid accusations of excessive generosity on the part of researchers which have been levelled at earlier, conventionally constructed budget standards.

Third, the budget standards can be regularly updated to reflect changes in prices and, from time to time, by reconstructing the budgets in order to reflect changing perceptions of minimum essential needs within society. In other words, the method can allow for the fact that poverty is not a concept which remains unchanged with the passing of time.

Fourth, although the budget standards so far derived suggest that benefit levels are inadequate, the differences are not so large as to make it unthinkable in policy terms that the standards could be met. For example, increases of between £3 and £12 per week would bridge the gap for children. This provides supportive evidence for those qualitative studies which have suggested that relatively small increases in benefit would make a great deal of difference to the lives of poor families. At the very least, some redistribution of benefits in favour of younger children would seem to be worth considering.

Finally, establishing agreed poverty lines for the UK as a whole using this methodology could lead to a much wider consensus about the meaning and measurement of poverty in our society. This might help us to move away from the somewhat sterile debates of recent years about whether poverty exists at all in the UK towards agreement about ow best to tackle its manifestations. Until we can agree some definition of what poverty is, we cannot debate sensibly its nature, extent or, indeed, how best to improve the living standards of those experiencing it.

Notes

1   The research to develop the methodology was funded in the first instance by the Joseph Rowntree Foundation for whose support the author is extremely grateful.

2   Family premium is not, of course, intended necessarily to be spent directly on children. The decision to include it was in order to reflect the inclusion in the budget standard of some household goods, such as televisions and washing machines.

References

Bradshaw, J. (ed) (1993), *Budget Standards for the United Kingdom*, Avebury, Aldershot.

Dobson, B. and Middleton, S. (1998), *The Financial Cost of Childhood Disability*, Joseph Rowntree Foundation, York.

Gordon, D. and Pantazis, C. (1997), *Breadline Britain in the 1990s*, Ashgate, Aldershot.

Hagenaars, A. and de Vos, K. (1988), 'The Definition and Measurement of Poverty', *Journal of Human Resources,* vol. 23, pp. 211-21.

Middleton, S. (1997), 'Household Budgetary Requirements in Jersey: Report of a Pilot Project', CRSP Working Paper 296a, Centre for Research in Social Policy, Loughborough.

Middleton, S. (1998), 'Perceptions of Poverty and Social Exclusion: Report of a Development Project', Centre for Research in Social Policy, Loughborough.

Middleton, S., Ashworth, K. and Braithwaite, I. (1997), 'Small Fortunes: Spending on Children, Childhood Poverty and Parental Sacrifice', Centre for Research in Social Policy, Loughborough.

Middleton, S., Ashworth, K. and Walker, R. (1994), *Family Fortunes: Pressures on Parents and Children in the 1990s*, Child Poverty Action Group, London.

Oldfield, N. and Yu, A. (1993), *The Cost of a Child: Living Standards for the 1990s*, Child Poverty Action Group, London.

Roll, J. (1992), *Understanding Poverty: A Guide to the Concepts and Measures,* Family Policy Studies Centre, London, p. 5.

Rowntree, S. (1902), *Poverty: A Study of Town Life*, Macmillan, London.

Sawrey, R. and Waldegrave, C. (undated), 'Minimum Adequate Income: Maori and Pacific Island Focus Group Study', Social Policy Unit, The Family Centre, Lower Hutt, New Zealand (mimeo).

Townsend, P. (1979), *Poverty in the United Kingdom: A Survey of Household Resources and Living Standards*, Allen Lane and Penguin Books, London.

Walker, R. (1987), Consensual Approaches to Poverty Lines and Social Security', *Journal of Social Policy*, vol. 16, pp. 213-26.

5 Developing the Use of Administrative Data to Study Poverty

GEORGE SMITH and MICHAEL NOBLE

Background

There are, no doubt, many ways of studying poverty and the poor. What is so impressive in looking back at landmark enquires such as Seebohm Rowntree's 'investigation into the social and economic conditions of the wage-earning classes' in York at the turn of the century (Rowntree, 1902), is the number of different methods that were used. Thus Rowntree himself argues against the 'extensive' method of drawing simply on official and other statistics on the grounds that these would produce a picture that 'would be very incomplete and of doubtful service', in favour of the 'intensive' study of a single town. Along with that of Booth, Rowntree's work has been claimed as one of the precursors of statistical surveys (Grebenik and Moser, 1962) through its direct collection and analysis of data at the individual level. It could also be placed firmly in the line of detailed geographical mapping studies, or into the series of case studies of towns and cities, that have continued to be a feature of social research in Britain. The enquiry is also a source both of qualitative case studies of individual families and their budgets, as well as the very quantitative setting of a poverty line. It might also, to squeeze in our own particular interests, be claimed as an early example of using administrative data. Thus Rowntree makes clear that while some data on income was obtained directly from the households, in the majority of cases it was estimated - 'the information' he rather coyly notes -'at the disposal of the writer enabling him to do this with considerable accuracy' (Rowntree, 1902, 1905). He was of course referring to the wages paid at a large factory in York with which he had 'an intimate acquaintance'.

Since Rowntree's time these different methods have grown out of all recognition and become specialist fields in their own right. The dry and unwieldy official statistics of that period, often the result of successive aggregation of data from the local level upwards, have become far more user friendly and capable of further analysis. And they have been increasingly complemented in the post war period by the development of large-scale social surveys, such as the Family Expenditure Survey (FES) (from 1957), the General Household Survey (GHS) (from 1971), Labour Force Survey (LFS) (from 1984) and most recently Family Resources Survey (FRS) (from 1992). This development was itself heavily dependent on the growth of computing power since the 1960s to process and analyse such survey data routinely. Case study and qualitative methods also continue to form an important contribution to the study of poverty (Kempson, 1996).

In this paper we want to draw attention to the recent developments in the use of administrative data to throw light on many aspects of poverty and low income. We will draw mainly on our own work since 1988, though we are by no means the only group involved in this development. Nor is it restricted to the UK. By 'administrative data' we mean information that is not *primarily* collected for research or analysis purposes, but directly for use in providing services, assessments or administrative record keeping. Administrative data has of course often been used in research studies, for example research that has sampled or researched files or other records by hand, but this has always been highly labour intensive (and therefore by definition cannot be routine). It often raises questions of sampling - how is the 'population' defined and information selected? Administrative data also raises questions of access - how is this obtained and by whom? We should concede immediately that there is a continuum between many of the traditional sources of official statistics and 'administrative data'. Thus until at least the 1980's the official monthly unemployment 'headline' count in Britain was based on aggregating up information on 'lodged NI (national insurance) cards' at Department of Employment local offices, and the quarterly 'age and duration' unemployment statistics based on a more elaborate (hand) count. These were then aggregated up from the local returns to the district, regional and national data.

The latter part of the 1980's was marked by the growing use of computer held information for administrative purposes. The increasing sophistication of both hardware and software over this period meant that the power to access, manipulate and routinely link this information to other sets of data developed rapidly. Some legislative changes in the late 1980's also gave impetus to computerisation, particularly with data which can be used to study poverty and low income.

Thus prior to the implementation of the Social Security Act in 1986 in

April 1988, individual housing (HB) record forms tended to be held on computers in a *static* 'card index' format (that is, simply recording the relevant information and the benefit currently in payment). Very few systems provided for the computerised calculation of benefit. The 1988 reforms increased the complexity of the housing benefit calculation whilst making it eminently more reducible to a computer algorithm. The reason was that the amount of discretion in what could be paid had been virtually eliminated in these reforms. Thus since April 1988 HB records have increasingly been held in a *dynamic* format where the information held on individual claimants provides the basis for *automatic* calculations of benefit, with the end product being the printing of cheque in payment or some form of credit transfer.

Such developments are not restricted to HB. Thus in education, centrally held teacher pension records have been analysed to give much more information about the age and working profile of teachers. The secondary school league tables published each year for England are now the result of exam boards streaming all individual pupil data to a central point where they can be merged at individual pupil level and aggregated by school or exam centre through the national Department for Education and Employment (DfEE) (replacing an earlier sample 'survey' of schools). Her Majesty's Inspectors (HMI) of schools have always 'retrieved' information from school inspection reports to throw light on issues of educational concern. From the 1980's this became semi-automated through the 'key-word' searches, but from 1992 onwards with the development of the OFSTED inspection system, a searchable on-line Educational Information System (EIS) has built up containing text and data on all inspections and reports in England, in literally tens of thousands of documents.

These developments, particularly that of data or record linkage, raise '1984' type questions. We have something to say on this aspect, but the main purpose of this paper is to draw the attention of the researchers to the uses of such administrative data. We do this first by tracing briefly the development of our own work from the late 1980's onwards. We then look at some of the advantages and disadvantages of using administrative data, including some of the 'data protection' issues, before concluding that such administrative data is an increasingly important resource for the study of poverty and low income. Researchers probably lag well behind administrative and certainly commercial usage of this form of information gathering - the very first outside group to contact us over our earlier mapping work on low income (Noble and Smith, 1996) was an association of mortgage brokers wanting to know whether it would help them identify doubtful areas of mortgage lending. Like all information there is potential for good or ill usage. But with increasing computing power, ease of access and record linkage, we doubt it can be ignored.

Developing the Use of Administrative Data

Most of the examples used in this paper are drawn from our work on housing benefit/council tax benefit (HB/CTB) data. Though these are effectively national benefits covered by standard rules, they are administered by local district authorities. Housing Benefit is paid to anyone who is responsible for rent like payments and is on a low income. Council tax benefit is paid to both tenants and owner-occupiers on a low income. People receiving the basic 'social assistance' benefit income support (referred to as 'IS cases') receive these benefits by virtue of this fact. People not on IS but otherwise on a low income can receive these benefits if their income and capital falls within prescribed limits (referred to as 'non-IS cases).

Amendments to the housing benefit scheme in 1988 provided the impetus for local authorities, which had not already done so to computerise their HB systems. In 1988 we still had property tax known as 'general rates' and housing benefit (and the systems to administer it) covered both rent and rates. Local authorities were free to develop whatever software they wished 'in-house' or purchase it from a burgeoning number of commercial vendors. The advent of the 'Poll Tax' under Mrs Thatcher (and hence Community Charge Benefit) in 1991, and its replacement by Council Tax in 1993 meant that major software revisions were required. It also meant that a few authorities developed separate systems for housing benefit and (now) council tax benefit. A recent survey we have undertaken jointly with the Local Government Management Board (LMGB) Anti Poverty Unit gives an idea of the diversity of such software. There are currently 475 HB/CTB authorities using their own 'in house' systems. Put another way London with its 33 Boroughs uses 18 different systems. Metropolitan boroughs in England (36) use 21 different systems while non metropolitan districts and unitaries in England (297 authorities) use 66 different systems. In Scotland the 71 authorities use 34 different systems while the 38 authorities in Wales use 17 systems. Of the proprietary systems the 'brand leader' is ICL with 118 users, followed by CAPITA with 52 users and Mcdonnell Douglas with 38.

The HB/CTB data set includes both tenants and owner-occupiers, people on IS and people whose income is slightly above IS levels. As well as people living in their own or rented accommodation, the data also contain people living in bed and breakfast or hostel accommodation. These are very large data-sets. Thus in Oxford and Oldham where we have done extensive work, typically about 25 per cent of the *total* population is accounted for on the HB system; in 1993/4 there were over 15,000 claimants in Oxford, representing with dependents 26,000 people, and in Oldham 29,000 claimants representing 52,000 people.

The HB/CTB system is thus a powerful source of information on those on low income. Not only is the data set wide in its coverage of those on low income, it also has a large number of variables. It contains information on the age and sex of the claimant, partner and any dependent children. It contains details of housing costs, council tax liability as well as details of HB/CTB in payment. For non-IS cases, it contains full details of income sources, including other benefits in payment, to whom payable, amounts etc. It also contains limited information on hours worked.

The data for our analyses are extracted from these benefit calculator programs. Anonymised (but postcoded) individual records of 'live cases' are extracted. Care is taken to avoid double counting especially where separate systems are used for both HB and CTB. The actual variables extracted will vary depending on the systems in use, how the systems hold the data and what tools or programs are available for extraction.

1.   When we began these studies we used these extracts to establish the numbers and categories of claimants on the system, and also to calculate the impact of changes in benefit levels following the 1988 changes and later reforms in benefit (Noble, Smith *et al.*, 1989; Noble, Knights *et al.*, 1989; Noble *et al.*, 1990; Smith *et al.*, 1991; Noble *et al.*, 1997). Subsequently we used extracted data to assess the take-up of benefits such as family credit or disability benefits (Noble *et al.*, 1992; Daly and Noble, 1996). In principle these research mechanisms could be, and have been, converted to action by local authorities. Thus the calculations can be used to notify a 'prima facie' eligible group of a particular benefit in a form of 'targeted take-up' - and they can be sent relevant 'take-up' information. Or it could be used to identify non-IS claimants who have 100 per cent rebates on their housing and council tax and may therefore be eligible for some income support.

2.   In the early 1990s we began to experiment with geographical mapping of this HB/CTB data as much as of the data was by then postcoded. This was again the result of a combination of technical developments (such as the availability of Geographical Information Systems (GIS) packages) and the HB/CTB data being increasingly postcoded (that is the addressed line ended with a full 6/7 digit code), as the Post Office introduced incentives for bulk mail users such as local authorities, postcoding their mail. Critically, this postcoding enabled us to relate the HB/CTB data to a number of other data sources available at local level, such as the 1991 census (Noble and Smith, 1996) and other administrative data (Social Services data) (Noble and Smith, 1994) and particular local facilities and estimations of 'saturation' in relation to particular service provision (Noble and Smith, 1994); that is, we could look to see how far the number of nursery places in a particular locality fitted with the actual numbers of pre-school children in a relevant age group in low in come households.

3.   The increasing availability postcoded HB/CTB data lead on to a number of studies helping local authorities identify potential 'poverty priority areas'. Though this began in urban areas and conurbations such as Oldham and Birmingham, a significant development has been in the mapping of rural poverty with 'shire counties such as Dorset, Oxfordshire, Shropshire and Wiltshire. Further developments in mapping have involved systems that include information on additional variables, for example on ethnic groups in the Birmingham area (such as a project underway on 'Race, Place and Poverty').

4.   A further development emerges in areas where we have undertaken repeated extracts of the HB/CTB data. This is the possibility of longitudinal analysis. This might be possible simply using repeated 'time cuts' as is done with something like the FES trend analysis over time (Goodman and Webb, 1994). However, in some HB/CTB systems 'person reference numbers' are retained even if there is a period not claiming. It is thus in principle possible to track claimants over time. This we have done in the latest study to address the question of movement on and off low income benefits particularly by lone and couple parents (Noble *et al.*, 1998).

We take up these two last developments in more detail later in this chapter.

Analysing Administrative Data: Some Advantages and Disadvantages

So far we have demonstrated something of the range of work possible using administrative data of this type. An obvious advantage is access at relatively low cost to very large amounts of information which has been collected and verified. As this is dynamic information it is normally right up to date. We are, at the time of writing (mid 1998), already analysing 1998 data. Because of its 'population' (rather than sample) nature it is also possible to study groups that are relatively rare and would normally require complex screening surveys to pick up. For example two groups we have studied are male lone parents, who comprise about five to six per cent of lone parents on low income benefits, and those in board and lodging or hostel accommodation, another relatively small group. The obvious limitations of the data are that is restricted to those on the system and to information collected for benefit purposes only. Here we explore two major objections that have been made to the e use of this data.

Do HB/CTB Data Capture All Those on Income Support?

It has been argued that a major weakness of the HB/CTB data is that it will fail to capture all those in receipt of income support. We have seen that the combined use of HB and CTB data captures both tenants and owner occupiers. But what of those who are **not** responsible for either housing costs or council tax? Important groups here would be people living in tied or rent/council tax free accommodation. Another group of 'missed' income support claimants would be those potentially eligible for HB or CTB but who have non dependents whose circumstances are such that any entitlement to HB/CTB is extinguished by 'non dependent deductions'.

These groups undoubtedly exist. How big are they? To what extent does using HB/CTB data underestimate those in receipt of income support?

We have undertaken a small validation study using Department of Social Security (DSS) income support data from the August 1995 100 per cent scan of cases. We have had limited access to individual level (but anonymised) 1995 100 per cent scan IS data from the DSS. This covered a large area of southern England, including several districts for which we had HB/CTB data. In one area in particular we had HB/CTB data for 30 June 1995 representing a close temporal match to the DSS data.[1]

Although we could not (nor had any wish to) match the data at individual level, we were able to make comparisons at a district (and, indeed at a sub district level).

For the area in question the DSS data revealed 11222 claimants, whereas the HB/CTB data revealed 8,804 claimants (78.4 per cent). We cannot necessarily assume that one data set is wrong and the other right - at this point we have only limited information about the nature of the DSS data and its extraction. It may be that it uses less tough criteria for inclusion than we employ with HB/CTB data where only 'live' cases in payment are counted not those in process or under deliberation.

However we can obtain more insight by looking at particular claimant groups. Thus for lone parents the HB/CTB data actually shows slightly **more** claimants than the DSS data (2,095 as against 2,035). This is easily accounted for by the fact that the DSS classification is through receipt of the lone parent premium, whereas the HB/CTB classification uses actual family configuration (i.e. single person plus dependent child(ren). An examination of the age distribution of lone parents on IS from each data source is shown in Figure 5.1. From this we see a remarkable fit between the two distributions (Pearson.988 Spearman.983 p<.01).

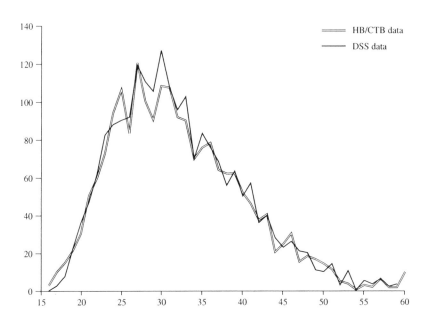

Figure 5.1   Lone parents in test area. Income support cases from both DSS and local authority HB/CTB. Age distribution

If we look at two parent families 812 are represented in the DSS data as compared to 696 in the HB/CTB data - 85.7 per cent. If we look at the age distributions we again get excellent correlations (Pearson .941; Spearman .915 p<.01); and a good match between the two age distributions (Figure 5.2).

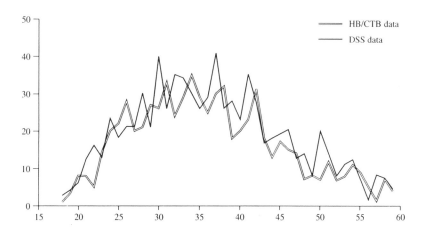

Figure 5.2   Two parent families in test area. Income support cases from both DSS and local authority HB/CTB. Age distribution

The fact that the DSS data runs ahead of the HB/CTB data for middle aged claimants suggests that we may be looking at the effect of 'grown up' children extinguishing entitlements to HB/CTB through non-dependent deductions.

The HB/CTB data is, as we might predict, at its weakest with single non pensioners. We find the fewest (3,412 - 58.4 per cent) in the HB/CTB system when compared to the DSS data (5,839). If we examine the age distributions the correlations are also weakest with the rank correlation better (Pearson.927; Spearman.941). The plot (Figure 5.3) shows the distributions we would expect from the presence of non dependent IS claimants, typically teenagers or early 20 year olds remaining at home.

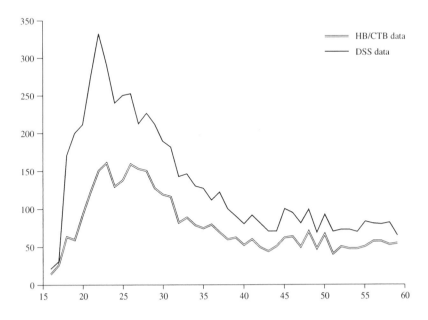

Figure 5.3   Single non-pensioners in test area. Income support cases from both DSS and local authority HB/CTB. Age distribution

For pensioners, 2,354 are represented on the HB/CTB data as compared to 2787 on the DSS data (84.5 per cent). The pensioners distribution (Figure 5.4) is interesting in several ways. First, correlation between the two data sets is good (Pearson.978; Spearman.964 p<.01). Second, as one might expect, with some pensioners living as non dependents with their children or other relatives, the HB/CTB data slightly lags behind the DSS data. Third, the shape of the curve shows the effect of the premium thresholds for the pensioner groups, with a rise in the numbers falling into entitlement as each premium threshold is reached despite the declining numbers of pensioners with advancing age.

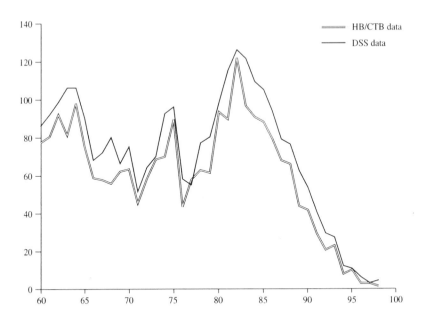

Figure 5.4   Pensioners in test area. Income support cases from both DSS and local authority HB/CTB. Age distribution

To What Extent are Non-income Support Cases Comparable in Different Areas?

One major advantage of the HB/CTB data is that it includes people on low incomes who are not receiving IS. As we have seen, this includes a variety of groups: those whose income is above income support level, those who work and whose hours take them outside the IS eligibility level, those who work and whose hours take them outside the IS eligibility level criteria irrespective of income; those who would otherwise be able to maintain a claim for IS but have not so claimed. As we can see from Table 5.1 as many as 50 per cent of HB/CTB claimants in many areas are receiving HB/CTB benefits other than as income support claimants. As the table shows for some groups (especially pensioners) the percentage on the data as non IS claimants may be considerably higher than this.

Table 5.1   Per cent of non-income support claims in total HB/CTB system; selected areas

	Old	Dav	Chr	Pur	Osw	Ken	Bir
Single pensioner	51	55	50	56	41	54	42
Couple pensioner	68	75	63	67	53	75	61
Single non pensioner	34	38	31	42	29	36	18
Lone parent	27	25	19	22	21	24	15
Couple parent	51	49	43	56	34	54	28
Overall	45	49	44	50	36	49	32

Key: Old = Oldham; Dav = Daventry; Chr = Christchurch; Pur = Purbeck; Osw = Oswestry; Bir = Birmingham

Data on non-income support cases thus adds considerable depth to the analysis of low income households, particularly with the current policy emphasis on moving claimants from basic social assistance to in-work benefits. However, what about comparability? Entitlement to both HB and CTB varies with rent and council tax levels. In a high rent area people with higher levels of income will be entitled to *more* help than similar income groups in a low rent area. Even after 'netting off' benefit entitlement and housing costs there will still be a disparity. This is not to suggest that in high rent areas some of the people falling within the HB/CTB envelope are in any sense **not** on a low income. It is simply to say that in another low rent area someone with the same similar 'after housing costs' (AHC) income may not appear on the data set at all.

As we (and others) have argued elsewhere this makes inter district comparisons (and, arguably some intra-district comparisons) using non income support data difficult (Kempson and Bennett, 1997). However the different shape of this 'envelope' is calculable. If we know the income distribution in an area and rent levels for equivalent properties it is possible to estimate the extent to which the populations in different local authority areas are comparable. The chart below (Figure 5.5) shows the amount of housing benefit for different incomes (net of housing costs) at rent levels of £30 and £60 per week. This shows graphically that those with an AHC income between £149.45 and £165 will appear on the data set if the rent for a particular property is £60 per week but would not appear on it if the rent were £30 per week.

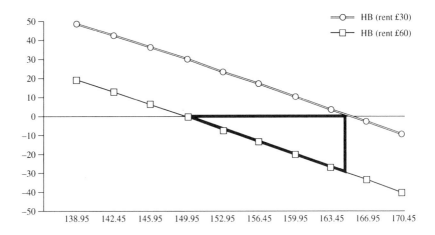

Figure 5.5   The non income support housing benefit 'envelope'

The Use of Administrative Data in Studying Poverty and Deprivation

While the administrative data we have used has limitations, and in some studies we have carried out has had to be supplemented by other sources of information such as postal questionnaires and interviews, in several important areas it offers unique possibilities for research purposes, policy and practise. We illustrate two examples from our own work.

Mapping Income Deprivation

Area measures of poverty have an important role in post war social policy. Successive governments from the mid 1960s have recognised the attraction of targeting resources at areas of poverty and low income. We have thus seen a succession of programmes from the Education Priority Areas in the 1960s through the Community Development Projects, the Urban Programme, the Single Regeneration Budget and now Health and Education Action Zones in 1998 which have relied (or still rely) to a greater or lesser extent on the ability to identify deprivation at the small area level. Normally data to estimate deprivation at this local level consistently between different areas has had to use census data usually formulated into indices. Perhaps the most important in policy terms (if not academically) have been the 'official' DoE (Department of the Environment) (now DETR - Department of the Environment, Transport and Regions) 'z' scores derived from 1981 census data and the Index of Local Conditions derived from the 1991 census data and the Index of Local Conditions derived from the 1991 census data. Typically these indices seek to measure a number of aspects of 'multiple deprivation' but at small area level these usually resolve themselves into income deprivation and housing stress. For income deprivation, the 1981 index relies heavily on the inclusion of 'at risk' groups such as 'single parent households' and 'pensioners living alone'. By contrast the 1991 index sought more direct variables such as 'no access to car' and 'children living in low earning households' (DoE, 1994).

However, even the more sophisticated 1991 index has been heavily criticised, particularly for its capacity to identify areas of income deprivation outside the major conurbations (Noble, Cheung *et al.*, 1995 Lee *et al.*, 1995; West Midlands Low Pay Unit and West Midlands Joint Data Team, 1996). Administrative data by contrast provides up to date measures of income deprivation at the very local level.

First, the comprehensive postcoding of the HB/CTB data has meant that for a number of authorities we have been able to map the whereabouts of claimants of income support and other means tested benefits. The data has allowed us to distinguish various types of claimant, for example, pensioners, lone and couple parents, those claiming disability benefits etc. This can have some very important policy advantages over a more general index of deprivation, for example in the targeting of resources for specific groups (Noble and Smith, 1994).

Second, using the known distributions of claimants we have been able to construct indices using census variables which better predict deprivation than the DETR Inex of Local Conditions (Noble, Cheung *et al.,* 1995; Bishops Advisory Group on Urban Priority Areas, 1995). This has enabled local authorities which do not have access to HB/CTB or other direct measures of income deprivation to map low incomes in their areas. Furthermore the index has been used by the Church of England to aid in its distribution of the Church Urban Fund to deprived areas (Bishops' Advisory Group on Urban Priority Areas, 1995).

The availability of nationally referenced data sets giving robust and up to date information on income deprivation must surely be an important supplement to, if not supplant, indices measuring 'multiple deprivation'. 1996 national income support data is now becoming available from the DSS at ward level and discussions are in train to make to make available ED level data.

The Time Dimension: Longitudinal Data

Apart from the direct measures of low income provided, one of the significant advantages of both HB/CTB data and (to a lesser extent) DSS IS data over data derived from the decennial census of the population, is potentially out of date by the time of publication normally some two years after the census is taken. By contrast HB/CTB extracts may be taken at regular intervals a year or even six months apart, giving up to date information on patterns of claiming which is invaluable to those devising anti-poverty policies.

There is another way in which the dynamic nature of the HB/CTB data can be harnessed to inform studies of poverty. As we have noted, in some areas the HB/CTB calculator programmes assign a unique number to each person referenced on the system whether claimant, partner, dependent child or non-dependent. Once assigned, this number is retained indefinitely even when the person is no longer claiming benefit. Such a system allows the tracking of individuals in and out of the system and allows a study of social security benefits which parallels studies of 'welfare dynamics' in the United States. We have used these techniques to examine the claiming patterns of lone mothers (Noble, Cheung and Smith,1998; Noble, Smith and Cheung, 1998) and are currently examining the claiming patterns of other parent groups - lone fathers and couple parents over a four year period. While there are problems in tracking cases who move out of the benefit envelope altogether, and issues of geographical mobility out of the area, administrative data allows large numbers of cases to be tracked over time. Thus, in a single urban area, we typically have data at any one time on more than 3,000 lone mothers, 200 lone fathers and 1,800 couple parents on IS, plus another large group on NS. These numbers are substantially larger than could be achieved except at enormous costs by specially mounted survey, and compare with something like 140 lone mothers on benefit in the British Household Panel Study (BHP) (August1992) and 550 lone parents in total in the follow-up to the 1958 birth cohort (NCDS).

Data Protection

The Data Protection Act (DPA) 1984 establishes principles on the use of computerised data. These principles cover the collection of data, the holding of data and the uses to which data can be put. It gives individuals limited but important protection from mis-application of data held about them (Birkinshaw, 1990). The DPA applies only to 'personal information' held in 'soft' form. Thus, the use of HB/CTB data for research purposes appears to come within the scope of data protection. In particular, data extracted at an individual level would seem to fall within the remit of the legislation. However, all extracts of the data are made without name or address (except postcode) and there is some doubt therefore as to whether this is 'personal information' within the meaning of the legislation. Certainly, early consultations with the Data Protection Registrar suggested that there was a 'key' whereby individuals could be named from the data, then this extract from the HB/CTB data did not constitute 'personal information' in DPA terms.

The situation has now changed. The current view of the Data Protection Registrar would seem to be that postcoded data - particularly that which contains dates of birth would, in certain circumstances allow the identification of individuals, if released at individual level. However, even in these circumstances, the DPR is content provided the data are processed with a view to releasing information only at the aggregate (DPR, 1997).

Where we have linked HB/CTB with other data this has been at the local area aggregate level. The use of the 'postcode to ED' look-up table itself also effectively blurs the position. Postcode areas do not exactly match to EDs and therefore it is not possible to be sure from the presentation of ED or other aggregate level data, for example, grid squares, whether any individual case in fact lies within the area or just outside.

Conclusion

In this paper we have set out to demonstrate the value of using administrative data in the study of poverty and low income at the local level. In particular we have focused on the use of local authority housing benefit/council tax benefit data, though we are also working with data from national agencies at one end and individual school level data at the other. We have illustrated the way this data can be used by describing developments in our work since 1988. We have underlined the way that technical developments in both hardware and software have made use of administrative data increasingly possible. The initial extract of HB/CTB data from a local authority took many long hours to decipher and check. Now extracts from systems with which we have previously worked can be quite routine. We have also reviewed the scope of the information held on low income households in local authority HB/CTB systems with comparable data held by national agencies and we have explored the problems of comparing HB data from non-income support cases between different local authority areas. We draw attention to particular uses of this administrative data in providing ways of identifying priority areas at the local authority level, and to its use as a possible longitudinal data-base in studying 'benefit dynamics'. Finally we review briefly the data protection question.

In conclusion we would underline the advantages of using such administrative data for research purposes. First, it has already been collected and much of the information is directly verified, that is claimants have to provide documentary evidence as part of their claim (only the FRS survey, in our experience, includes benefit data of a comparable quality). Second, it is up to date; and third there are large enough numbers of cases for local area cases for local area studies or the study of otherwise elusive groups, such as lone fathers. Finally, the cost of collection and data mounting has already been met. There are of course no reasons why the administrative data needs to be from the local level, and we have already undertaken work for a national agency where we had data on approximately 140.000 cases in one conurbation. All this is not to say that there are not limitations to this data. Clearly the major one is the question of the administrative 'envelope'; that is cases only fall within the scope of a particular system because they currently meet its requirements (and decide to apply). The information recorded is normally only that required for a specific purpose (though there is often a surprising amount of redundant information).

Clearly administrative data forms only part of the information necessary to study poverty and low income. It does not rule out the need for detailed surveys, case studies or other statistics. However, as we have shown, it is a rapidly moving field with new options and possibilities emerging. We would underline again that academic researchers probably lag behind the use of administrative data within central government and certainly within the commercial sector, though here the interest in poverty and low income is often to develop more sophisticated ways of 'redlining' or identifying risky groups or areas, so that they can be avoided.

If Rowntree had been studying York at the end of the 20th rather than the 19th century, we have little doubt that he would have used such administrative data along with other sources of information, as his able successors (Huby and Bradshaw, 1998 or this volume) have done in their contemporary study of York. He might, of course, have had rather more difficulty getting hold of the income data from a certain large factory in York, as it is no longer a family business but part of multi-national corporation.

Note

1   In addition to its Quarterly Statistical Enquiry (QSE) which is based on a five per cent sample of cases, the DSS takes a 100 per cent scan of its income support caseload on an annual basis. The last such scan was taken in August 1996. These scans contain limited individual level data. The data are very reliably postcoded.

References

Birkinshaw, P. (1990), *Government and Information: The Law relating to Access, Disclosure and Regulation*, Butterworths.

Bishops' Advisory Group on Urban Priority Areas (1995), *Staying in the City: Faith in the City Ten Years On*, Church House Publishing, London.

Daly, M. and Noble, M. (1996), 'The Reach of Disability Benefits: An Examination of the Disability Living Allowance' *Journal of Social Welfare and Family Law*, vol. 18, no. 1, pp.37-57.

Data Protection Registrar (DPR) (1997), Personal Communication. 11th Feb 1997.

Department of the Environment (DoE) (1994), *Index of Local Conditions: An Analysis Based on 1991 Census Data*, London.

Goodman, A. and Webb, S. (1994), *For Richer, For Poorer: The Changing Distribution of Income in the United Kingdom 1961 - 1991*, Institute for Fiscal Studies, London

Huby, M. and Bradshaw, J. (1998), *A Study of Town Life: Living Standards in the City of York 100 years after Rowntree*, Social Policy Research Unit, University of York, York.

Kempson, E. (1996), *Life on a Low Income*, York Publishing Services, York.

Kempson, E. and Bennett, F. (1997), *Local Variations in the Costs Borne by Low Income Households*, Policy Studies Institute, London.

Lee, P., Murie, A., and Gordon, D. (1995), *Area Measures of Deprivation*, Centre for Urban and Regional Studies, University of Birmingham, Birmingham.

LGMB (1995), *Combating Local Poverty: The Management of Anti-poverty Strategies by Local Government*, London.

Noble, M., Knights, E., Wilkinson, J. and Smith, S. (1989), *Changing Housing Benefit: Who Gains? Who Loses?*, Department of Social and Administrative Studies, University of Oxford, Oxford.

Noble, M., Smith, G., Payne, J. and Roberts, J. (1989), *The Other Oxford: Low Income Households in Oxford*, Department of Social and Administrative Studies, University of Oxford, Oxford.

Noble, M., Wilkinson, J., Knights, E., and Smith, G. (1990), *Changing Housing Benefit in Oldham?*, Department of Social and Administrative Studies, University of Oxford, Oxford.

Noble, M., Smith, G. and Munby, T. (1992), *The Take-up of Family Credit*, Department of Applied Social Studies and Social Research, University of Oxford, Oxford.

Noble, M. and Smith, T. (1994), 'Children in Need: Using Geographical Information Systems to Inform Strategic Planning for Social Service Provision', *Children and Society*, vol. 8, no. 4, pp. 360-76.

Noble, M., Cheung, S.Y. , Smith, G. and Smith, T. (1995), 'Using Census Data to Predict Income Support Dependency', *Policy and Politics*, vol. 23, no. 4, pp. 327-33.

Noble, M. and Smith, G. (1996), 'Two Nations? Changing Patterns of Income and Wealth in Two Contrasting Areas', in J. Hills (ed.), *New Inequalities*, Cambridge University Press.

Noble, M., Platt, L., Smith, G. and Daly, M. (1997), 'The Spread of Disability Living Allowance', *Disability and Society*, vol. 12, no.5, pp. 741-51.

Noble, M., Cheung, S. Y. and Smith, G. (1998), 'Origins and Destinations - Social Security Claimant Dynamics', *Journal of Social Policy*, vol. 27.

Noble, M., Smith, G. and Cheung, S.Y. (1998), *Lone Mothers Moving in and Out of Benefits*, York Publishing Services, York.

Rowntree, S. (1902), *Poverty: A Study of Town Life*, Macmillan, London.

Smith, G., Noble, M., Smith, S. and Munby, T. (1991), *The Impact of the 1989 Social Security Changes on Hostel and Board and Lodging Claimant*, Department of Applied Social Studies and Social Research, University of Oxford, Oxford.

Townsend, P. (1987), 'Deprivation', *Journal of Social Policy*, vol. 16, part 2, pp. 125-46.

West Midlands Low Pay Unit and West Midlands Joint Data Team (1996), *Measuring Deprivation in the West Midlands Region (A Critique of the Index of Local Conditions)*, West Midlands Low Pay Unit and West Midlands Joint Data Team, Birmingham, July.

6 Analysis of Low Income Using the Family Resources Survey

LIZ TADD

Introduction

The arrival of the Family Resources Survey (FRS), with its very much larger sample compared with the Family Expenditure Survey, opens up new avenues for analysis. Editions of Households Below Average Income (HBAI) prior to 1993/94 used family type and economic status of family as the primary axes of analysis, supplemented by tenure. The last two volumes of HBAI have introduced a summary analysis of the incomes of ethnic minority groups; incomes by gender; by age; and by region. Such analyses present different perspectives on the data and raise new methodological issues.

This paper presents some of the key findings based on the new FRS analyses and discusses the associated methodological issues.

Background

Measuring Living Standards

Households Below Average Income (HBAI) provides estimates of patterns of personal disposable income[1] in the United Kingdom (UK), and of changes over time. It attempts to measure people's potential living standards derived from goods and services financed from disposable income.

The income measures used in HBAI also take into account variations in the size and composition of the households in which individuals live. This reflects the common sense notion that a household of five adults will need a higher income than a single person living alone in order for them to enjoy a comparable standard of living. The process of adjusting income in this way is known as equivalisation and is needed in order to make sensible income comparisons between households.

One of the most important assumptions underlying all HBAI analyses is that income received by every household member is shared equally within each household. HBAI attempts to measure living standards and the assumption of equal sharing is adopted as a simplistic measure in the absence of usable information on how income is actually shared between household members. For discussion of within-household sharing see for example Jenkins (1991) and Davies and Joshi (1994).

For all HBAI analyses, the income allocated to each individual within the household is the total household net income after equivalisation.

Sources of Data

Until very recently, HBAI information has been derived mainly from the Family Expenditure Survey (FES). The FES is a continuous survey which covers a sample of the UK population living in households. The responding sample covers about one in 3,000 households and historically has given information on about 7,000 households annually.

In October 1992, the Family Resources Survey (FRS) was launched by the Department for Social Security (DSS) to meet the information needs of DSS for policy analysis and development. Also a continuous survey, its larger sample size, currently approximately 26,000 responding households in Great Britain, allows HBAI to present information at a finer level of disaggregation.

Methodogical Issues

Households Below Average Income has always had to address methodological issues. The most important of these is how should income be defined, and what costs and deductions should be allowable when determining living standards. This is a matter that is kept under review as society changes and different sources of income, or costs, or benefits become increasingly more or less important to different groups of people. Also important is that only robust and appropriate analyses are presented.

One methodological issue which has always been recognised in HBAI is the role and effect of housing costs. Over the years, housing costs have fluctuated widely and affected the disposable income of households to a significant extent without necessarily reflecting a change in the quality of housing and thus living standards. The difficulty is that it is not known how much of the change in real terms costs is due to quality and how much to other factors (e.g. the introduction of market rents in the local authority sector). HBAI therefore presents income analyses on two bases: Before Housing Costs (BHC) and After Housing Costs (AHC). Some further detail on the issue of housing costs is provided in the Technical Appendix but for detailed discussion see Johnson and Webb (1992), Harris and Davies (1994) and Crawford (1996).

During 1996, a review of methodology was undertaken, in consultation with external experts, the recommendations of which were published. The review recommended various changes to the definitions used in HBAI which are incorporated in the definitions detailed in the Technical Appendix. The review recommended that information from the Family Resources Survey be introduced into the HBAI series, and in future years the FRS replace the Family Expenditure Survey as the main source of information. HBAI datasets based on FRS data are currently available for the financial years 1994/5 and 1995/6.

The methodological review also recommended that, because of the difficulty measuring income for the self-employed, results should be presented both including and excluding the full-time self-employed, and that prominence should be given to those **excluding** the self-employed. This recommendation, and the uncertainty over income measures for the self-employed, has implications for any analyses where the self-employed are a significant group.

Advantages of the Family Resources Survey

The FRS has several advantages for the analysis of income data:

- the increased sample size enables us to look at smaller sub-groups of the population, for example to look at data by regions;
- because of the larger sample size, the HBAI analysis can be based on a single year's data. This improves its timeliness compared with HBAI analysis based on FES when it was necessary to combine two years of data;
- the timeliness in the future will also be improved due to a reduction in the processing required to derive HBAI specific variables from the main survey data;
- improved data on receipt of benefits particularly for families in receipt of more than one benefit;
- the ability to change questions in response to methodological reviews;

- more information available on the editing and imputation carried out on the data.

The main disadvantage for HBAI analysis of the FRS compared with the FES is that there are no associated expenditure data to compare with the income data for surveyed households. Also it only covers Great Britain (GB) and not the UK. An analysis of the 1994/95 FES, which compared results for GB and UK, showed that the geographical coverage made very little difference to the results.

The New Analyses Published in HBAI

HBAI will continue to present analyses by family type and economic status. These are basic analyses which illustrate which parts of society are living on low incomes, which groups are becoming more numerous and who is becoming relatively worse or better off over time. However, with the FRS it is also possible not only to look at the types of families in which people live and *separately* the economic status, but to look at how these two factors *combine* at different points of the income distribution. For example, to look at the low income unemployed and examine how many are these are couples with children, singles without children, etc.

The last two editions of HBAI have also included some completely new analyses which start to exploit the potential of the FRS data. The 1993/94 edition included analyses by ethnicity and by country, and in the 1994/95 edition were included analyses by gender, by age and of income related benefit recipients.

The sections below examine the results of these new analyses and, for each topic, discuss the methodological issues the analysis raises without necesarily providing the answers; in some cases the answers require considerably more analysis and research.

Ethnicity

The data collected in the FRS follow the standard ethnic groupings. Sample sizes allow income distribution analysis for the White, Black and Indian groups separately, for Pakistani and Bangladeshi people combined and for 'Other' groups (including the Chinese) combined. For HBAI analysis, individuals have been classified according to the ethnic background of the head of household. The analysis does not distinguish those in a particular ethnic group who were born in the UK from those born overseas.

Overall, the white population make up 94 per cent of all individuals but form a larger proportion of the top two quintiles, and a smaller proportion of the bottom one. The white population only make up 89 per cent BHC (87 per cent AHC) of the bottom quintile. Conversely, the ethnic minority population are over represented at the bottom of the distribution and under-represented at the top. In particular, Pakistanis and Bangladeshis make up five per cent of the bottom quintile but only one per cent of the overall population.

Table 6.1 shows the income distribution for each ethnic group. Sixty-five per cent of Pakistani and Bangladeshi had incomes in the bottom quintile; few had incomes which would place them in the top 5 deciles.

Other ethnic minority groups are also over-represented at the bottom of the income distribution, but not to the same extent. On the BHC measure, just over a quarter of people in Black, Indian and 'Other' families were in the bottom quintile. These groups are more evenly distributed across the rest of the income range although only about a quarter of Blacks and Indians have incomes in the top two quintiles. On the AHC measure, the proportion of Black and 'Other' individuals in the bottom quintile rose to 38 per cent.

In examining the incomes of households, it must be borne in mind that household composition, employment patterns and participation of women in the work force may vary between the ethnic groups. In particular the higher proportion of Indians who are self-employed compared with other groups (see Table 6.2 below) and the high proportion of Pakistanis/Bangladeshis who are not working. Compared with other groups, Whites have a higher proportion of individuals living in families where the head or spouse is aged 60 or over.

Table 6.1a   Ethnic group by quintile (BHC)

Individuals (incl. self-employed)	Net equivilised disposable household income					Total grossed number =100% millions
	Bottom quintile %	Second quintile %	Third quintile %	Fourth quintile %	Top quintile %	
White	19	20	20	21	21	52.3
Black	29	28	19	13	11	0.9
Indian	26	25	24	13	13	0.9
Pakistani/ Bangladeshi	65	21	9	3	2	0.8
Other	26	19	18	17	19	0.8

Source: FRS 1995/6

Table 6.1b   Ethnic group by quintile (AHC)

Individuals (incl. self-employed)	Net equivilised disposable household income					Total grossed number =100% millions
	Bottom quintile %	Second quintile %	Third quintile %	Fourth quintile %	Top quintile %	
White	19	20	20	21	21	52.3
Black	38	25	17	11	10	0.9
Indian	28	24	21	14	13	0.9
Pakistani/ Bangladeshi	65	21	9	5	1	0.8
Other	38	16	14	17	15	0.8

Source: FRS 1995/6

Table 6.2   Proportion of each ethnic group in each economic status group of family

	White	Black	Indian	Pakistani/ Bangladeshi	Other
Self-employed	10	3	16	9	13
Single or couple, all in full-time work	23	27	25	5	21
One in full-time work, one in part-time work	13	3	8	2	6
One in full-time work, one not working	12	8	14	23	13
One or more in part-time work	7	8	4	3	6
Head or spouse aged 60 or over	18	10	10	8	4
Head or spouse unemployed	6	15	10	25	11
Other	10	26	12	25	27

Source: FRS 1995/6

Methodological Issues

The first methodological issue raised by this analysis is how to treat households which include members with different ethnic origins. The decision was taken for HBAI analysis to classify all individuals within the household according to the ethnic background of the head of household. In doing this, it is ackowledged that information about households of mixed composition is lost.

Other methodological issues relate to the effects of possibly different lifestyles of different ethnic groups. For example, approximately one in six of individuals in Indian families are self-employed compared with one in twenty of Blacks and broadly one in ten of other groups. The difficulties associated with measuring the income of the self-employed are already acknowledged in the HBAI series but the effects could be exaggerated for groups where self-employment is more common.

In addition, if the self-employment is linked with family businesses there may also be issues related to the transfer of money within households (and also between households) that are not captured in the FRS data.   Living arrangements also vary by ethnic group: around two in five of individuals in Indian and Pakistani/Bangladeshi families live in multi-benefit unit households, leading to a sharing of resources, compared with around one in four of White and Black people. The methodological question for HBAI is whether a survey which is best designed to capture accurate income data in general is best suited to collecting information from groups with potentially different financial habits. Different money management traditions e.g. relating to housing tenure and costs might also affect the BHC and AHC measures differently for each ethnic group.

A more detailed study of the incomes of ethnic minorities linked with their social and economic circumstances has been conducted by Berthoud (1998). This study uses data from the FRS and also from the Fourth National Survey of Ethnic Minorities.

Regional Analysis

The FRS can also provide information by country of residence within Great Britain and an analysis for 1994/5 was published in HBAI 1979-1993/94.[2] A regional analysis for regions within England was published in Regional Trends 1997.   Table 6.3 shows regional and country distributions of income for 1995/6.

Those who live in Wales were slightly over-represented in the bottom quintile. On the Before Housing Costs basis, a quarter of residents of Wales were in the bottom quintile together with 22 per cent of residents of Scotland. Only 13 per cent of those in Wales were in the top quintile compared with 17 per cent of those in Scotland and 21 per cent of those in England.

On the After Housing Costs measure there is a shift up the income distribution in both Wales and Scotland, with the proportion of those in Wales in the bottom quintile dropping to 23 per cent and in Scotland to 19 per cent. The results for Wales and Scotland are broadly compatible with those provided by the Institute for Fiscal Studies.

Looking at the regions in England, on the BHC measure those in the north and central regions of England are over-represented in the lower two quintiles and under-represented in the top quintile. The reverse is generally true for the south of the country (although the South West is more concentrated in the middle three quintiles). However on the AHC measure, the picture over the country is more mixed and, particularly in London, the proportion in the bottom quintile is substantially higher reflecting the high cost of housing in the capital.

Table 6.3a   Income distribution of households for each income quintile in Great Britain, split by region (AHC)

Government office region	Net equivilised disposable household income					Total grossed number =100% millions
	Bottom quintile %	Second quintile %	Third quintile %	Fourth quintile %	Top quintile %	
North East	26	22	24	16	12	2.6
North West	20	22	21	21	17	5.6
Merseyside	22	24	21	18	14	1.3
Yorks. & Humberside	20	22	22	20	16	4.7
East Midlands	19	22	22	20	17	4.1
West Midlands	20	20	22	21	17	5.1
Eastern	16	18	19	22	25	5.4
London	26	18	14	16	26	6.9
South East	17	15	18	22	27	7.4
South West	19	22	21	19	19	4.7
England	20	20	20	20	21	47.9
Wales	23	21	22	20	14	3.1
Scotland	19	21	21	21	18	4.7
Great Britain	20	20	20	20	20	55.8

Source: FRS 1995/6

Table 6.3b   Income distribution of households for each income quintile in Great Britain, split by region (BHC)

Government office region	Net equivilised disposable household income					Total grossed number =100%
	Bottom quintile %	Second quintile %	Third quintile %	Fourth quintile %	Top quintile %	millions
North East	26	24	22	16	12	2.6
North West	21	22	19	22	16	5.6
Merseyside	24	25	19	18	14	1.3
Yorks. & Humberside	23	21	21	19	16	4.7
East Midlands	21	21	22	19	16	4.1
West Midlands	22	21	21	19	17	5.1
Eastern	16	17	19	23	25	5.4
London	19	19	17	17	28	6.9
South East	15	16	19	22	29	7.4
South West	19	22	21	20	19	4.7
England	19	20	20	20	21	47.9
Wales	25	22	21	19	13	3.1
Scotland	22	19	21	21	17	4.7
Great Britain	20	20	20	20	20	55.8

Source: FRS 1995/6

Methodological Issues

The FRS uses a stratified clustered probability sample. The first level of stratification is by 24 regions (17 in England, two in Wales and five in Scotland) and so the proportion of the sample falling into each region reflects the population numbers. Each regional sample is further stratified using information on socio-economic group, unemployment and owner occupancy. Analysts therefore have confidence that the income data by region is robust and reliable.

However, no adjustment is made for regional differences in the cost of living and thus the regional data being presented may not truly reflect the relative living standards of people in different regions. For further discussion of this issue see Borooah *et al.* (1996).

Ideally the data would be adjusted using a regional price index. However, in the absence of such an index, one possibility might be to sensitivity test various assumptions about regional differences.

Men and Women

There is increasing interest in analysis by gender for many topics and the Government Statistical Service is introducing a policy of making analyses by gender available, wherever possible, for main statistical series. Income is no exception but the traditional HBAI methodology, which uses household income as the basis for all analysis, is not well-suited to this disaggregation.

Households Below Average Income 1979-1994/5 published some analyses of men's and women's incomes on the usual HBAI definitions and conventions. Some examples of these analyses and commentary on the results are given below. Both partners in a couple appear at the same position in the income distribution.

HBAI data for 1995/6 showed that men were under-represented at the bottom of the income distribution: whilst adult males formed 38 per cent of the whole population in Great Britain, they made up only 32 per cent of the bottom quintile, but 45 per cent of the top quintile. Adult women were evenly distributed. In the bottom quintile, 55 per cent of adults were women, but in the top quintile, the situation was reversed with only 47 per cent of adults being women.

However, particular groups of women and men were more likely to have low incomes (Table 6.4). Large proportions of single women with children were in the bottom two income quintiles (71 per cent BHC), as were single female pensioners (62 per cent BHC), and both women and men in pensioner couple families (53 per cent BHC). Single male pensioners were disproportionately in the second quintile. Both women and men in couples, and singles without children, were under-represented in the bottom two quintiles. A similar picture is presented in the AHC data.

Table 6.4   Percentage distribution of income by family type and gender (BHC)

Family type	Net equivilised disposable household income					Total grossed numbers =100% millions
	Bottom quintile %	Second quintile %	Third quintile %	Fourth quintile %	Top quintile %	
Pensioner couple	27	26	21	15	11	5.3
Single pensioner						
male	20	35	23	13	10	0.9
female	28	34	19	14	6	3.3
Couple with children	18	18	23	22	19	10.6
Couple without children	11	11	16	25	37	11.6
Single with children						
male	29	28	19	12	13	0.1
female	32	39	19	8	3	1.5
Single without children						
male	17	17	19	23	24	6.2
female	17	17	21	22	22	3.6
All men	17	17	20	22	24	20.9
All women	20	21	20	20	20	22.1
All adults	18	19	20	21	22	43.0

Note: For couples, both partners appear at the same place in the income distribution: eg. the percentage distribution for men in couples is the same as that of women. Totals for couples count both partners.

Source: FRS 1995/6

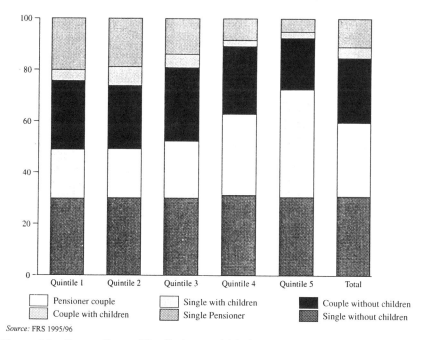

Source: FRS 1995/96

Figure 6.1a Proportions of family types within income quintiles: men (BHC)

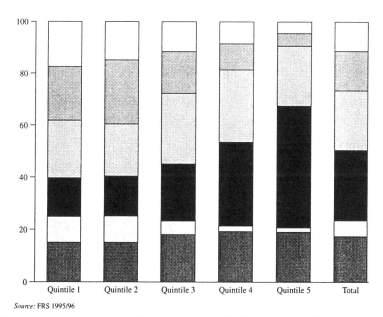

Source: FRS 1995/96

Figure 6.1b Proportions of family types within income quintiles: women (BHC)

Table 6.5 **Percentage distribution of income by economic type and gender (BHC)**

Economic type	Net equivilised disposable household income					Total grossed number =100%
	Bottom quintile %	Second quintile %	Third quintile %	Fourth quintile %	Top quintile %	millions
Men						
Self-employed	20	13	18	18	31	2.2
Single/ couple all in full-time work	2	6	16	32	45	5.9
Couple, one in full-time work, one in part-time work	3	12	28	31	26	2.2
Couple, one in full-time work, one not working	10	20	25	25	19	2.3
One or more in part-time work	22	22	20	19	17	1.2
Head or spouse aged 60 or over	28	30	21	13	9	3.8
Head or spouse unemployed	54	24	12	7	3	1.7
Other	30	31	21	11	7	1.6
All men	**17**	**17**	**20**	**22**	**24**	**20.9**

Table 6.5 (continued)

Economic type	Net equivilised disposable household income					Total grossed number =100%
	Bottom quintile %	Second quintile %	Third quintile %	Fourth quintile %	Top quintile %	millions
Women						
Self-employed	20	14	18	18	30	1.9
Single/ couple all in full-time work	2	7	17	31	43	4.8
Couple, one in full-time work, one in part-time work	3	12	28	31	26	2.2
Couple, one in full-time work, one not working	10	20	25	25	19	2.3
One or more in part-time work	21	27	23	16	13	1.6
Head or spouse aged 60 or over	29	31	20	13	7	6.0
Head or spouse unemployed	58	22	9	7	3	1.0
Other	37	33	18	8	4	2.3
All women	**20**	**21**	**20**	**20**	**20**	**22.1**

Source: FRS 1995/6

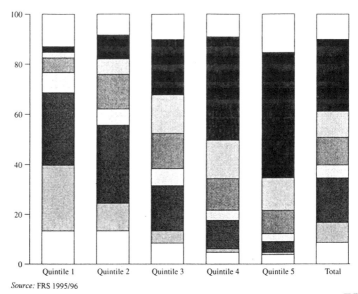

Source: FRS 1995/96

Figure 6.2a Proportions of economic types within income quintiles: men (BHC)

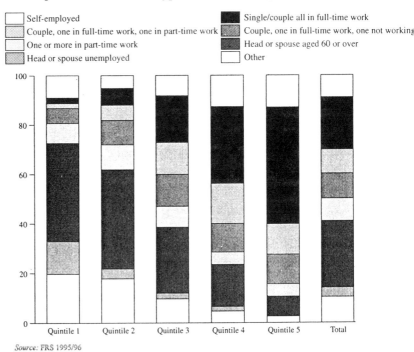

Source: FRS 1995/96

Figure 6.2b Proportions of economic types within income quintiles: women (BHC)

The economic status of women within quintiles differed from that of men. Figure 6.2 shows the distribution of economic status of the families in which men lived within income quintiles and separately the distribution of women. In the bottom quintile BHC, men were predominantly in benefit units with an unemployed head or with a retired head or spouse. By comparison, women were more likely to be in benefit units with a retired head or spouse or in families classed as 'Other' which includes many lone parents. They were less likely to be in families with an unemployed head.

Methodological Issues

The main methodological issue that needs to be considered in this context is that in HBAI all individuals within the same household - men, women and children - are credited with the same income level. This methodology reflects the assumption in HBAI that every individual in the household enjoys the same standard of living. If this assumption is generally true, then women's living standards are well represented in these analyses. However, there is some evidence which questions this asumption. (See the work of Jenkins, Vogler and Pahl, and Sutherland.)

An alternative analysis would be to look at women's incomes in their own right. However, a woman with a very low income because she does not work, might be truly poor or she might be the partner of a wealthy man and have no need to work. Also many women experience temporary periods when they have little or no personal income, for example because of child care responsibilities at home. At these times, they rely on the income of the other members of the household and intra-household transfers take place. These are not captured as the woman's income in HBAI (or from other survey data). In these cases the woman's living standards derive from the household's living standards and would be mis-represented by looking at their income alone.

A move away from the normal HBAI treatment of household income would also raise questions about how some benefits income should be allocated between partners. Examples are housing benefit and council tax benefit which could not easily be divided between partners. Again the underlying survey data provide no information on sharing of income within households.

The analyses presented here have highlighted the incomes of male and female adults. There is also the question of how children should be treated in male/female analyses. For all HBAI analyses it is assumed that children share in the fruits of their parents' income and their position in the income distribution reflects this assumption. This assumption can be maintained for gender analyses; the alternative being to allocate children only that income which is their's in their own right. This alternative approach has similar disadvantages to not allocating women a share in the household income.

Age

The most recent edition of HBAI included an analysis by age. It found that in 1995/6, young people, and in particular children, were over-represented at the bottom of the income distribution. A quarter of children lived in households where the household income was in the bottom quintile BHC. Young adults aged under 25 were slightly over-represented in the fourth quintile and under-represented in the top quintile.

Individuals aged between 25 and 59 were over-represented in the upper quintiles. This is most marked for individuals aged 45-59, where only 14 per cent were found in the lowest quintile and 29 per cent (BHC) in the highest quintile. For all these age groups, a broadly similar pattern is seen in the AHC income. For those aged 60 or over, 25 per cent had incomes (BHC) in the bottom quintile and 28 per cent in the second quintile. On the AHC measure 19 per cent had incomes in the bottom quintile and 31 per cent in the second quintile. This difference between the two measures is because pensioners tend to have lower housing costs than non-pensioners.

Table 6.6a   Percentage distribution of income by age (BHC)

Age	Net equivilised disposable household income					Total grossed number =100%
	Bottom quintile %	Second quintile %	Third quintile %	Fourth quintile %	Top quintile %	millions
Children	26	23	21	17	13	12.7
Adults under 25	19	20	20	23	18	5.2
25-44	16	16	19	22	27	15.9
45-59	14	14	19	24	29	10.6
60+	25	28	21	15	11	11.3

Source: FRS 1995/6

Table 6.6b   Percentage distribution of income by age (AHC)

Age	Net equivilised disposable household income					Total grossed numbers =100%
	Bottom quintile %	Second quintile %	Third quintile %	Fourth quintile %	Top quintile %	millions
Children	28	23	21	16	12	12.7
Adults under 25	23	17	19	23	17	5.2
25-44	18	16	20	22	25	15.9
45-59	14	14	19	24	31	10.6
60+	19	31	21	17	13	11.3

Source: FRS 1995/6

Methodological Issues

The age analyses do not raise any major methodological issues. In these analyses individuals (including children) have been allocated an income level based on the household income and then allocated to an age band based on their own age.

Multi-generation households, either those where an adult child is living with parents or where elderly relatives are living in the same household as younger people, may cause some individuals to shift up or down the income scale compared with analysing the benefit unit income by age. In the FRS, people are classified as being in the same household if they either share one meal a day together or share the living accommodation (i.e. living room). Relations living in the same dwelling but in separate accommodation (e.g. in 'granny' flats) are counted as separate households.

Families in Receipt of Income Related Benefits

For the purposes of HBAI analyses, beneficiaries of income related benefits are defined as members of a family where someone in that family is in receipt of Income Support, Housing Benefit, Council Tax Benefit or Family Credit. In the following analysis and Tables 6.7 and 6.8, the income which determines the quintile groups includes income related benefit. Of all individuals in Great Britain, 26 per cent were beneficiaries; however, four fifths of single parents and half of single pensioners were beneficiaries.

Table 6.7a   Percentage distribution of income by receipt of income related benefits

	Net equivilised disposable household income					Total grossed number =100%
	Bottom quintile %	Second quintile %	Third quintile %	Fourth quintile %	Top quintile %	millions
BHC						
Non receipt	12	15	22	25	26	41.5
Receipt	44	35	14	5	2	14.3
AHC						
Non receipt	10	16	23	25	26	41.5
Receipt	49	33	12	5	2	14.3

Source: FRS 1995/6

Table 6.7b   Receipt of income related benefits by distribution of income

	Net equivilised disposable household income					Total grossed number =100%
	Bottom quintile %	Second quintile %	Third quintile %	Fourth quintile %	Top quintile %	millions
BHC						
Non receipt	44	55	82	93	98	41.5
Receipt	56	45	18	7	2	14.3
AHC						
Non receipt	37	58	85	94	98	41.5
Receipt	63	42	15	6	2	14.3

Source: FRS 1995/6

Just over a tenth of non-recipients had a BHC income in the bottom quintile whereas over two-fifths of benefit recipients had incomes in the same range. Of beneficiaries, more than 60 per cent of those in families comprising a couple with children were in the bottom quintile whereas almost twice as many single pensioners appeared in the second quintile as in the bottom quintile (but it should be noted that these results may not be robust to the choice of equivalence scale). For all family types very few benefit recipients were found in the top two quintiles. The same patterns can be seen when the AHC distribution is examined.

Table 6.8a Percentage distribution of income by family type and whether receiving income related benefits (BHC)

Whether receiving benefits and family type	Net equivilised disposable household income					Total grossed numbers =100% millions
	Bottom quintile %	Second quintile %	Third quintile %	Fourth quintile %	Top quintile %	
Receipt						
Pensioner couple	46	35	13	5	1	1.3
Single pensioner	26	45	19	9	1	2.1
Couple with children	63	27	8	2	1	3.7
Couple without children	42	32	15	7	3	1.1
Single with children	40	42	14	3	1	3.7
Single without children	34	31	20	10	5	2.3
All beneficiaries	44	35	14	5	2	14.3
Non receipt						
Pensioner couple	21	24	23	18	14	4.0
Single pensioner	27	24	20	18	12	2.1
Couple with children	10	16	26	26	22	16.7

Table 6.8a (continued)

Whether receiving benefits and family type	Net equivilised disposable household income					Total grossed numbers =100% millions
	Bottom quintile %	Second quintile %	Third quintile %	Fourth quintile %	Top quintile %	
Couple without children	7	9	16	27	40	10.4
Single with children	15	14	30	26	15	0.8
Single without children	12	13	20	26	29	7.5
All beneficiaries	12	15	22	25	26	41.5

Source: FRS 1995/6

Table 6.8b   Percentage distribution of income by family type and whether receiving income related benefits (AHC)

Whether receiving benefits and family type	Net equivilised disposable household income					Total grossed numbers (=100%) millions
	Bottom quintile %	Second quintile %	Third quintile %	Fourth quintile %	Top quintile %	
Receipt						
Pensioner couple	45	37	13	4	1	1.3
Single pensioner	21	52	15	11	2	2.1
Couple with children	64	26	8	2	1	2.1
Couple without children	47	28	15	7	3	1.1
Single with children	54	35	9	2	1	3.7

Table 6.8b (continued)

Whether receiving benefits and family type	Net equivilised disposable household income					Total grossed numbers (=100%) millions
	Bottom quintile %	Second quintile %	Third quintile %	Fourth quintile %	Top quintile %	
Single without children	46	24	17	9	4	2.3
All beneficiaries	49	33	12	5	2	14.3
Non receipt						
Pensioner couple	21	24	23	18	14	4.0
Single pensioner	27	24	20	18	12	2.1
Couple with children	10	16	26	26	22	16.7
Couple without children	7	9	16	27	40	10.4
Single with children	15	14	30	26	15	0.8
Single without children	13	12	19	26	30	7.5
All beneficiaries	10	16	23	25	26	41.5

Source: FRS 1995/6

Methodological Issues

Benefits are paid to benefit units (families). However, in HBAI, individuals are ranked by household income so some beneficiaries' position in the income distribution will reflect the income of other household members. This is particularly an issue in this analysis which might be used for judging how well the benefits are being targeted towards those in need. The analysis assumes total sharing of income within a household but the information is not available to judge how well that reflects reality.

Another factor relevant to the interpretation of this analysis is that the income related benefit system gives additional money in premiums to some groups, in particular the elderly and the disabled, in part to reflect a perceived need for additional money in order for them to reach the same standard of living as other groups. Measuring 'need' is particularly difficult and, in HBAI, we do not make any adjustments for these additional needs. This increases the difficulty of drawing strong conclusions from the position of beneficiaries in the income distribution. Analyses of benefits paid entirely to meet additional needs or costs (e.g. Disability Living Allowance and Attendance Allowance) are correspondingly more affected.

The analysis uses income after receipt of benefit for the distribution: income excluding income related benefit could be used but for many households that income is very low or zero.

Other Examples of the Family Resources Survey Being Used in Income Studies

The FRS, as well as being used as a data bank for direct analysis, can also be used as a sampling frame for more detailed studies of particular sub-groups of the population. One example is a study of 'Households with Minimal Incomes' which was conducted in 1996 and is reported on briefly below.

The FRS can also provide a data source for other research and analysis, and secondary analysis of the FRS and HBAI data is currently being undertaken as part of a Joseph Rowntree Foundation funded study.

A Study of 'Households with Minimal Incomes'

In order to examine the reasons for, and duration of, periods of very low income, a two-stage project was commissioned,[3] going back to interview respondents of the FRS who were identified as having minimal incomes of £40 or less per week After Housing Costs (AHC).

Qualitative Research

The first stage of the project consisted of qualitative interviews with a sample of seventeen, to investigate possible explanations relating to the reasons for, and duration of, periods of low income.   There was then a following quantitative stage of face-to-face re-interviews with the remaining FRS low income respondents to quantify the scale of such explanatory factors.

The aims of the qualitative research were to explore a number of hypotheses concerning the reasons for, and durations of, minimal incomes recorded among households in the FRS:

- minimal income is a transitional phase;
- income is understated (or withheld) intentionally, or unintentionally as a result of questionnaire design;
- households are living off capital for extended periods;
- housing costs are not actually paid (accruing debts).

One finding of the research was that households recorded as having minimal incomes in the survey encompassed diverse living standards and circumstances.   Deliberately under-reported incomes did not appear to be a feature of minimal income households.

Quantitative Research

The second stage consisted of second interviews with 165 households who at the time of the original FRS interview had AHC equivalised income of less than £40 per week.

The main findings from this second stage were:

- half of the households on 'minimal incomes' had no member who worked;

- round half of the households surveyed were, at the original interview, estimated to be entitled to income-related benefits which they were not receiving, and only a minority were awaiting the outcome of a claim;
- apart from the in-work group, the main source of income was state-funded: retirement pension for pensioners, grants for students and benefits for those not in work;
- nearly 40 per cent of the households interviewed had no capital on which to draw;
- about one-third of households had AHC income below £40 a week at both the original interview and the follow-up; just under 40 per cent had incomes exceeding £100 a week by the second interview (the interval between the two interviews ranged from nine to 21 months);
- half of households experiencing improved incomes saw an increase in earnings and for two-thirds of these households the increase was due to more workers in the household;
- one-third of those who were on a low income at both interviews said that they had borrowed money from family and friends in the last six months.

Methodological Issues

One issue which was identified during the qualitative study was that the full range of resources and strategies used by households were not recorded in the FRS, but these made an important contribution in the absence of other income - in some cases being responsible for putting food on the table. Among student households or where members are self-employed, a fuller range of alternative resources needs to be considered. Examples of these included: family help in the form of money, food or clothes; drawings on savings and selling possessions. These resources made an important contribution to how well households survived periods of minimal income, but these resources were not always financial.

However, the recording of resources which are unreliable, have a limited potential and can reduce the expenditure capacity of subsequent higher income periods, is not without problems. There is a danger that inclusion of such resources in calculations of households' incomes may produce an inflated view of household incomes and overshadow the extent to which some households struggle to make ends meet. Further, should such resources as gifts and meals from family and friends be included in calculations of minimal incomes when, among better-off households, such items are not routinely used to supplement income and are usually reciprocated.

An earlier study of data on low incomes was made by Davies (1995).

Technical Appendix

Family Resources Survey

The FRS was launched in October 1992 to meet the information requirements of DSS analysts. The large sample of the FRS (in 1995/6, 26,435 households were interviewed in Great Britain) makes it possible for HBAI to present information for single years without increasing sampling errors, and thereby to present more up-to-date information.

Definition of Income

The income measure used in HBAI is weekly net (disposable) equivalised household income. Income is the total income of all members of the household, including dependants.

Income is adjusted for household size and composition by means of equivalence scales, which reflect the extent to which households of different size require a different level of income to achieve the same standard of living. This adjusted income is referred to as 'equivalised income'.

Income is the current usual income of household members at the time of the Family Resources Survey interview. This is generally the income being received in the period when the interview takes place, except for employees whose last pay was not the amount they normally receive, in which case the income measure uses their normal pay.

Income (Before Housing Costs (BHC)) includes the following main components:

- usual net earnings from employment;
- profit or loss from self-employment (losses are treated as a negative income);
- all social security benefits (including Housing Benefit but excluding Social Fund loans);
- income from occupational and private pensions;
- investment income;
- maintenance payments;
- Social Fund, maternity, funeral or community care grants;

- income from educational grants and scholarships (including 'top up' loans for students);
- the cash value of certain forms of income in kind (free school meals, free welfare milk and free school milk).

Income is net of the following items:

- income tax payments;
- National Insurance contributions;
- contributions to occupational pension schemes including all additional voluntary contributions (AVCs) to occupational pension schemes, and any contributions to personal pensions;
- all maintenance and child support payments (deducted from income of the person making the payments);
- domestic rates/community charge/council tax.

Income After Housing Costs (AHC) is derived by deducting a measure of *housing costs* from the above income measure.

Housing Costs

These include the following:

- rent (gross of housing benefit);
- water rates, community water charges and council water charges;
- mortgage interest payments (net of tax relief);
- structural insurance premiums (for owner occupiers);
- ground rent and service charges.

Negative incomes BHC are reset to zero, but negative AHC incomes calculated from the adjusted BHC incomes are possible. Where incomes have been adjusted to zero BHC, income AHC is derived from the adjusted BHC income.

Before Housing Costs and After Housing Costs Income Measures

The need for the two measures arises from the variation in housing costs: in part this reflects variations in the quality of housing, but there are also significant cost variations which do not reflect quality variations. Also the growth in BHC income is likely to overstate improvements in the living standards of low-income groups, because it counts, as an income rise, higher Housing Benefit which merely offsets higher rents. Conversely income growth AHC will tend to understate improvements in living standards where higher housing costs reflect improved housing. Because of this each measure has advantages and disadvantages. Therefore it is HBAI practice to give results both BHC and AHC.

Equivalisation in HBAI

The income measures used in HBAI take into account variations in the size and composition of the households in which individuals live. This reflects the common sense notion that a household of five adults will need a higher income than a single person living alone in order for them to enjoy a comparable standard of living. The process of adjusting income in this way is known as equivalisation and is needed in order to make sensible income comparisons between households.

Equivalence scales conventionally take a couple as the reference point, with an equivalence value of one; equivalisation therefore tends to increase relatively the income of single person households (since their incomes are divided by a value of less than one) and to reduce relatively the incomes of households with three or more persons, which have an equivalence value of greater than one.

Household

A single person or group of people living at the same address as their only or main residence, who either share one meal a day together or share the living accommodation (i.e. living room). A household will consist of one or more benefit units.

Benefit Unit

A single adult or couple living as married and any dependent children. An adult living in the same household as his or her parents, for example, is a separate benefit unit from the parents and would be assessed separately for Income Support or Family Credit.

Notes

1   See the Technical Appendix for the definition of income.
2   In HBAI, the notation 1994/95 is used to represent the combined financial years 1994/5 and 1995/6 for Family Expenditure Survey data.
3   Social and Community Planning Research (SCPR) and the Office for National Statistics (ONS) were commissioned by the Department of Social Security (DSS) to carry out a two stage study to investigate the circumstances and incomes of very low, or 'minimal' income households. A summary of the results was published in HBAI 1979-1994/95 and the section included in this paper quotes from that summary. The full findings of this project were published during 1998.

References

Berthoud, R. (1998), 'The Incomes of Ethnic Minorities' an unpublished working paper, University of Essex.

Borooah, V.K., McGregor, P.P.L., McKee, P.M. and Mulholland, G. (1996), 'Cost-of-living Differences Between the Regions of the United Kingdom', in J. Hills (ed), *New Inequalities*, Cambridge University Press, Cambridge.

Crawford, I. (1996), 'UK Household Cost-of-living Indices, 1979-92', in J. Hills (ed), *New Inequalities*, Cambridge University Press, Cambdrige.

Davies, M. (1995), *Household Incomes and Living Standards: The Interpretation of Data on Very Low Incomes*, DSS Analytical Note No 4, DSS, London.

Davies, H. and Joshi, H. (1994), 'Sex, Sharing and the Distribution of Income', *Journal of Social Policy*, vol. 23, pp. 301-40.

Johnson, P. and Webb, S. (1992), 'The Treatment of Housing in Official Low Income Statistics', *Journal of the Royal Statistical Society*, no. 155, part 2, pp. 273-90.

Harris, G. and Davies, M. (1994), 'Income Measures for Official Low Income Statistics: The Treatment of Housing Benefit Costs and Local Government Taxes', *DSS Analytical Note No. 2*, DSS, London.

Goodman, A. and Webb, S. (1994), 'For Richer, For Poorer: The Changing Distribution of Income in the UK 1961-91', Institute for Fiscal Studies, London.

Households Below Average Income: Methodological Review Report of a Working Group, DSS, May 1996, DSS, London.

Jenkins, S.P. (1991), 'Poverty Measurement and the Within-household Distribution: Agenda for Action', *Journal of Social Policy*, vol. 20 pp. 457-83.

Regional Trends (1997), The Office for National Statistics, London.

Rowlingson, K *et al.* (1998), 'Securing a Future: The Links Between Income, Assets and Life Cycle', Policy Studies Institute, London.

Sutherland, H. (1997), 'Women, Men and the Redistribution of Income', *Fiscal Studies (1997)* vol. 18, no. 1, pp. 1-22.

Vogler, C. and Pahl, J. (1993), 'Social and Economic Change and the Organisation of Money Within Marriage', *Work, Employment and Society*, vol. 7, pp. 71-95.

7 A Century of Poverty in England and Wales, 1898-1998: A Geographical Analysis

IAN GREGORY, HUMPHREY SOUTHALL and DANIEL DORLING

This paper analyses geographical trends in relative poverty and inequality in England and Wales between 1898 and the present by assembling statistics for infant mortality, overcrowded housing and unemployment for Rowntree's times (1898 or 1901), the inter-war depression (1928 or 1931), the 'never-had-it-so-good' post-War boom (1951, 1958 or 1961) and the present (in practice, 1990 or 1991). Geographically, all variables display a relatively stable north-south divide and, in general, worse conditions in the great conurbations. Both infant mortality and overcrowding show clear long-run upwards trends in inequality, just as absolute levels fell; the history of unemployment is more complex. While the detailed findings may reflect the limitations of the current methodology, these overall conclusions appear robust.

Introduction

The paper is concerned with long-run trends in poverty in England and Wales between the publication of Rowntree's (1902) report on poverty in York and the present, and seeks in particular to provide a tentative quantitative answer to the question of whether relative poverty, measured geographically, has become more or less extreme. Such a study is only possible through the application of novel methods for data analysis based around a Geographical Information System (GIS), which is used to make data for different dates as closely comparable as possible. Even then the range of variables available for use is inevitably limited. Work on the underlying GIS is very much still in progress and there will eventually be considerable scope for refining the methodology and, hopefully, employing a finer spatial resolution. Even so, it is believed that both the methodology and the results are sufficiently interesting to justify this paper.

Three indicators of poverty, chosen to be consistently available for the whole of England and Wales over the past 100 years, were interpolated onto a standardised spatial framework to allow direct comparison, both over time and one with another. This raises three issues that are addressed in this introduction: the geographical scale of the analysis, the choice of poverty indicators, and the periodisation employed.

The research of Rowntree and his contemporaries was strictly local in focus, studying poverty in a single town such as York (Rowntree, 1902) or a single district of the metropolis (Booth, 1889). Such a focus permitted them and later researchers following up their work (see for example McKendrick, 1998 or Shepherd, 1998) to combine qualitative and quantitative methods, but meant that they seldom developed a very clear grasp of the overall geography of poverty: much research concentrated on the East End of London simply because many researchers were London-based, and similarly Rowntree studied York for mainly personal reasons. The analysis is strictly quantitative, but permits us not only to make some broad generalisations concerning trends in relative poverty but also to clearly define the geography of relative poverty in different periods. In other words, the study is concerned with establishing which geographical areas experienced the worst hardship, and then with how much worse off they were relative to the best-off areas. The limitations of early data mean that the areas used are relatively large, thus placing the analysis at the top of a multi-scale approach to the study of poverty (Shepherd, 1998) but complementing more localised studies.

The debate about how best to define poverty is as old as the study of poverty itself and many different methods have been put forward (Burrows and Rhodes, 1998). As the study compares areas over the long-term against a background of wide social change it has used a relative rather than an absolute definition of poverty (Harris, 1998). Very few statistical indicators of poverty are available over the last century as a whole, and what follows is limited to three key indicators, each of which is discussed in more detail in the subsequent sections:

• **Infant mortality**: the death rate for children aged under 1, an essentially demographic variable and therefore one calculable for different periods with few problems of consistency. Infant mortality rates today are far lower than in Rowntree's time, but the deaths of young children are still a deep trauma for the families concerned. The rate remains a useful indicator of broader poverty, being particularly influenced by the mother's health and nutrition, and the environment into which the child was born.

- **Overcrowded housing**: The data concern the number of persons in each household relative to the number of rooms, information gathered by every census this century. The definition of a household and the method of counting rooms are both problematic, and today greater emphasis might be given to other aspects of poor housing, such as available amenities and environmental issues including condensation. However, patterns prove remarkably enduring, and space and privacy are still greatly valued in society.

- **Unemployment**: An obvious measure of economic hardship, but the most problematic of the indicators used. Most available data derive from the operation of specific schemes for its relief, and are inevitably heavily influenced by their rules which have been constantly changed and adjusted. Instead the census is used as it is a relatively constant measure of under- and un-employment. Unfortunately the first census to provide this information was that of 1931.

Ideally, this paper would be concerned with continuous time series, but quite apart from the sheer volume of data that would be required much of the information used comes from the census, carried out only once every ten years; there was no 1941 census, and the collection of many other statistical series was interrupted by the two world wars. The census is particularly important for a complete coverage of the country at sub-county scale, sample surveys such as the Labour Force Survey include too few people from any one locality to provide reliable results. This study is therefore limited to comparing four key dates:

- **The turn of the century**: A period of prosperity relative to other nations, but also perceived as having great disparities between rich and poor. The focus of this paper is on 1898, but the 1901 census is often used.

- **The inter-war recession years**: A time which saw unemployment, especially in the north, first entering the political agenda but also the foundations of modern consumer society being laid. The paper focuses on 1928, and the 1931 census.

- **The 'never had it so good' 1950s**: In 1957, Macmillan continued 'Go around the country, go to the industrial towns, go to the farms and you'll see a state of prosperity such as we have never had in my lifetime.' 1958 and 1961 are used.

- **The present - Booming Britain?**: The 1991 census is the main source, while not ideal this provides regular 30-year intervals. Infant mortality data come from the period 1990 to 1992.

The Historical GIS

The most recent data are available for very small geographical areas: wards, enumeration districts (EDs) or even, in the case of the mortality data, the precise postcode of the individual fatality's home (Dorling, 1997). However, for most of the century the data are limited to those that appeared in published reports: of the census, the Registrar General, and other organisations. The type of area used depends largely on date:

1. Until the First World War **Registration Districts** (RDs), of which there were around 630, were the principal publishing areas of the Registrar General and thus the census. They were originally defined in terms of towns and their spheres of influence (Lipman, 1949) giving some similarities to modern Travel-to-Work areas. Major provincial cities such as Norwich, Bristol, and Newcastle were generally RDs in their own right; the great cities of Liverpool, Manchester, and Birmingham each consisted of small clusters of RDs, and London contained over 30 RDs.

2. RDs were replaced by **Local Government Districts** (LGDs) which consisted of county and municipal boroughs and urban and rural districts. There were around 1,500 LGDs although as noted below this fluctuated considerably. When originally formed LGDs were typically subdivisions of RDs; the urban areas were designated as boroughs or urban districts while the rest of the RD became a rural district. This means that although LGDs provide a much more distinct rural/urban pattern than the RDs, their original pattern was nested within the RD structure.

3.   Modern data are frequently published for **Wards** or **Enumeration Districts** (EDs). This gives vastly more spatial detail than the other two measures: in 1991 there were around 8,000 wards and 110,000 EDs in England alone (Coombes, 1995). Unit postcodes provide a similar spatial resolution.

Even comparing the same types of area at different dates is problematic as a constant trickle of boundary changes has taken place. LGDs provide an example: in 1901 there were 1,834 of them but by 1961 there were only 1,466, and even the areas which remained in existence throughout often experienced major alterations to their boundaries.

To cope with this the study was able to draw on a major project based at Queen Mary and Westfield College which is constructing a historical (GIS) which will contain a full record of the changing boundaries of the statistical reporting units of Britain from parish-level upwards (Gregory and Southall, 1998). Work to date has been limited to England and Wales, which is the only reason for the limited geographical focus of the study. When the system is complete, it will be possible to use the simple population counts which are available for the individual parishes to estimate the size and characteristics of the populations transferred by boundary changes (as in Dorling and Atkins, 1995), but for now the methods must assume that the population transferred is simply proportional to the area transferred (Goodchild and Lam, 1980).

The data sources and the areas used to map each data set are shown in Table 7.1. The need for standardisation is driven by two considerations: most obviously, it allows direct comparison between one date and another for each area. Perhaps even more importantly however, it allows the data to be compared consistently; the value given for any area is the average value within that area and therefore, as reporting units become geographically larger, local extremes are increasingly averaged away and the range of values is reduced. Data collected for the three different types of areas listed above are thus not comparable unless standardised onto a single type. As an example of this, using the raw LGD data for 1928, the infant mortality inequality ratio between the best ten per cent and worst ten per cent of the population is 6.3. However, standardising the data onto RDs reduces this to only 2.7, reflecting the removal of many of the urban/rural contrasts found among LGDs.

Table 7.1   Data sources and base maps used

Data set	Source	Collection areas	Mapped onto
Infant Mortality 1891-1900	The RG's Decennial Supplement, 1901	RD	RDs
Infant Mortality, 1928	The RG's Statistical Review, 1928	LGD	1928 LGDs for the North, 1910 LGDs for remainder
Infant Mortality, 1958	The RG's Statistical Review, 1958	LGD	Approximated 1951 LGDs
Infant Mortality, 1990-92	Individual Death Records	Postcodes	1981 wards
Overcrowding, 1901	1901 Census County Reports	LGD	1901 LGDs for the North, 1910 LGDs for remainder
Overcrowding, 1931 (both counts)	1931 Census County Reports	LGD	1931 LGDs for the North, 1910 LGDs for remainder
Overcrowding, 1961	The 1961 Census	LGD	Approximated 1951 LGDs
Overcrowding, 1991	1991 Census Small Area Statistics	EDs	1981 wards
Unemployment, 1931	1931 Census Employment Report	LGD	1931 LGDs for the North, 1910 LGDs for remainder
Unemployment, 1951	1951 Census Employment Report	LGD	Approximated 1951 LGDs
Unemployment, 1991	1991 Census Small Area Statistics	ED	1981 wards

Note: RG's stands for Registrar General's. 'North' in the 'Mapped onto' column refers to the four Northern counties of England plus Lancashire and Cheshire, and the East and North Ridings of Yorkshire.

Standardisation must be based on the least detailed set of areas for which data was collected. For this reason RDs as they existed in 1898 were used. The basic problem can be summarised as the need to redistribute a variable Y from a set of source zones S onto a set of target zones T. The estimated values of Y for each target area can then be calculated as:

$$\overset{\wedge}{y_t} = \sum_s \frac{A_{st} y_s}{A_s} \quad (1)$$

where A_s is the area of the source zone, A_t is the area of the target zone, A_{st} is the area of the zone of intersection and Y is the variable being modelled (Flowerdew & Green, 1994). The GIS allows this to be done in a very straightforward manner using an overlay operation where two 'maps' have a geometric union operation applied and new areas are calculated based on the results.

The modern data required a slightly different methodology based on using either a corrected ED centroid or unit postcode centroid to aggregate up to 1981 wards (Dorling, 1993). The resulting ward level data were then re-allocated to 1898 RDs based on the entire value being allocated to the RD which contained the largest part of the ward. Until the entire GIS is finished it is felt that this is acceptable given the large degree of aggregation at each stage, from over 100,000 EDs or unit postcodes to around 10,000 wards to 630 RDs.

For both methodologies it is believed that the effect of the interpolation is likely to reduce contrasts due to the smoothing effects that the homogeneous population assumption will cause.

Once the data were in this standardised form, the districts containing the worst-off ten per cent of the population, and the best-off ten per cent could be identified: the measure of relative poverty is simply the ratio of the average rate for the relevant indicator in the worst-off districts to the average for the best-off districts. Note that the worst-off districts will by no means contain all the individuals or households in the worst-off ten per cent of the population as a whole: many, and probably the majority of the people in these districts will not be that badly off, while some people in better-off districts will be among the ten per cent worst-off individuals. However, so long as the most detailed data available concerns geographical aggregates, not individuals, the focus is necessarily blurred and there are advantages to such an ecological approach in that it allows us to observe ecological processes such as de-industrialisation, migration to areas with a better climate or, more abstractly, Thatcherism.

Mapping is a tool that has a long history in research on poverty. Booth for example used mapping for both presentational purposes, and to a more limited extent, for interpretative analysis (Shepherd, 1998). The advent of GIS has freed cartography from many of its traditional constraints and it provides us with a range of visualisation techniques (Hearnshaw and Unwin, 1994). Most people are familiar with the choropleth map where geographical areas are shaded according to the intensity of a value or rate recorded across them. The problem with these is that they emphasise often sparsely populated rural areas while cities can all but disappear therefore, in addition to a choropleth, the maps included all provide an area figure. These are derived from conventional maps by a process in which the area of each district is made proportional to its population, or some other measure of its significance, while trying as far as possible to keep adjacent units together (Dorling, 1994, 1996). The result may be unfamiliar, but the shape of the country is broadly retained. One key feature of the population-based figures is that when the units are divided into five bands or quintiles, indicated by different shades of grey, each quintile covers one-fifth of the total population, and therefore there will be an equal area of each shade in each map. Conversely, the conventional maps often contain quite small areas of the darkest shade because the worst-off were concentrated into major cities.

The remainder of the paper consists of discussions of the three indicators of poverty in turn, and a short conclusion. Maps of each indicator at each date are also included. Although the techniques used are complex, the results are simple and best presented graphically, so the commentary is quite limited.

Infant Mortality

In many ways the infant mortality data permit the most straightforward comparisons as definitions have changed little. To represent 1898 data from the Registrar General's *Decennial Supplement* for the 1890s were used. These give rates of death per 1,000 births for ten years from 1891 to 1900, collected at RD level. For 1928 and 1958 the data were taken from the Registrar General's *Statistical Reviews* for the individual year in question, again expressed as deaths per 1,000 births. These were collected for LGDs. The 1990s data are slightly different in that they are based on actual death records for the years 1990 to 1992 with the postcodes used to provide a spatial reference which permitted them to be grouped by 1898 RD. Three years were used because modern rates are so low that small numbers can become a major statistical problem. The rate is expressed as deaths per 1,000 babies, based on the 1991 census and corrected both for normal under-recording and by using the national count of birth certificates to allow for the extra under-reporting typical of census counts of babies. The reason number of babies rather than births is used in the 1990s is to remove the impact of people migrating in the year that their baby is born, thus skewing the rates. This has become important as migration around the time of birth has become more common in the 1990s and families are now much smaller.

The century saw a massive fall in infant mortality, the rate for the median RD falling from 121 per thousand in the 1890s to 3.73 per thousand in 1990. The geographical pattern in the 1890s is very clear: high rates in the industrial districts of South Wales, the West Midlands and the North. Figure 7.1 shows clearly that the worst districts were concentrated in Lancashire and the West Riding; Tyneside was relatively healthy, and in London the worst conditions were in a small number of central districts. Rural areas were almost uniformly much healthier. By 1928, Lancashire and the West Riding had experienced significant improvement and some rural districts had fallen back in the ranking, particularly in parts of Wales and East Anglia. It seems that conditions in urban areas were improved by large scale public health measures, while rural areas were beginning to be penalised for poorer medical care.

The maps for 1958 and for 1990 are more difficult to summarise except on a regional scale. The north-south, or rather core-and-periphery divide is particularly clear in 1958, with almost uniformly low relative rates in the south east, and still strongly present in 1990. If anything, the urban-rural divide is clearer in the most recent map. Turning to the measure of relative inequality, tabulated in the conclusion, this is not concerned at all with how far the worst-off areas are grouped together, only with how they compare with the best-off areas. In the 1890s, the worst-off areas had only twice as high a mortality rate as the best-off areas, but by the 1990s they had seven-and-a-half times the rate of death.

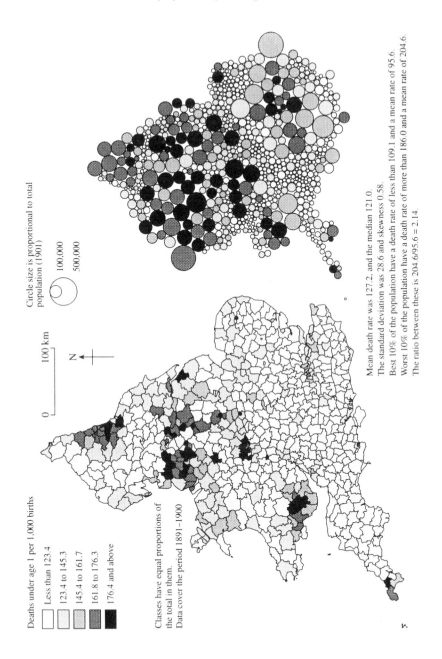

Figure 7.1   Infant mortality, 1898 on 1898 RDs

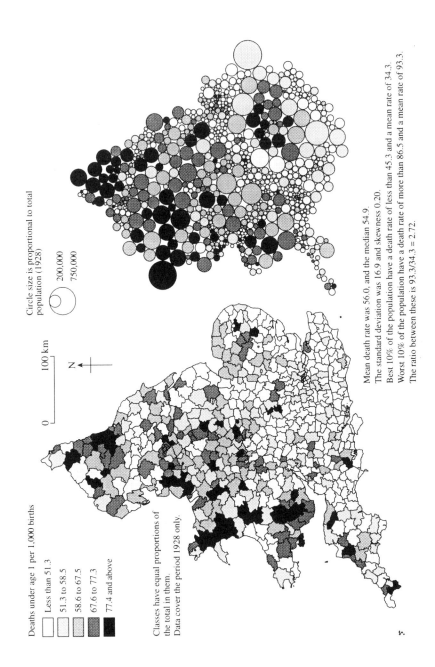

Circle size is proportional to total population (1928)

200,000
750,000

Deaths under age 1 per 1,000 births

Less than 51.3
51.3 to 58.5
58.6 to 67.5
67.6 to 77.3
77.4 and above

Classes have equal proportions of the total in them.
Data cover the period 1928 only.

100 km

N

0

Mean death rate was 56.0, and the median 54.9.
The standard deviation was 16.9 and skewness 0.20.
Best 10% of the population have a death rate of less than 45.3, and a mean rate of 34.3.
Worst 10% of the population have a death rate of more than 86.5 and a mean rate of 93.3.
The ratio between these is 93.3/34.3 = 2.72.

Figure 7.2   Infant mortality, 1928 on 1898 RDs

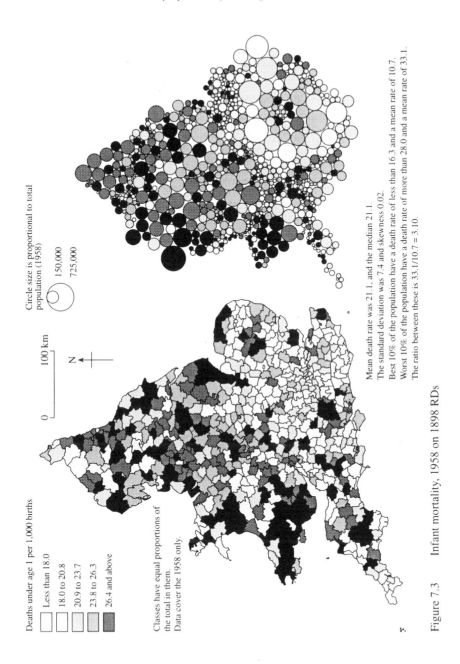

Deaths under age 1 per 1,000 births

☐ Less than 18.0

☐ 18.0 to 20.8

☐ 20.9 to 23.7

☐ 23.8 to 26.3

☐ 26.4 and above

Classes have equal proportions of
the total in them.
Data cover the 1958 only.

Circle size is proportional to total
population (1958)

◯ 150,000
◯ 725,000

0 ___ 100 km

N

Mean death rate was 21.1, and the median 21.1.
The standard deviation was 7.4 and skewness 0.02.
Best 10% of the population have a death rate of less than 16.3 and a mean rate of 10.7.
Worst 10% of the population have a death rate of more than 28.0 and a mean rate of 33.1.
The ratio between these is 33.1/10.7 = 3.10.

Figure 7.3   Infant mortality, 1958 on 1898 RDs

Figure 7.3   Infant mortality, 1958 on 1898 RDs

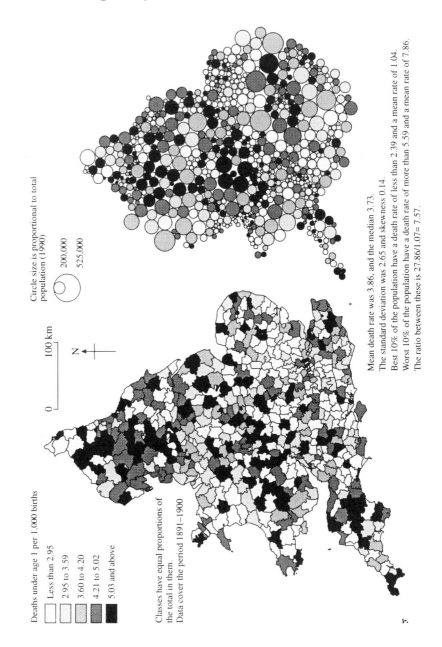

Figure 7.4   Infant mortality, 1990 on 1898 RDs

Overcrowded Housing

This section examines the changing geography of housing via census statistics of overcrowding. Overcrowding is usually summarised in terms of persons per room: in the nineteenth century, overcrowding meant rates of over two persons per room, but now over one person per room is seen as unacceptable. A compromise definition of over 1.5 persons per room has been used in this paper, the same standard as used by the 1931 census. For the three later dates the percentage of each district's population living at over 1.5 persons per room was calculated. For 1901 however the available data did not permit this calculation, the report tabulating numbers of persons only for 'tenements' of four rooms or less; the *General Report* of the 1901 census [Cd. 2174] describes (p.39) tenements as 'separate occupations', or in other words a dwelling with a separate front door. From this data the number of persons living at over 1.5 persons per room in these small dwellings could be calculated, and as no population figures were available this total had to be used to calculate a rate **per tenement**. The 1931 census allowed the calculation of a similar measure, based on taking the number of 'private families' living in four rooms or less and working out the density of occupation of these in terms of persons per room. This is slightly different to the 1901 definition because of the possibility of more than one family living in a single tenement: in 1931, where more than one family was enumerated within a 'structurally separate dwelling', each was classified in terms of the rooms the family occupied and not the total number of rooms in the dwelling. From this the number of families occupying less than five rooms could be calculated and this is given as a ratio of the number of families. There are therefore two sets of results included for 1931, the first permitting the closest possible comparison with 1901, the second with 1961 and 1991.

Overall, the most striking feature of the conventional maps is the concentration of the worst housing in both urban and rural districts in the north-east of England. This remains little changed from 1901 to 1961, but disappears completely by 1991. It has been suggested that these poor conditions were an extension of the very poor conditions that prevailed over the border in Scotland, and partly reflected the nature of the housing stock, with the distinctive and small 'Tyneside flat'; certainly, in 1901 a much higher proportion of all 'tenements' were of four rooms or less than in any other region. The transformation since 1961 may indicate the impact of specific policies. The figures show surprisingly low rates of overcrowding in the north-west and

Yorkshire, with the exception of Liverpool, while the West Midlands conurbation and London had large areas of overcrowding at their cores. With the exception of the north-east, these patterns changed relatively little over the period as a whole.

Turning to the inequality ratio, this again rises consistently, so that by 1991 the worst-off districts contained nearly 30 times the proportion of people living in overcrowded conditions as did the best-off areas - although of course that proportion was now far lower than in 1931: 5.78per cent versus 40.6 per cent.

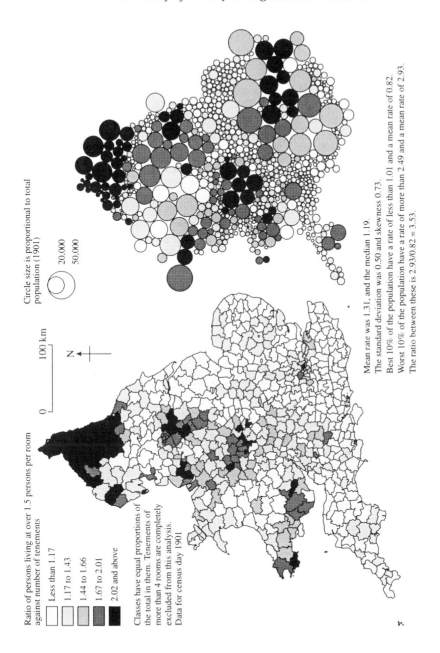

Circle size is proportional to total population (1901)

20,000

50,000

Mean rate was 1.31, and the median 1.19.
The standard deviation was 0.50 and skewness 0.73.
Best 10% of the population have a rate of less than 1.01 and a mean rate of 0.82.
Worst 10% of the population have a rate of more than 2.49 and a mean rate of 2.93.
The ratio between these is 2.93/0.82 = 3.53.

0   100 km

N

Ratio of persons living at over 1.5 persons per room against number of tenements

Less than 1.17

1.17 to 1.43

1.44 to 1.66

1.67 to 2.01

2.02 and above

Classes have equal proportions of the total in them. Tenements of more than 4 rooms are completely excluded from this analysis.
Data for census day 1901

Figure 7.5 Overcrowding, 1901 on 1898 RDs (for tenements with less than five rooms)

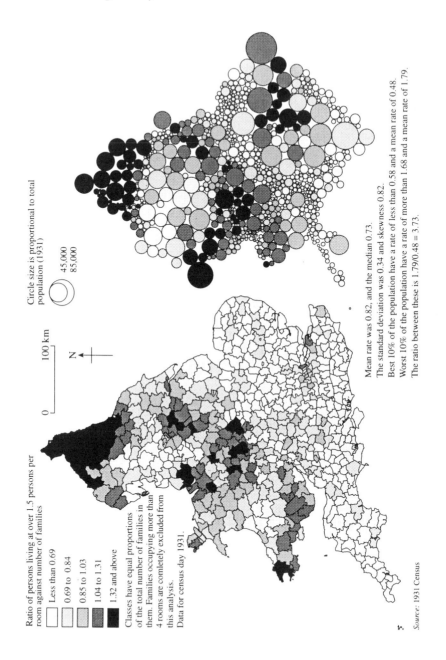

Circle size is proportional to total population (1931)

45,000
85,000

Ratio of persons living at over 1.5 persons per room against number of families

Less than 0.69

0.69 to 0.84

0.85 to 1.03

1.04 to 1.31

1.32 and above

Classes have equal proportions of the total number of families in them. Families occupying more than 4 rooms are comletely excluded from this analysis.
Data for census day 1931.

0   100 km

N

Mean rate was 0.82, and the median 0.73.
The standard deviation was 0.34 and skewness 0.82.
Best 10% of the population have a rate of less than 0.58 and a mean rate of 0.48.
Worst 10% of the population have a rate of more than 1.68 and a mean rate of 1.79.
The ratio between these is 1.79/0.48 = 3.73.

Source: 1931 Census

Figure 7.6   Overcrowding, 1931 on 1898 RDs

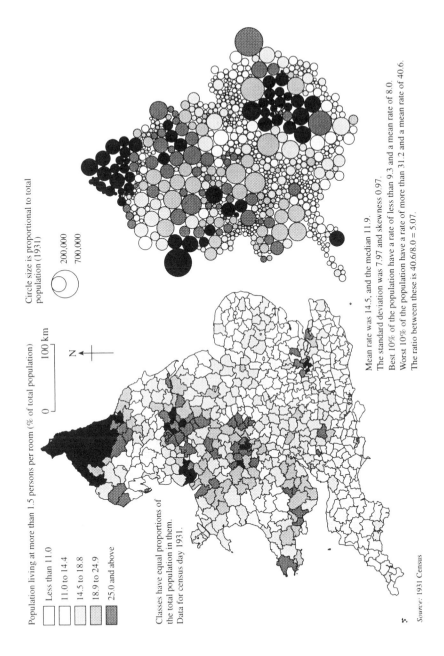

Circle size is proportional to total population (1931)

200,000
700,000

Population living at more than 1.5 persons per room (% of total population)

0   100 km

N

Less than 11.0
11.0 to 14.4
14.5 to 18.8
18.9 to 24.9
25.0 and above

Classes have equal proportions of the total population in them. Data for census day 1931.

Mean rate was 14.5, and the median 11.9.
The standard deviation was 7.97 and skewness 0.97.
Best 10% of the population have a rate of less than 9.3 and a mean rate of 8.0.
Worst 10% of the population have a rate of more than 31.2 and a mean rate of 40.6.
The ratio between these is 40.6/8.0 = 5.07.

Source: 1931 Census

Figure 7.7   Overcrowding, 1931 on 1898 RDs (for families in less than five rooms)

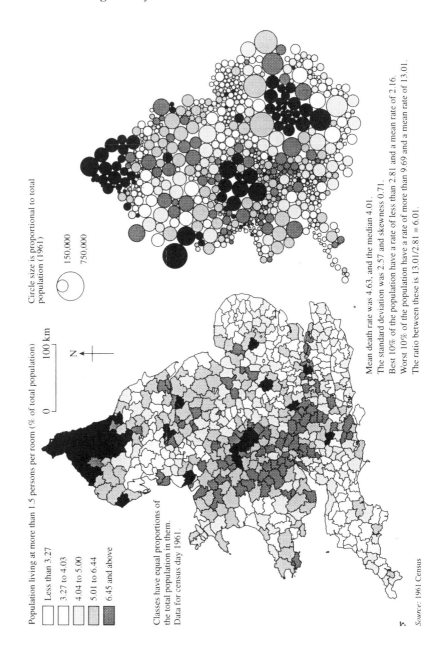

Population living at more than 1.5 persons per room (% of total population)

☐ Less than 3.27
☐ 3.27 to 4.03
☐ 4.04 to 5.00
☐ 5.01 to 6.44
■ 6.45 and above

Classes have equal proportions of
the total population in them.
Data for census day 1961.

0   100 km

N

Circle size is proportional to total
population (1961)

○ 150,000

◯ 750,000

Mean death rate was 4.63, and the median 4.01.
The standard deviation was 2.57 and skewness 0.71.
Best 10% of the population have a rate of less than 2.81 and a mean rate of 2.16.
Worst 10% of the population have a rate of more than 9.69 and a mean rate of 13.01.
The ratio between these is 13.01/2.81 = 6.01.

Source: 1961 Census

Figure 7.8   Overcrowding, 1961 on 1898 RDs

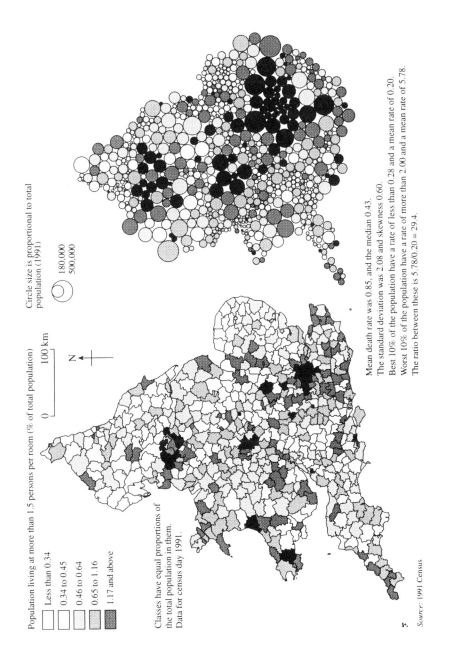

Figure 7.9   Overcrowding, 1991 on 1898 RDs

Unemployment is the most problematic of the indicators studied here - to avoid the problems of the ever-changing definitions used by government schemes the census measure is used for three of the four periods to provide some standardisation over time. Green (1995) compares the 1991 census definition of unemployment with other modern definitions, namely the National Insurance-based 'claimant count' (now based on the 'Jobseekers Allowance') and the Labour Force Survey and concludes that all three have their merits and are best used in combination. In a similar way data for the inter-war years are available from several sources including the Poor Law and Ministry of Labour's 'Local Unemployment Index' (LUI), as well as the 1931 census, and it is believed that the unemployment pattern shown by the census definition is broadly similar to that given by the other sources although further research to investigate this is intended. The study was unable to go back to the turn of the century as there were no straightforwardly comparable data available (Garside, 1980).

The 1991 data attempt to reflect recent debates by including not only those classified as unemployed by the census but also those people classed as being either unavailable for work due to permanent sickness or on a government training scheme; it is believed that many of these people would have been classified as unemployed in earlier censuses. Accordingly, the 1991 denominator used is the number of people who are economically active plus the long-term sick (excluding those over 65 for men and 60 for women). The results show unemployment as concentrated in the old industrial regions and, as the figure shows, London.

Census data in 1961 could not be used as the reporting areas were too crude, so 1951 data have been used to provide the snap-shot of the post-War boom. This provides data on those 'out of work' as the numerator and the economically active population, calculated as the total population aged between 15 and retirement age, as the denominator. By combining two tables this could be calculated for all LGDs but due to data limitations no account could be taken of the long-term sick. The most striking feature of the pattern is the very low rates - the maximum rate is only 8.1 per cent of the economically active population and the mean is under two per cent. This compares with means of 9.0 per cent and 11.2 per cent in 1931 and 1991 respectively. The spatial pattern, particularly on the figure is quite striking with higher rates concentrated in South Wales, the North East, London, and in coastal areas especially in the South. The reason for the coastal bias is probably that the census was taken in early April and classed seasonal workers in sea-side towns as unemployed. The low rates in other industrial areas such as Birmingham, South Yorkshire, and Lancashire excluding Merseyside is also a clear feature.

As far as the authors are aware this is the first study to use the 1931 census at a national level in a study of unemployment. The measure used includes those classed by the census as unemployed as the numerator with the economically active population providing the denominator. A striking feature is that even though this was near the trough of the inter-war recession the average rates are still noticeably lower than they are today. There is however a much clearer North-South divide which is not necessarily obvious on the choropleth - high rates are concentrated in areas from South Wales through Birmingham to the Industrial North. Compared to these rates, those in the south, even for inner London, are not particularly bad.

Measuring unemployment prior to the First World War is highly problematic with sources of data being limited to the Poor Law and trades union unemployment schemes. Neither of these provide the basis for a sensible comparison with the later data; the rules concerning Poor Relief at this time meant that workers from the industrial areas were very unlikely to claim, while the unions only provided relief to their members who were usually skilled workers in artisan trades, meaning mainly engineering, shipbuilding and building workers rather than miners, textile workers or unskilled labourers (Southall, 1986). For this reason relative inequality in unemployment could only be compared for 1931, 1951, and 1991.

The pattern for both infant mortality and overcrowding shows a rapid decline in average rates but at the same time inequality seems to rise. Unemployment provides a more complex pattern: mean rates were high during the depression in 1931 and in 1991 but very low in 1951. The inequality ratio is the inverse of this, starting at 5.03 in 1931, rising slightly in 1951 and dropping to only 3.59 in 1991.

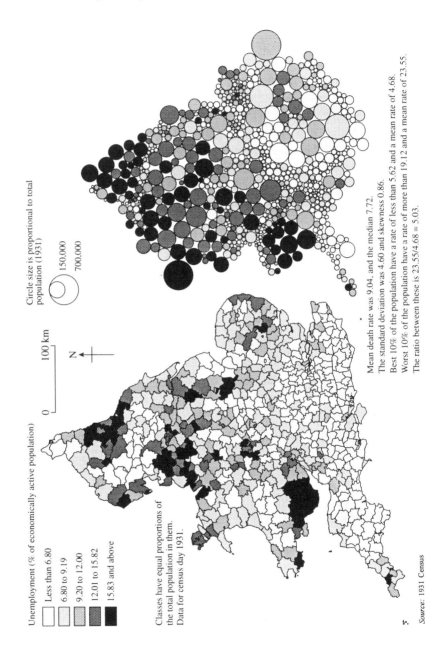

Circle size is proportional to total population (1931)

150,000
700,000

Unemployment (% of economically active population)

Less than 6.80
6.80 to 9.19
9.20 to 12.00
12.01 to 15.82
15.83 and above

Classes have equal proportions of the total population in them. Data for census day 1931.

0   100 km

N

Mean death rate was 9.04, and the median 7.72.
The standard deviation was 4.60 and skewness 0.86.
Best 10% of the population have a rate of less than 5.62 and a mean rate of 4.68.
Worst 10% of the population have a rate of more than 19.12 and a mean rate of 23.55.
The ratio between these is 23.55/4.68 = 5.03.

Source: 1931 Census

Figure 7.10   Unemployment, 1931 on 1898 RDs (census definition of unemployment)

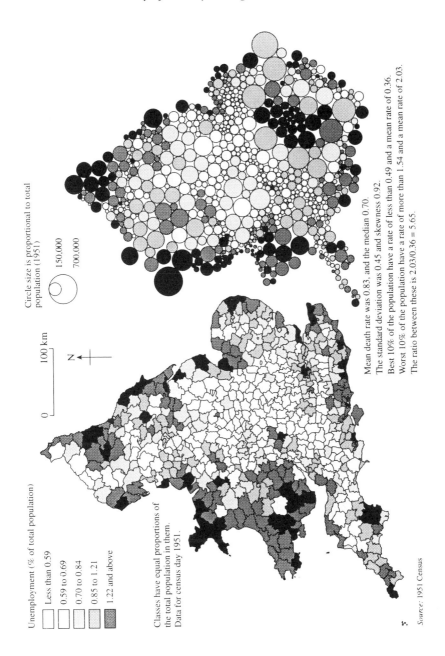

Circle size is proportional to total population (1951)

150,000

700,000

Unemployment (% of total population)

Less than 0.59

0.59 to 0.69

0.70 to 0.84

0.85 to 1.21

1.22 and above

Classes have equal proportions of the total population in them. Data for census day 1951.

0   100 km

N

Mean death rate was 0.83, and the median 0.70.
The standard deviation was 0.45 and skewness 0.92.
Best 10% of the population have a rate of less than 0.49 and a mean rate of 0.36.
Worst 10% of the population have a rate of more than 1.54 and a mean rate of 2.03.
The ratio between these is 2.03/0.36 = 5.65.

Source: 1951 Census

Figure 7.11   Unemployment, 1951 on 1898 RDs (census definition of unemployment)

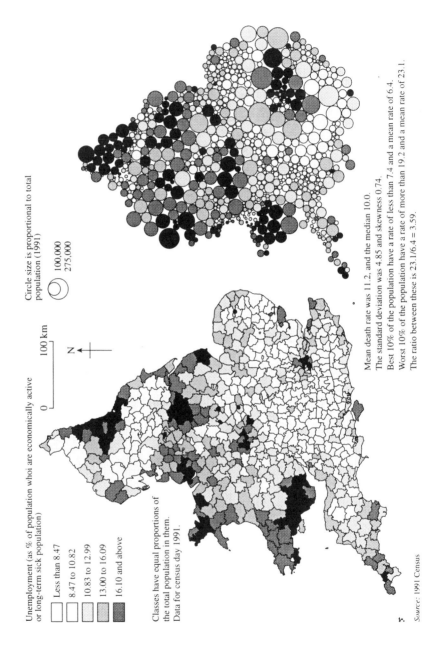

Figure 7.12   Unemployment, 1991 on 1898 RDs (based on census data

Conclusion

Table 7.2 summarises the statistical findings on poverty in England and Wales in the 100 years to 1998. Two sets of very general conclusions can be drawn. Firstly, the geographical patterns show a marked persistence of higher poverty in the periphery - the North, but also South Wales and often the remoter parts of the South West. In most maps, the major conurbations are worse off than adjacent rural areas, although in the mid-20th century significant areas of rural deprivation are apparent. London generally contained substantial deprived areas while surrounded by the affluent South East, but even so the worst conditions were to be found further north.

Secondly, the calculation of an index of relative poverty is inevitably crude but it is believed that for infant mortality and housing it is fairly robust. In particular, it must be emphasised that there is no statistical reason why lower absolute levels of the measures of poverty should inevitably lead to higher levels of relative poverty; that this seems to have happened says something about our society. What can be said is that the results may in part reflect the particular scale of analysis used: while this is at sub-county level, over much of the country, rural areas cannot be distinguished from towns, and if a century ago social segregation was primarily at the micro-scale, one street or neighbourhood versus another, the calculations used will tend to minimise it. However, as the figures show, much of the population was concentrated into the large urban centres where RDs covered relatively small and homogenous urban areas, so this problem should not be exaggerated. Completion of the full parish-level GIS should permit a more thorough investigation of these issues.

Overall, it is believed that despite its current limitations this paper provides significant evidence that over the last century an overall improvement in living standards has been accompanied by a steady rise in relative deprivation.

Table 7.2   Relative poverty in England and Wales, 1898 to present

Variable	Descriptive Measures:				Best 10%:		Worst 10%:		
	Mean	Median	St Dev	Skew	Cut-off	Mean	Cut-off	Mean	Ratio
Inf. Mort. 1890s	127.2	121.0	28.6	0.58	109.1	95.6	186.0	204.6	2.14
Inf. Mort. 1928	56.0	54.9	16.9	0.20	45.3	34.3	86.5	93.3	2.72
Inf. Mort. 1958	21.1	21.1	7.4	0.02	16.3	10.7	28.0	33.1	3.10
Inf. Mort. 1990s	3.86	3.73	2.65	0.14	2.39	1.04	5.59	7.86	7.57
O'crowd. 1901[1]	1.31	1.19	0.50	0.73	1.01	0.82	2.49	2.93	3.53
O'crowd. 1931[1]	0.82	0.73	0.34	0.82	0.58	0.48	1.68	1.79	3.73

Table 7.2 (continued)

O'crowd. 1931[2]	14.5	11.9	7.97	0.97	9.3	8.0	31.2	40.6	5.07
O'crowd. 1961[2]	4.63	4.01	2.57	0.71	2.81	2.16	9.69	13.01	6.01
O'crowd. 1991[2]	0.85	0.43	2.08	0.43	0.28	0.20	2.00	5.78	29.4
Unem. 1931	9.04	7.72	4.60	0.86	5.62	4.68	19.12	23.55	5.03
Unem. 1951	1.89	1.58	1.04	0.89	1.05	0.87	3.46	4.55	5.23
Unem. 1991	11.2	10.0	4.85	0.74	7.4	6.4	19.2	23.1	3.59

Notes: The 'cut-off' is the rate above or below which the top or bottom districts containing ten per cent of the population are found.   The two 'means' to the right of the table refer to areas falling respectively above and below these cut-offs. The 'ratio' is the mean for the worst ten per cent divided by the mean for the best ten per cent.   The measure of skewness is calculated by subtracting the median, multiplying this by three and dividing by the standard deviation. Overcrowding is calculated by two different methods that are not directly comparable.

[1] Method 1 for 1901-31 is based on households living in four rooms or less.

[2] method 2 for 1931-91 is based on the entire population.

Acknowledgements

The construction of the historical GIS which made this research possible was funded by the Aurelius Trust, the British Academy, the ESRC, the Joint Information Systems Committee, the Leverhulme Trust, the Pilgrim Trust, the Roehampton Institute and the Wellcome Trust. Research into pre-1914 and inter-war unemployment and pauperism was a joint project between Humphrey Southall and David Gilbert, now of Royal Holloway, University of London; pre-1914 work was funded by the Leverhulme Trust and inter-war data entry by the Nuffield Foundation. We are deeply grateful for Eileen Longland for entering the infant mortality and housing data, and this work was funded by the participants on a GIS training course at Queen Mary and Westfield in September 1997.

References

Booth, C. (1889), *Labour and Life of the London People. Volume I: East London with a Coloured Map*, William and Norgate, London.

Burrows, R. and Rhodes, D. (1998), 'The Geography of Misery: Area Disadvantage and Patterns of Neighbourhood Dissatisfaction in England', Paper Presented to the Rowntree Poverty Conference, University of York, March 1998.

Coombes, M. (1995), 'Dealing with Census Geography: Principles, Practices and Possibilities', in S. Openshaw (ed), *Census Users Handbook*, GeoInformation International, Cambridge.

Dorling, D. (1993), 'Map Design for Census Mapping', *The Cartographic Journal*, vol. 30, no. 2, pp.167-83.

Dorling, D. (1994), 'Cartograms for Visualising Human Geography', in H. Hearnshaw and D. Unwin (eds), *Visualisation in GIS*, John Wiley and Sons, Chichester, pp.85-102.

Dorling, D. (1996), 'Area Cartograms: Their Use and Creation', *CATMOG*, University of East Anglia, Environmental Publication.

Dorling, D. (1997), Death in Britain: How Local Mortality Rates Have Changed: 1950s-1990s, Joseph Rowntree Foundation, York.

Dorling, D. and Atkins, D. (1995), *Population Density, Change and Concentration in Great Britain 1971, 1981 and 1991, Studies on Medical and Population Subjects No. 58*, HMSO, London.

Environmental Systems Research Institute (1994), *Arc/Info version 7.0.4*.

Flowerdew, R., and Green, M. (1994), 'Areal Interpolation and Types of Data', in S. Fotheringham and P. Rogerson (eds), *Spatial Analysis and GIS*, Taylor and Francis, London, pp.121-46.

Garside, W. (1980), *The Measurement of Unemployment in Great Britain 1850-1979: Methods and Sources*, Basil Blackwell, Oxford.

Goodchild, M. and Lam, N. (1980), 'Areal Interpolation: A Variant of the Traditional Spatial Problem', *Geo-Processing*, vol. 1, pp.297-312.

Green, A. (1995), 'A Comparison of Alternative Means of Unemployment', *Environment and Planning A*, vol. 27, pp.535-56.

Gregory, I. and Southall, H. (1998), 'Putting the Past in its Place: The Great Britain Historical GIS', in S. Carver (ed), *Innovations in GIS 5*, Taylor and Francis, London, pp.210-21.

Harris, B. (1998), 'Seebohm Rowntree and the Measurement of Poverty, 1899-1951', Paper Presented to the Rowntree Poverty Conference, University of York, March 1998.

Hearnshaw, H. and Unwin, D. (eds) (1994), *Visualisation in GIS*, John Wiley and Sons, Chichester.

Lipman, V. (1949), *Local Government Areas 1834-1945*, Basil Blackwell, Oxford.

McKendrick, J. (1998), 'Recovering Lost Geographies of Poverty: From Kay and Rowntree to Spatial Science ... and Back Again', Paper Presented to the Rowntree Poverty Conference, University of York, March 1998.

Rowntree, B. (1902), *Poverty: A Study of Town Life (2nd edition)*, Macmillan, London.

Shepherd, I. (1998), 'Mapping the Poor: The Micro-Geography of Poverty in Late-Victorian London', Paper Presented to the Rowntree Poverty Conference, University of York, March 1998.

Southall, H. (1986), 'Regional Unemployment Patterns Among Skilled Engineers in Britain, 1851-1914', *Journal of Historical Geography*, vol. 12, pp.268-86.

Southall, H. (1988), 'The Origins of the Depressed Areas: Unemployment, Growth, and Regional Economic Structure in Britain before 1914', *Economic History Review, II*, vol. XLI, pp.236-58.

Southall, H. (1991), 'Poor Law Statistics and the Geography of Economic Distress' in J. Foreman-Peck (ed), *New Perspectives on the Late Victorian Economy. Essays in Quantitative Economic History 1860-1914*, CUP, Cambridge, pp.180-217.

8   Urban Deprivation and Government Expenditure: Where Does Spending Go?

GLEN BRAMLEY and MARTIN EVANS

Introduction

The British government spends money on everyone in the country, but how much is spent in deprived areas? Some spending, such as fire, police, roads, provides public goods. Universal services such as education and health care serve the population according to their position in the life cycle and their need. Income transfers provide a range of benefits geared to meet risks and contingencies, spread income over the life cycle or prevent income poverty. We know a significant amount about how much is spent on the welfare state and who benefits at the national level (Glennerster and Hills, 1998), but very little about the profiles of spending in small areas. In this chapter we outline how public spending flows into local and small areas can be measured and the patterns of spending which are revealed, particularly between deprived and other areas.

Much previous research has highlighted spatial concentrations of poverty and multiple deprivation, particularly in cities (Holterman, 1975; DOE, 1995; Hills, 1995) and there is some evidence of growing polarisation (Green ,1994, 1996; Noble and Smith, 1996). Housing tenure plays an important if disputed role in this (Murie and Lee, 1997). However, there is great uncertainty about the extent to which an area itself worsens deprivation for given groups of households. Do concentrations of poor people hold back the individual poor? Even in the US there is growing realisation that, despite the heavy emphasis on inner-city ghettos, the reality of poverty is more widespread:

> The ongoing discussion of the American 'underclass', and the images of ghetto poverty ... have made the poor seem increasingly alien to many Americans... In reality, the poor are much more like 'us' than 'them'. The majority of poor live in mixed-income neighbourhoods. (Blank, 1997, p.5)

Successive policy responses have focused on areas through the Inner Cities and Urban Programmes and more recently City Challenge and Single Regeneration Budgets (SRB). Special area-based spending programmes are common but often spend quite modest amounts, especially when put alongside main spending programmes such as social security, health and education. This means that the potential role of public services and spending in countering deprivation is very high, but the issue may be how to 'bend' main programmes. Effective 'bending' is difficult without better knowledge of what is spent, where and on whom. Discrimination in some programmes may be swamped or offset by the unintended effect of different distributions in parallel spending streams. A local strategic awareness would seek to package expenditure so that the inter-departmental budget going into deprived areas would have better outcomes.

The evidence on local public spending presented here relates to three study areas, the London Borough of Brent, The City of Liverpool and The City of Nottingham. These are all local authorities that have had recent experience of SRB programmes. The small area analysis is based on Census wards and our emphasis is on the residence of service users or beneficiaries of government spending. Our spending totals make no assumptions about the local economic impact; the service provider may be situated elsewhere and the employment generated by public funds may benefit another local economy. Our spending figures are net spending for the financial year 1995/6. Wherever possible we employed a broad range of approaches, depending on the nature of services and data available. Readers interested in the detailed methodology of the research are advised to read the full descriptions elsewhere (Bramley *et al.*, 1998).

Not all government spending can be meaningfully related to small areas. Spending on defence, foreign affairs and national goods such as research and development are obvious examples. Other expenditure excluded as national include agriculture, trade and industry, the legal system, prison services and financing items (for example, privatisation).

Deprivation in the Three Study Areas

We use as ward-level deprivation measures the DETR's Index of Local Conditions (ILC),[1] based on 1991 Census data (DOE 1995). Table 8.1 shows the wards in each area by their position in four ILC deprivation bands. Our three areas each have wards with very high deprivation (ILC scores over 12). Brent has just under half of its wards in this most deprived band, Liverpool around 40 per cent, and Nottingham 15 per cent. Liverpool also has another 40 per cent of its wards in the next highest band of deprivation. Under this index, Granby in Liverpool is the 2nd most deprived ward in England, and St Raphael's, Carlton, Kilburn in Brent are all in the top most 50 of deprived wards. Lenton, the most deprived ward in Nottingham, is 183rd in ranked deprivation in England.

Table 8.1   Deprivation by 1991 index of local conditions in Brent, Liverpool and Nottingham (count of wards)

ILC score in bands	Brent	Liverpool	Nottingham	Total
4 very high (ILC >12)	14	13	4	31
3 high (ILC 6-12)	7	13	7	27
2 moderate (ILC 0-6)	3	1	13	17
1 low (ILC <0)	7	6	3	16
Ward totals	31	33	27	93

Source: DOE (1995)

Britain's economy has recovered since 1991 and hence our 1995/6 spending figures may not fully match the ILC deprivation pattern in the middle of the 1991 recession. We compare deprivation from 1991 ILC scores to data obtained for this study from the Department of Social Security (DSS) on receipt of Income Support (IS) in 1995. IS is the means-tested 'safety net' of social assistance, and hence the proportion of the population who claim can be seen as a cross-sectional measure of income deprivation. These provide area profiles similar to those produced by Noble *et al.* (1994) for Oxford and Oldham, and Dobson *et al.* (1996) for Leicester.

IS is paid to 17.2 per cent of the British population (DSS, 1996). Figures 8.1 and 8.2 give the ward ILC deprivation scores ranked from left to right by descending levels of deprivation for two of our study areas. Superimposed on the ILC scores shown in the histograms (which relate to the left-hand Y scale) are three lines showing the proportion of population receiving IS (and which relate to the right-hand Y scale). The three measures of IS claiming are (a) the

proportions of 18 to 59 year olds who claim IS; and (c), the proportion of over 60 year olds who claim.[2]

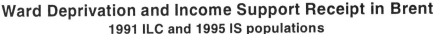

Ward Deprivation and Income Support Receipt in Brent
1991 ILC and 1995 IS populations

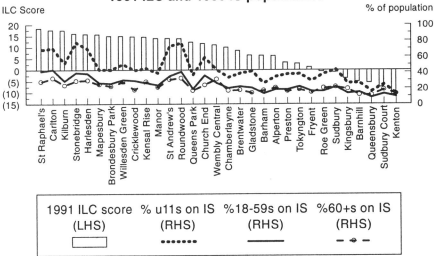

Figure 8.1 Ward deprivation and income support receipt in Brent

Figures 8.1 and 8.2 show that there is no very close correspondence between the ranking of 1991 ILC deprivation and ranking of IS claims in 1995. However, the ILC is more of a multivariate measure of deprivation and exact correspondence is not expected. The overall underlying rankings are similar, however, with the most deprived wards having the highest proportions receiving IS, and the least deprived having the lowest. However, there are fairly obvious peaks and troughs in ward-based IS claims which mean that some wards have higher or lower levels of IS claimants than their ranked deprivation from 1991 would suggest. This may be due to changes in the incidence and location of poverty since 1991, and/or to other local demographic/economic/spatial factors affecting claiming (for example, differential take-up) or the base population. Further explanation of ward-based differences such as these is beyond this chapter but will be pursued in further research.

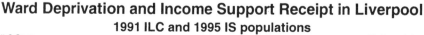
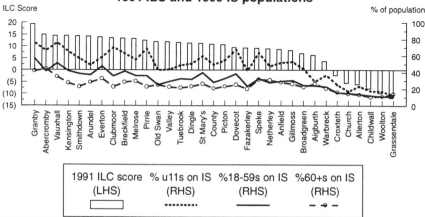

Figure 8.2   Ward deprivation and income support receipt in Liverpool

Spending Results for Selected Services

Social Security

Social security results are based on 100 per cent case counts and amounts for all of the main national benefit programmes. These are either from an annual 100 per cent IS scan, or from scans of current caseloads using the Generalised Matching System (GMS), a new cross-benefit database. Housing Benefits were obtained from local authority computerised records, and several 'small' spending national benefits - Industrial Injury Benefits, War Pensions, Social Fund, and Independent Living Fund - which are based on regional estimates.

Table 8.2 shows that all three of our study areas have far higher rates of IS claiming and spending than the national average. For the over 60s, Brent has a 35 per cent higher claim rate than the average, Liverpool 51 per cent higher, and Nottingham 22 per cent higher. The working age population in Brent claim 98 per cent more than average, in Liverpool 142 per cent more and in Nottingham 102 per cent more. Children are worst affected: across the board nearly one-quarter of British children are in families claiming IS; in Brent, however, they are 74 per cent more likely, in Liverpool 95 per cent more, and in Nottingham 110 per cent more likely to be in families receiving IS than the national average. Table 8.2 also shows the large range of IS claiming and spending within our three areas. In the highest spending wards, around 70 per cent of children rely on IS. In the lowest spending wards, in Liverpool and Brent, around 16 to 17 per cent of children are also reliant, below the national average. In Nottingham, however, even the lowest spending ward has a proportion of children fairly close to the national average of 25 per cent.

Income Support is strongly skewed towards deprived areas. At the extreme, Granby in Liverpool spends 360 per cent of the national average, while Carlton in Brent spends 337 per cent, and Radford in Nottingham 305 per cent. But even in the least deprived wards in all three of our study areas, IS represents significant government spending. This finding means that it is potentially misleading to equate differences in deprivation with the presence or absence of poverty. Poverty, or in this case, its proxy IS, is spread across areas of high and low deprivation in our study areas as well as being very concentrated in the most deprived areas. This important finding qualifies all of our results that follow.

Table 8.2   Spending on and proportion of population groups claiming income support in three urban areas, 1995/6

IS spend Ward and ILC rank percentage of population			with IS		IS spend
Category					
Per capita IS spend		% > 60	% 18-59	% <11	£ per capita
Brent					
Highest	Carlton: 2nd of 31	32.6	43.4	70.1	986
Lowest	Queensbury: 30th of 31	11.1	8.2	16.0	205
Average		20.5	23.9	43.4	556
Liverpool					
Highest	Granby: 1st of 33	41.7	56.7	75.8	1060
Lowest	Woolton: 32nd of 33	11.1	11.1	17.2	236
Average		22.9	29.3	48.6	617
Nottingham					
Highest	Radford: 3rd of 27	29.1	44.8	69.0	894
Lowest	Wollaton: 27th of 27	9.4	10.3	26.5	227
Average		18.6	24.5	52.2	508
GB National Average		15.2	12.1	24.9	293

Sources: DSS Income Support 100 per cent sample, DSS 1997 and unpublished population estimates

Retirement pension spending suggests that more is spent on the least deprived wards on a per-capita basis. However, these differences lessen when the spending is taken on a per elderly resident basis. Even so, retirement pensions illustrate a common theme, which is that the main spending programmes may 'bend' away from, as well as towards, deprived areas. Incapacity Benefit (IB) is currently a controversial area of social security spending because incapacity has grown so much, especially among working age men . Our results show much higher rates of claiming in Liverpool than in the other areas, and it is tempting to suggest that this reflects long term weak labour market conditions. Other research on IB claiming at local authority level supports this interpretation (Beattie and Fothergill, 1998). The overall effect of IB was moderately biased to deprived wards. The non-contributory disability benefits showed a rather flat profile when placed alongside ward deprivation - a result we expected for benefits that aim to ensure horizontal equity. We also found that a very high proportion of over 70 year olds in Merseyside receive War Pensions. Overall, Table 8.3 shows social security spending is geared to the most deprived wards and much of this is because of means-tested delivery. The non-means tested benefits provide a much flatter distribution, and deliver a lot of spending to non-deprived as well as deprived wards.

Table 8.3   Total social security spending and proportion means tested per head by ward deprivation level in Brent, Liverpool and Nottingham, 1996

Deprivation ILC bands	Average £ per capita	% means tested
4 very high (ILC >12)	2,337	61
3 high (ILC 6-12)	1,894	50
2 moderate (ILC <6)	1,570	43
1 low (ILC <0)	1,449	34

Notes: ILC bands explained above

Source: Authors' calculations

Health

Health spending is mostly to individual patients and hence, as in social security, should in principle be identifiable to private addresses and postcodes. However, the data on patient activity is very uneven. It is best for hospital in-patient activity. GP's lists provide a good estimate of geographical coverage of practices, but are less indicative of the intensity of service usage by different patients. Community Health Service data offered least in locality profiling. Added to this difference of data quality by service area are differences between our study areas in health authority (HA) methods for identifying locality spending. This means that our methodology differed and we had to resort to population-weighted or other proxy estimates in several areas. These methodological difficulties may explain, in part, the surprisingly flat per capita distribution, which is slightly more pro-deprived wards when we allow for age. Table 8.4 shows our results. They seem less skewed to reflect the poorer health of the poor than expected; this pattern has been shown by other analyses of General Household Survey and other data (Sefton, 1997). Our methodology could not link actual uptake for some parts of the Health Service to individuals and hence to locality, unlike national surveys of individuals, and this 'smoothing' effect may have had significant effect on the results. Age-weighted per capita spending shows somewhat more of a skew to deprived areas, but to a varying degree.

Table 8.4   Health service expenditure per head: summary of ward level estimates by ward deprivation, 1995/6

	Brent	Liverpool	Nottingham
Mean	563	711	673
Coefficient of variation %	13%	12%	9%
CV expenditure per age-wtd population %	13%	17%	17%
Range % of mean	66%	59%	40%
Highest wards	Preston 799	Everton 968	St Anne's 842
	Stonebridge 686	Abercromby 817	Trent 766
	Queens Park 459	Broadgreen 569	Wollaton 572
	Kenton 426	Dovecot 548	Abbey 571
Ward deprivation level			
Non deprived	524	695	587
Slightly deprived	636	742*	665
Fairly deprived	557	690	696
Most deprived	569	737	726
Ratio: Most - non deprived	1.08	1.06	1.24
Ratio: Age weighted expend	1.09	1.28	1.47

Note: * Based on differing methods and coverage, so not fully comparable; age-weighted expenditure allows for different health service utilisation rates by age groups
Source: Authors' calculations based on Health Authority data

Personal Social Services

In the case of Personal Social Services (PSS) we obtained the most complete results for children's services, with partial results for elderly people and patchy evidence for all other clients. PSS is a more moderate spending sector in scale: it operates under a statutory basis that varies between clients, and is controlled and managed by local government.

We had area data on key categories of children (e.g. children looked after) but spending per client figures were generally restricted to authority-wide average unit costs. We found a strong skew to poor areas in two of our three areas, but not Nottingham.[3] Wards in the most deprived group in all three areas had an average spend of £103 per capita compared with £38 per capita in the least deprived wards, a difference of 173 per cent. This might be seen as an example of the costs of dealing with the casualties of poverty.

Children's PSS spending is distributed between wards in a more pro-poor way than other PSS. Spending on elderly PSS per capita was 70 per cent higher in the most deprived wards, but this skew would be greater once allowance is made for the fact that elderly people in our study areas tend to live more in the less deprived wards. For other clients the difference appears to be in the order of 50-100 per cent.

Education

Higher education (HE) provides relatively good data from both Local Education Authority student grant databases and Higher Education Funding Council student data, and similar data are available for Further Education (FE). We had to model student loans, and in doing so, found high levels of home-based HE study in poorer areas. A finding that suggests the need for further research. Our results confirmed the expected 'pro-rich' bias of HE, with spending heavily leaning towards the least deprived wards (50 per cent above average) and generally low levels of spending in our two provincial case study cities (under half the national average). We found differences in the direction of slope of FE between our different case study areas; pro-rich in Liverpool, pro-poor in Brent.

Schools are the largest element of spending in education. Spending can be disaggregated to school level fairly readily because of the common accounting framework provided by the Local Management of Schools (LMS) system. The preferred methodology for allocating school spending to pupils' ward of residence depends on interrogating school-based information systems, which if successful (as in Liverpool) generate large data volumes. Cruder methods rely more on updated demographic numbers and assumptions about local catchments.

Table 8.5 Expenditure on schools in Liverpool based on full pupil location data (summary of ward analysis, pounds per head)

	Primary		Secondary & GM		Special	
Mean	159		132		27	
Range % of mean	107%		97%		158%	
Highest Wards	Pirrie	240	Church	207	Everton	52
	Valley	233	Everton	194	Clubmoor/ Speke	44
Lowest Wards	St Marys	140	County	96	Aigburth	10
	Vauxhall	70	Speke	79	Woolton	10

Ward Deprivation Level	*Primary*			*Secondary & GM*
Non Deprived	128	Non Deprived		142
Slightly Deprived *	129	Slightly Deprived*		101
Fairly Deprived	166	Fairly Deprived		123
Most Deprived	170	Most Deprived		139

*only one ward in this band in Liverpool

The results show a modest pro-poor skew for primary schools (17 per cent difference between most and least deprived wards in Liverpool), flat or marginally pro-rich for secondary/Grant Maintained, and a moderately pro-poor distribution for special education (most deprived wards 47 per cent above least).

The results for mainstream schooling are largely explicable by LMS formula funding rules. These allow only limited weight on educational disadvantage, while giving extra weight to older pupils staying on over 16. School size also has some effects, which may tend to favour deprived areas. There are important policy issues and opportunities here, but these are constrained by a tight overall budget.

Housing

Housing raises conceptual issues about how to measure capital and subsidy, which we skate around by appealing partly to public expenditure conventions and partly to practical data limitations. We did not attempt to measure 'economic subsidy', unlike Sefton (1997) and some earlier writers (e.g. Hills, 1995). We were able to measure recent public capital expenditure by local authorities and housing associations (HAs), actual housing benefit expenditures or take-up, and either gross expenditure or general subsidies to Housing Revenue Account (the latter crudely apportioned to wards pro rata stock). This service showed one of the strongest concentrations of spending in the most deprived wards, with capital spending per capita around five times the level in the least deprived, Housing Benefit over three times, and total housing public spending about four times. This pattern is strongly associated with the coincidence of most deprived wards with predominance of social rented tenure. However, spending per social renter does not rise systematically with deprivation level or predominant tenure. Two reasons for this are the rise of HB in the private rented sector and the fact that some new HA investment may be in areas not previously having much social housing.

The housing results arguably raise some issues about cost-effectiveness, at least in extreme cases where there are concentrations of very high spending (of the order of £2,000 per head in two cases). Very high private sector HB spending per private tenant was noted in some Brent wards, for example, while in certain other wards the expenditure on capital investment was very high and some doubts might be raised about whether this investment would always prove to be worthwhile.

Police

The police service is quite different in character. Policing is essentially a 'public good' and some of its effects (relating to general security, reassurance and risk reduction) are diffused across the whole population of an area. The police mainly deal with individuals as either the victims or perpetrators of crime, but it is unclear to what extent the benefits of policing should be attributed to these individuals. Much of the service is organised to cover geographic areas, and this includes the coverage of transport networks, public spaces and commercial areas, which may well be used by people from further afield. Significant chunks of expenditure are attributable to national and public order functions (e.g. policing major national events) and to general overheads. Ways of splitting expenditure between these and local policing functions, and between local patches, vary markedly between different police forces. Some of these characteristics apply to certain other services, for example fire protection.

Nevertheless, spending on policing has grown, and attention to crime and security in regeneration strategies is increasing. Any analysis of spending by location may at least describe the first order cost of policing different kinds of area; questions about the resulting distribution of benefits are perhaps more difficult to answer. We were able to make such an allocation for Brent and Liverpool; figures for Nottingham are allocated on proxy indicators. The results indicate an apparently strong skew to deprived wards, where per capita spend is 120 per cent higher than least deprived wards. However, this is undoubtedly complicated by a central city effect, particularly in Liverpool. Similar effects operate in a range of other services in the public protection and environmental field. Nevertheless, the association of crime and poverty/deprivation is well established, and is for example now reflected in the formulae used to distribute the police grant and the Standard Spending Assessment (SSA) between police authorities. This association could be seen as an aspect of the social cost of deprivation and exclusion, or of the failure of other policies to tackle them.

Other Services

A range of other services are also examined in the study, including transport, leisure and local environmental services. Although these analyses reveal some distinctive features and contribute to the overall picture, lack of space prevents a full discussion here (see Bramley *et al.*, 1998).

Government Spending: The Overall Picture

Overall Spending by City/Borough

Locally relevant public spending, when added up across programmes, is very significant in all wards. The average for the 91 wards in our three areas is just under £4,300 per head of population, which equates to about £10,750 per household. For a typical ward in Brent spending averages £30 million, while in Liverpool (where wards are larger) the figure is £60 million.

Spending is highest in absolute terms in Liverpool (£4,602 per head) and lowest in Nottingham (£3,826). The Brent figure (£4,372) would be markedly less in real terms if deflated for 'London costs' (a 15 per cent deflation would reduce it to £3,712, below the Nottingham level. For our three cities together, average spending is only 17 per cent above national average per capita spending for the range of public programmes covered by our analysis. However, since Liverpool is about 20 per cent above the other two, we can say that Liverpool spends about 29 per cent above the average, while Nottingham spends about seven per cent above and Brent only about four per cent in real terms. Thus, of the three cities/boroughs, it is Liverpool that really stands out as a relatively high spender. Of course, such spending differences might be regarded as rather modest, given that these are some of the most deprived local authority areas in England (this is undoubtedly true of Liverpool).

We have tried to calculate measures of public expenditure dependence relative to proxy-based measures of household income. Figure 8.3 shows three such measures for our three cities: transfer payments over gross income; in-kind expenditures over gross income; total measured public expenditure over enhanced income (gross income plus in-kind expenditure). The dependence of local household real incomes on public expenditure appears to be much greater in Liverpool, with the broader measure approaching 60 per cent and the transfer payment measure approaching 40 per cent. Transfer payments are particularly high in Liverpool. The ratios are lower for Brent partly because modeled incomes are significantly higher.

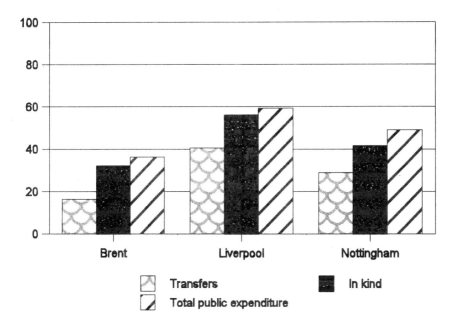

Figure 8.3   Public expenditure dependence relative to income

Ward Level Variation

Public spending per head varies quite a lot at ward level (Table 8.6). Table 8.7 shows the estimated total spending for each ward in the three areas, ranked in descending order of ILC deprivation score. The range of variation in spending is from under £3,000 to over £9,000. However, it is clear that there is one outlier in the dataset: Everton (in Liverpool, £9382), whose spending is £2,850 higher than the next nearest ward (Carlton, in Brent, £6,538). Many factors contribute to the Everton phenomenon, including a small population and central city location. It is not obviously a product of error, but it remains something of a puzzle. In general, although particular spending heads may show lumpy distributions across wards, when adding up across all the spending programmes these tend to average out. Even so, there is clearly a good deal of variation, of the order of £1-2,000 per head, between individual wards at the same deprivation levels. Figure 8.4 confirms this by showing a scatter diagram of the relationship between ILC and total spend per head.

Table 8.6   Total public expenditure per head by ward ranked by deprivation by city (identifiable locally relevant public expenditure 1995/6, £ per head of population)

	Brent			Liverpool			Nottingham	
Ward	*ILC*	*£/head*	*Ward*	*ILC*	*£/head*	*Ward*	*ILC*	*£/head*
St. Raphael's	18.34	5,497	Granby	19.40	5,500	Lenton	15.19	4,742
Carlton	17.60	6,538	Abercromby	14.90	6,313	St.Anne's	14.34	4,971
Kilburn	17.48	4,682	Vauxhall	14.52	6,305	Radford	14.00	4,246
Stonebridge	16.07	6,097	Kensington	14.49	4,310	Bridge	12.73	4,357
Harlesden	15.83	5,780	Smithdown	14.38	5,460	Forest	11.69	3,999
Mapesbury	15.65	4,448	Arundel	14.21	4,077	Trent	10.22	4,950
Brondesbury P	15.01	4,741	Everton	13.94	9,382	Manvers	9.91	4,555
Willesdon Gn	14.95	4,864	Clubmoor	13.58	4,692	Park	9.72	3,748
Cricklewood	14.69	4,324	Breckfield	13.41	4,633	Strelley	9.09	4,233
Kensal Rise	14.64	4,713	Melrose	13.38	4,532	Aspley	8.78	3,802
Manor	14.03	4,197	Pirrie	12.61	5,078	Bulwell East	6.74	3,684
St. Andrew's	13.97	5,304	Old Swan	12.01	4,430	Bulwell West	5.97	3,916
Roundwood	13.93	5,124	Valley	12.00	5,231	Bestwood Pk	5.63	3,825
Queens Park	12.35	4,288	Tuebrook	11.65	4,026	Byron	4.98	3,376
Church End	11.68	5,165	Dingle	11.51	4,602	Greenwood	4.88	3,682
Wembley Cen	11.09	4,370	St. Mary's	11.35	4,978	Clifton East	4.40	3,697
Chamberlayne	10.07	3,959	County	11.03	4,323	Robin Hood	4.37	3,596
Brentwater	8.58	3,888	Picton	10.72	3,822	Basford	3.92	3,304
Gladstone	6.52	3,791	Dovecot	9.58	4,234	Bilborough	3.67	3,922
Barham	6.41	4,402	Fazakerley	9.34	4,369	Portland	3.48	3,293
Alperton	6.30	3,701	Speke	9.23	4,850	Sherwood	3.31	3,334
Preston	3.35	3,847	Netherley	8.99	4,707	Clifton West	2.80	3,238
Tokyngton	2.85	3,695	Anfield	8.75	4,075	Mapperley	2.25	3,381
Fryent	1.23	3,683	Gillmoss	8.30	4,149	Beechdale	1.79	4,174
Roe Green	-0.62	4,066	Broadgreen	7.02	4,326	Wilford	-2.01	3,273
Sudbury	-0.91	3,287	Aigburth	6.40	3,853	Abbey	-3.92	3,004
Kingsbury	-3.60	3,846	Warbreck	3.83	3,543	Wollaton	-10.99	2,991
Barnhill	-5.01	3,601	Croxteth	-2.20	3,816			
Queensbury	-5.53	3,261	Church	-5.41	3,542			
Sudbury Court	-7.46	3,132	Allerton	-6.05	4,023			
Kenton	-10.94	3,253	Childwall	-7.80	3,328			
			Woolton	-9.68	3,680			
			Grassendale	-11.67	3,683			

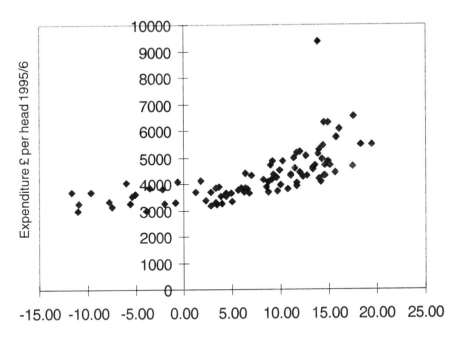

Figure 8.4   Total identifiable public expenditure by ward deprivation level in three cities

Figure 8.4 suggests that there is a positive relationship between spending and deprivation, albeit not a smooth or noiseless one. Indeed, it suggests a non-linear relationship, with spending rising more steeply in the most deprived wards. This is also shown in summary of spending by deprivation bands as described above and other variables in Table 8.7. Spending per head rises from £3,487 in the non deprived band to £3,618 and £4,243 in the next two bands, and then jumps to £5,124 in the most deprived band. The overall headline result is that the most deprived group of wards spend 45 per cent above the least.

Table 8.7   Total identifiable public expenditure by ward deprivation level by city, 1995/6

| | City/Borough | | | |
| | Brent | Liverpool | Nottingham | 3 Cities |
	£	£	£	£
1 Non Deprived	3,492	3,679	3,090	3,487
2 Slightly Deprived	3,742	3,543	3,595	3,618
3 Fairly Deprived	4,182	4,332	4,139	4,243
4 Most Deprived	5,043	5,380	4,579	5,124
All wards	4,372	4,602	3,826	4,294
Index most/least deprived	144	146	148	147

Source: Based on authors' calculations

The non-linearity of the relationship is confirmed by a regression analysis across the 90 wards (excluding Everton), where a simple model including a quadratic term in ILC (positive values only) and a tenure (social renting) dummy variable can account for 72 per cent of the variance. Cross-tabulations suggest that, after allowing for deprivation (ILC), the most significant other independent variable is housing tenure, predominantly social renting areas attracting systematically higher spending across a wide range of services. There are some signs of a central city effect, but this is somewhat skewed by Everton and Brent does not contain a central business district in the full sense. Exploratory regressions suggest that there may be some other effects at work for sectors of expenditure, but overall the key correlates which we have established are deprivation and tenure.

Spending Patterns by Programme Area

The relationship of spending with ward deprivation level varies substantially and systematically between different programme areas. Many of these patterns are broadly as would have been predicted on the basis of previously available evidence from household surveys or other sources. Some are perhaps more surprising, especially for programmes that have rarely been analysed in this way before.

A number of programmes target spending heavily in favour of deprived wards, with most deprived wards receiving more than double the per capita spend of least deprived. These include the major means-tested social security benefits (IS, HB), PSS for children, some ancillary education (e.g. free meals), housing investment and subsidy, police, regeneration programmes (SRB) and some environmental capital spending.

Programmes which discriminate moderately in favour of deprived wards on average include disability-related benefits, elderly and other PSS, primary and (more strongly) special needs education, further education (with some caveats mentioned above), fire protection, and bus subsidies.

The pattern of spend per capita is relatively flat for the following services: health, secondary education, some contributory social security, most environmental services, and some transport. The health spend is rather more pro-poor when divided by age-weighted population.

The following service areas generally deliver more expenditure per capita to affluent/non-deprived wards: higher education; roads; rail subsidies; pensions; some local environmental services (e.g. parks). The case of pensions refers to per capita expenditure; deflating by elderly population totals gives a slightly pro-poor slope. This arises because elderly people in these three areas tend to live less in the most deprived wards and more in the suburban wards.

We can group spending together by broader sectors using the government departments responsible, as in Figure 8.5. This shows that the discrimination in favour of deprived wards is mainly practised by three departments: Social Security (DSS), Environment, Transport and the Regions (DETR), and Home Office (HO). Health (DOH) and Education and Employment (DfEE) carry out rather less discrimination. The same is true of high relative spending in these cities, with the exception of the Home Office services.

Although central government and its agencies control the lion's share of spending, local government appears to discriminate more sharply in its spending between deprived and non-deprived wards (81 per cent higher vs 29 per cent). The example of DOH illustrates this, with stronger targeting of PSS vs Health. Whether this is a pointer for policy might be a good subject for debate.

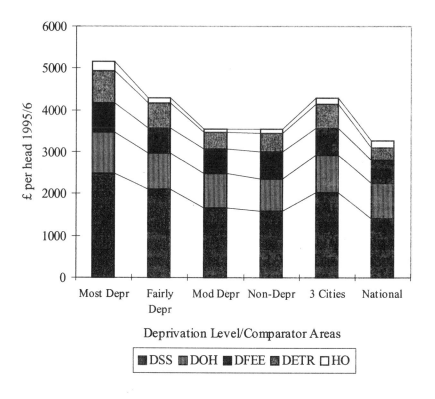

Figure 8.5   Expenditure per head by government department by ward deprivation level

Economic Categories

Figure 8.6 shows expenditure broken down by economic category. It shows that it is the means-tested part of social security that spends more in deprived areas; universal/contributory/categorical social security benefits spend on average around £1,000 per head in all types of ward, and the level of spend is slightly lower in the most deprived wards. Spending on the latter is largely driven by demographic differences in ward populations. Bending programmes more towards deprived areas would suggest increasing the proportion of spending that is means tested. We have already shown in Table 8.3 that the most deprived wards already have 61 per cent of spending so targeted. Other considerations are relevant to any debate about making social security more 'pro-poor': in particular, the wider taxation system and the accumulation of pension entitlements through contributions made in working life.

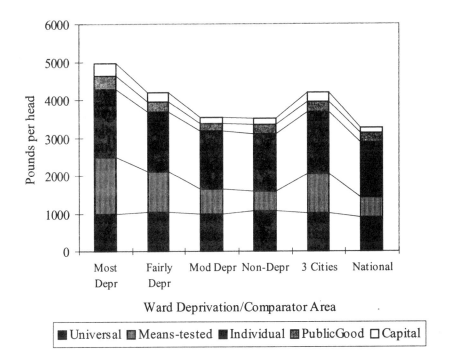

Figure 8.6 Expenditure per head by economic category by ward deprivation level

We spend more on individual services in-kind than on transfer payments. This rather broad category shows only a moderate tendency to spend more in deprived wards (18 per cent higher). A finer breakdown into needs-based and demand-based services in kind would probably reveal different profiles. Public goods spending appears rather surprisingly to be more skewed to deprived areas (45 per cent), but this result is driven by the findings on the workload/cost allocation of police and fire spending. Capital spending appears rather modest in the overall picture, although we have not been able to analyse some of the smaller capital spending components (e.g. in education) systematically. It is strongly skewed towards deprived areas (138 per cent higher), because the substantial element of housing together with the regeneration-related spends are strongly targeted, and these offset the opposing effect of investment in road and rail transport.

We can make a cruder economistic division of spending on 'economic investment' (education, employment/training, most transport and some local environmental expenditures). and payments made to sustain current levels of consumption, which might be labelled 'amelioration'. 'Investment' expenditure is only moderately targeted towards deprived areas (25 per cent higher); ameliorative expenditure is more targeted in proportional terms (54 per cent higher) and is clearly much larger in sheer volume terms. Thus one might say that in a typical deprived ward we are spending a lot of money, nearly £4,000, on amelioration for every £1,300 on investment; in an affluent ward these figures are £2,500 and £1,000. The policy question here is clear: could some of the large volume of ameliorative expenditure be redirected in some way which was more productive of an economic return in the medium or longer term, for both the individuals and the areas concerned? The New Deal policies of the current British government suggest that in the short term, investment spending on human capital and 'employability' in deprived areas must increase, alongside spending on benefits for unemployment, before any reductions on ameliorative spending can be made in the medium term.

The question of dependence on public expenditure relative to other sources of income is also perhaps relevant here. The calculations mentioned earlier suggest, at ward level, that the most deprived wards depend on public spending for about 56 per cent of their real income. The comparable figure for non-deprived wards is 36 per cent, while the national average figure is of a similar order of magnitude.

Client Group Analyses

It is possible to allocate many (but not all) spending programmes to one of four major client groups; children, young people, adult disabled people, and elderly people. Expenditure may then be compared both on a per capita basis and, more interestingly, on a per potential client basis. Potential clients are simply local populations broken down into bands by age (0-15, 16-24, 16-64, and 65+), with adult disability proxied by the 1991 Census measure of Limiting Long Term Illness (LTI). The results not wholly expected and quite striking in some instances.

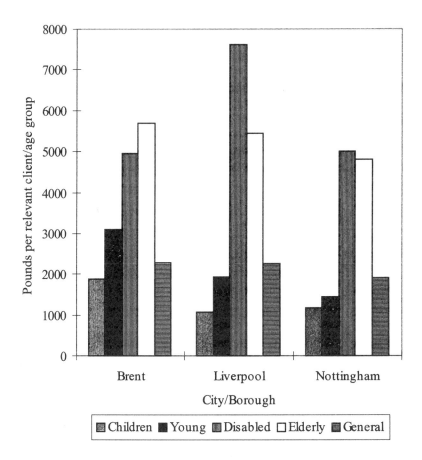

Figure 8.7   Expenditure per potential client by client group by city

Figure 8.7 shows that at city/borough level there is a remarkable discrepancy in client group spending between Brent and Liverpool. Brent spends much more on children and young people, while Liverpool spends very heavily on disability-related benefits and programmes (IB being one noteworthy example). This difference is after allowing for age and the incidence of LTI.

In Figure 8.8 we compare the population-weighted spending on the four specific client groups by dividing spending by their relevant populations, across the ward deprivation bands. For the elderly, this has the effect of restoring a modest pro-poor slope (13 per cent higher). However, for the other three client groups there is no overall tendency to spend more per potential client in the poorer areas, and in two cases (children and young) the spending is lower (by 14 per cent) in the most deprived compared with the most affluent wards. For these two client groups, Figure 8.8 reveals a U-shaped distribution, with the affluent end higher than the poor end. This suggests that there are two opposing sets of influences at work, each perhaps having a non-linear relationship with deprivation. Thus, poverty and deprivation-related elements of children's services pull up the left-hand end of the chart, but at the same time more universal demand-led elements pull up the right hand end.

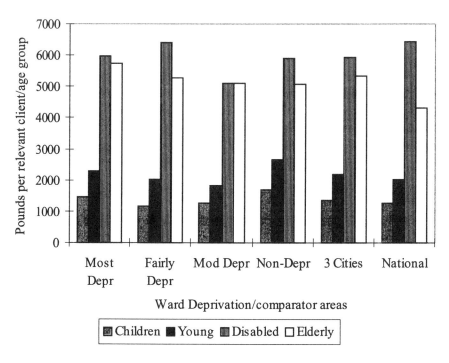

Figure 8.8   Expenditure per potential client by client group by ward deprivation level

These client group findings are, in our view, rather striking, and pose questions both for further investigation, and for policy. Put crudely, are we investing enough in the education and training of children and young people in our poorest areas, particularly in Liverpool?

A Tale of Two Wards

We have already shown that wards which are apparently at similar deprivation levels according to ILC may receive widely differing amounts of public spending. It is interesting to speculate about why this may be so, but a first step to understanding this is to identify the services which account for most of the differences. Table 8.8 presents such a comparison using particular pairs of comparably deprived wards in each of the three cities The higher spending of each pair is in each case a 'classic' inner city ward, Carlton (Brent) and Abercromby (Liverpool) being predominantly social rented but St Anne's (Nottingham) being relatively mixed in tenure. Services are selected if they exhibit a difference of more than £50 per head in two or more cases, or £100 per head in at least one case. It should be noted that this comparison is affected by how services are grouped together, as well as by any bias in the estimation method towards more lumpy or smooth distributions.

The eleven services identified in the table include pensions and three categories of income support, all the main housing expenditures, health, primary schools and police. These services appear because: (a) they account for large amounts of money; (b) they show significant discrimination between areas, in part at least on the basis of poverty; (c) they may also be significantly affected by local demography and/or housing tenure; and (d) they may also be affected by central city effects (e.g. police). The appearance of the income support measures really supports the points made earlier about current poverty versus broader deprivation measures (like ILC) based on dated census indicators. Housing Benefit is also a major discriminator; like housing capital spend, this is influenced by housing tenure and also by the concentration of problems on certain estates.

Table 8.8   Expenditures which vary most between pairs of comparably deprived wards in three cities (difference, £ per head)

Service/ expenditure category	Brent	Liverpool	Nottingham
	Carlton vs Mapesbury	Abercromby vs Kensington	St Anne's vs Radford
Retirement pension	18	-62	129
Income support - elderly	38	103	36
Income support - unemployed	57	166	-54
Income support - other	170	127	-42
Housing benefit	300	363	111
Health service	76	130	172
Primary schools	124	-50	-52
Housing corporation/HA capital	361	-147	173
LA housing capital	-160	562	-26
LA housing subsidy	482	40	0
Police	84	426	-16
Total identifiable expenditure	2,090	2,003	737

Implications

Estimating public spending totals at small area level is feasible, although difficult; it becomes easier over time as modern computerised databases with consistent postcoding/geocoding spread. Our results from this innovative exercise demonstrate a mixed picture of main programme spending; some is bent towards and some away from deprived areas. Government spending priorities tend to be set by national government looking down through its departmental views of the world. In this paper we have gone across government departments and looked up from three urban areas, each of which has a high incidence of deprivation. We have shown that spending overall is moderately in favour of deprived areas, but this picture differs markedly between different spending programmes and client groups (there are also some differences between cities). Simply reporting these findings may challenge some perceptions and assumptions about where the money is currently going. The findings certainly raise issues of whether the mix of spending is optimal and about whether it is delivered in the best way.

There is much talk about 'transforming' spending on social security into spending that is an investment in education or health. However, people currently dependent on state benefit income still have to live and the New Deal demonstrates some of the additional costs of moving into employment. Currently, as our figures show, many deprived areas are heavily dependent on such benefit spending, and removing or reducing it might weaken their fragile economies further, while worsening living standards for some of the worst off in our society. Once comprehensive local spending 'accounts' are available, the possibility of increasing costs of investment (e.g. through the New Deal, National Childcare Strategy and various Action Zones) being set off against local social security or other budgets may be possible.

Identifying the local budget flows and cross-departmental costs in 'Zones' may help to address some of the problems caused by many years of what has been described as 'benefit warehousing' - storing the problem in the cheapest (short-term) way while waiting for the market to restore economic growth and job creation. We have shown that in 1995/6, after several years of national economic recovery, in the deprived wards in all the areas studied, but most obviously in Liverpool, the level of dependence on 'dole' in all its forms remained high. But we have also shown that local authority spending programmes tend to target deprived wards more than central government programmes taken as a whole. This suggests that there were probably examples (e.g. community care) where locally-based needs assessment and service planning could lead to more effective targeting.

There are serious impediments to solving strategic problems of deprivation and poverty by becoming more local and cross-departmental in approach. There is an underlying functional logic to departmental boundaries and trying to overcome these may raise real technical as well as bureaucratic problems. Many benefits and services are available as of right to eligible individuals; removing such rights, in a shift from demand-led or universalistic provision to needs-rationed provision, would be difficult. Services have multiple goals, some of which, such as those geared to supporting economic competitiveness, may well be both important and in potential conflict with helping deprived areas and people.

We do not know, on the basis of this research, how much discrimination between affluent and deprived neighbourhoods is necessary: is 45 per cent the right number, or should it be 85 per cent? We have only looked at inputs, not outputs or outcomes. A central agenda for any follow-up work to this study must involve some linkage between expenditure and its effectiveness in different contexts.

Neither have we linked spending to taxation, including (as already mentioned) contributions to Health and National Insurance funds. Measures of redistribution between income groups, areas and demographic groups/cohorts need to take account of these aspects as well. It is clearly desirable that deprived areas be connected to the economy, wealth-generation and development and are able to benefit from general economic progress. Public expenditure distribution is only one aspect of this; employment generation, commuting patterns, and local/regional multiplier effects are other aspects which we have not examined at all in this study. Hopefully other parallel work evaluating regeneration programmes will shed more light on these aspects.

We also know that many of the poor do not live in very deprived areas. Our results illustrate some of the public expenditure implications of this, together with the fact that many public services are not specifically targeted on the poor. Any 'holistic approach' must mean more than just a re-juggling of services to the poor or to deprived areas, but is likely to involve a reconsideration of the nature, purpose and delivery of services more broadly.

Acknowledgements

This paper is based on research commissioned by the Department of Environment, Transport and the Regions as a pilot study to examine the feasibility of generating small area estimates of public expenditure across all main relevant programmes. A number of government departments were involved in the original commissioning of the research, in the course of the work itself, and in commenting on the draft findings. In addition, local authorities and other local and regional public agencies in the three study areas provided invaluable cooperation with the study in the form of staff time, guidance, contacts and, most importantly, data. The authors would like to acknowledge the contribution of all of these organisations and individuals, as well as of other members of the research team, particularly in the London Research Centre, in enabling the overall project to be undertaken and so providing the basis for this paper. The authors of the paper take full responsibility for any errors of fact or interpretation and for any opinions expressed here.

Notes

1   The ILC scores are based on 1991 incidence of unemployment, children in low-earning households, overcrowded households and households lacking basic amenities, households with no car, children in high rise accommodation, and the proportion of 17 year olds in full-time education (DOE, 1995).

2   It should be noted that we had no IS data on claimants' partners, only claimants and their children. This means that the claim rates for adults includes claims for both single and couple claimants. Hence, the overall proportion of the adult population who rely on IS will be higher than shown here.

3   Nottinghamshire can be shown to be untypical, on the basis of a study of children's PSS spending by ward in 26 local authorities, carried out by the University of York and others for DOH.

References

Beattie, C. and Fothergill, S. (1998), 'Registered and Hidden Unemployment in the UK Coalfields', in Lawless, P., Martin, R. and Hardy, S. (eds), Unemployment and Social Exclusion, Jessica Kinglsey/Regional Studies Association, London.

Blank, M. (1997), *It Takes a Nation: A New Agenda for Fighting Poverty*, Russell Sage Foundation, New York.

Bramley, G., Lancaster, S., Lomax, D., McIntosh, S., Russell, J., Evans, M., Atkins, J., Chell, M. and Flatley, J. (1998), *Where Does Public Spending Go? Report Of A Pilot Study To Analyse The Flows Of Public Expenditure Into Local Areas for the Department of the Environment,* Transport and the Regions, DETR, London.

Department of the Environment (DOE) (1995), *1991 Deprivation Index: A Review of Approaches and a Matrix of Results,* DOE Research Report, HMSO, London.

Dobson B., Trinder, P., Ashworth, K., Stafford, B., Walker, R. and Walker, D. (1996*), Income Deprivation in the City,* Joseph Rowntree Foundation, York.

Dorling, D. (1996), *Identifying Disadvantaged Areas: Health, Wealth and Happiness,* Position Paper for Joseph Rowntree Foundation Area Regeneration Programme.

DSS (1995), *Social Security Statistics 1995,* HMSO, London.

DSS (1996), *Social Security Statistics 1996,* The Stationery Office, London.

DSS (1997), *Social Security Statistics 1997,* The Stationery Office, London.

Giles, C., Johnson, P., McCrae, J. and Taylor, J. (1996), *Living with the State: The Incomes and Work Incentives of Tenants in the Social Rented Sector,* Institute for Fiscal Studies, London.

Glennerster, H. and Hills, J. (eds) (1998*), The State of Welfare: The Economics of Social Spending,* 2nd edition, Oxford University Press, Oxford.

Green, A. E. (1994), *The Geography of Poverty and Wealth,* University of Warwick, Institute for Employment Research, Coventry.

Green, A. E. (1996), 'Aspects of the Changing Geography of Poverty and Wealth', in J. Hills (ed), *New Inequalities: The Changing Distribution of Income and Wealth in the United Kingdom,* Cambridge University Press, Cambridge.

Hills, J. (1995), *Joseph Rowntree Foundation Inquiry into Income and Wealth,* Volume 2, Joseph Rowntree Foundation, York.

Holmans, A. (1995), 'The Changing Relationship Between Tenure and Employment', in H. Green and J. Hansbro (eds), *Housing in England 1993/4,* HMSO, London.

Holterman, S. (1975), 'Areas of Urban Deprivation in Great Britain: An Analysis of Census Data', *Social Trends,* 6, HMSO, London.

Lee, P., Murie, A. and Gordon, D. (1995), *Area Measures of Deprivation: A Study of Current Methods and Best Practices in the Identification of Poor Areas in Great Britain,* University of Birmingham, Centre for Urban and Regional Studies, Birmingham.

Murie, A. and Lee, P. (1997), *Poverty, Deprivation and Housing Tenure,* The Policy Press, Bristol.

Noble, M. *et al.* (1994), *Changing Patterns of Income and Wealth in Oxford and Oldham,* Department of Applied Social Studies and Social Research, Oxford.

Noble, M. and Smith, G. (1996), 'Two Nations? Changing Patterns of Income and Wealth in Two Contrasting Areas', in J. Hills (ed), *New Inequalities: The Changing Distribution of Income and Wealth in the United Kingdom,* Cambridge University Press, Cambridge.

Sefton, T. (1997), *The Changing Distribution of the Social Wage,* STICERD, LSE, London.

9 The Geography of Misery: Area Disadvantage and Patterns of Neighbourhood Dissatisfaction in England

ROGER BURROWS and DAVID RHODES

Introduction

Contemporary policy makers and social researchers are confronted with a confusing plethora of different measures of area disadvantage. As well as 'official' scales of deprivation such as the *Index of Local Conditions* we have many others, often developed with other purposes in mind, such as the *Jarman* Index, the *Townsend* Index and the *Breadline Britain* index. Although the construction of these various measures can be a matter of much technical and analytic complexity, the choice of which measure to use is anything but academic. To the extent that the spatial allocation of social resources can be influenced by variations in such measures the preference for one measure over another in the decision making process becomes a highly political matter. In the scramble for resources it would be very helpful if there could be at least some consensus as to the localities which should be prioritized. But which index - if any - should we use to identify such areas? There is, of course, no simple answer to this question (Lee *et al.*, 1995) and it is not our intention to contribute yet more work on indices of deprivation in order to tackle it. Instead we intend to approach the question in a rather different way. We suggest that if existing indices are to be used as a basis for the identification of disadvantaged areas *and* if policy makers are to take residents' views seriously, then it becomes important to know the extent to which the spatial variations in the views that residents have about their neighbourhoods coincide with the various maps of area disadvantage currently drawn upon by policy makers and social researchers. Such a strategy means that rather than (what will always be) 'essentially contested' conceptual and methodological issues determining which of the various indices we utilise, judgement should be determined by the

191

levels of dissatisfaction that residents express about the places in which they reside (see Burrows and Rhodes, 1998).

Ideally, of course, we would need to carry out a very large scale sample survey of the population designed to elicit residents' dissatisfaction with their neighbourhood of such a size and sample design that it would allow us to make small area estimates of the proportion of residents expressing dissatisfaction with their neighbourhood. This, however, is not practicable. How then can we generate estimates of the proportion of the population who are dissatisfied with the area in which they live at ward level, which would allow systematic comparisons with various of the existing deprivation indices on offer? In order to do this we draw upon nationally representative data explicitly designed to elicit residents' views of their areas contained in the 1994/5 *Survey of English Housing* (SEH). We use this data in order to examine in detail the socio-economic characteristics of those residents' who express high levels of dissatisfaction with the neighbourhoods in which they currently reside. We then use data from 1991 Census in order to estimate the likely spatial distribution of such residents' at ward and district level in England. This procedure allows us to generate crude estimates of the proportion of residents' likely to express high levels of dissatisfaction with their neighbourhoods. Finally, we systematically compare and contrast these estimated patterns of neighbourhood dissatisfaction with some of the measures of area deprivation noted above.

Measuring Neighbourhood Dissatisfaction

The SEH contains a large number of questions which are relevant to any analysis of residents' perceptions about their neighbourhoods (Green *et al.*, 1996). In the analysis which follows we have selected 17 different questions all of which relate to some aspect or other of a very general conceptualisation of area dissatisfaction. For our purposes here, each scale has been reduced to just three points: a positive or a satisfied response; a slightly negative or a slightly dissatisfied response; and a very negative or a very dissatisfied response. The full set of questions (with the key dimensions of potential sources of dissatisfaction italicised) are shown in Figure 9.1.

* How *satisfied generally* are you with this area as a place to live?
* Generally speaking, how *secure* do you feel when you are inside your home?
* On the whole, would you describe the people who live in this area as *friendly*, or not?
* Is *vandalism and hooliganism* a problem in your area?
* Is *graffiti* a problem in your area?
* Is *crime* a problem in your area?
* Are *dogs* a problem in your area?
* Is *litter and rubbish* in the streets a problem in your area?
* Are *neighbours* a problem in your area?
* Is *racial harassment* a problem in your area?
* Is *noise* a problem in your area?
* How good or bad do you think your area is for *schools*?
* How good or bad do you think your area is for *public transport*?

Source: Survey of English Housing, 1994/5

Figure 9.1 Questions concerned with area dissatisfaction

Table 9.1 shows that the most widespread source of high levels of area dissatisfaction relate to the issue of crime. Over one-fifth of respondents perceived crime to be a major problem in their area. Other major sources of area dissatisfaction which impact on over ten per cent of households were: problems with dogs; poor leisure facilities; high levels of vandalism; and litter and rubbish in the streets. Over five per cent of households reported high levels of dissatisfaction with: public transport; graffiti; noise; and poor street lighting. Just under five per cent of households were generally highly dissatisfied with their neighbourhoods. Over two per cent of households reported widespread problems with: the general appearance of the area; the behaviour of neighbours; and poor local schools. Over one per cent of households reported severe problems associated with: poor rubbish collection; feelings of insecurity when inside their homes; unfriendliness in their neighbourhood; and racial harassment.

Table 9.1   Rank order of sources of area dissatisfaction

Problem/issue	Rank order		Percentage who perceive as a major problem/issue
Crime		1	21.6
Dogs		2	16.3
Leisure facilities		3	15.3
Vandalism and hooliganism		4	14.0
Litter and rubbish		5	12.9
Public transport		6	8.6
Graffiti	=	7	6.1
Noise	=	7	6.1
Street lighting	=	7	6.1
Generally unsatisfied		10	4.9
General appearance		11	4.0
Neighbours		12	3.9
Schools		13	2.4
Rubbish collection		14	1.9
Securing		15	1.3
Unfriendliness	=	16	1.1
Racial harassment	=	16	1.1

Source: Survey of English Housing, 1994/95; Analysis by authors

It would be helpful to have some sort of summary measure to encapsulate the various dimensions of dissatisfaction within one index. We are fortunate that our data appears to be highly resistant to different scaling and index construction procedures in the sense that the conclusions that one reaches about which households are, and which households are not highly dissatisfied with their areas remain remarkably stable independently of which procedure is adopted. There is then no great advantage in using a complex scaling procedure when a very simple one will do. For this reason we have decided to adopt a simple counting procedure in order to construct a scale of area dissatisfaction. We have taken our 17 questions and counted the number of times each householder has rated a problem very negatively. This results in a simple scale running from a low of '0' (no problems or issues in the area considered to be very serious) to a possible high of '17' (all problems or issues in the area considered to be very serious). The frequency distribution of responses which results is shown in Table 9.2.

Table 9.2   Number of problems or issues (out of 17 possible) identified as being very serious by householder

Number of problems or issues relating to the area identified as serious	Number of households in England (000s)	Percentage	Cumulative percentage
None	8473	44.0	44.0
1	4859	25.2	69.3
2	2690	14.0	83.2
3	1353	7.0	90.3
4	765	4.0	94.3
5	492	2.6	96.8
6	297	1.5	98.4
7	133	0.7	99.0
8	70	0.4	99.4
9	59	0.3	99.7
10	28	0.1	99.9
11	18	0.1	100.0
12	6	0.0	100.0
13	2	0.0	100.0
14	2	0.0	100.0
N	*19246*	*100.0*	

Source: Survey of English Housing, 1994/95; Analysis by authors

Forty-four per cent of householders reported no problems or issues relating to their areas which they considered to be very serious. Some 25 per cent reported one problem that they considered to be very serious. Another 14 per cent identified two problems and seven per cent identified three problems.

This means that just over 90 per cent of households identified three or fewer problems or issues that they considered to be serious in their neighbourhoods and just under ten per cent of households identified four or more serious problems or issues with their area. In the spirit of keeping the operationalisation of area dissatisfaction as clear and as simple as possible we consider the ten per cent or so (some 1,924,600) of households who perceive that they have four or more serious problems or issues with their area as being unambiguously dissatisfied with their areas.

Using this simple measure of area dissatisfaction we are able to see which demographic and socio-economic characteristics of households are most strongly associated with high levels of area dissatisfaction. Table 9.3 shows the percentage of households with differing characteristics who perceive that they face four or more serious problems or issues in their area. The broad patterns may be summarised as follows:

- Households living in urban areas are more likely to be dissatisfied than households living in rural or semi-rural areas.
- Households living in the Northern regions of England and also in London are more likely to be dissatisfied than are households living in the rest of England.
- Households living in flats are more likely to be dissatisfied than are households living in houses. Of householders living in houses those living in terraces are more dissatisfied than are those in semi-detached accommodation who in turn are more likely to be dissatisfied than are those living in detached accommodation.
- In relation to tenure, those living in social housing are the most likely to be dissatisfied, followed by those living in the private rented sector (PRS). Amongst owner occupiers, those with a mortgage are more likely to be dissatisfied than are outright owners.
- Patterns of high levels of area dissatisfaction also possess a very clear social class gradient. Using the standard classification of the Registrar General, households in Social Class I are the least likely to be dissatisfied and those in Social Class V are the most likely to be dissatisfied with their areas.
- There is also a strong association with current economic status. Those who are retired or employed full-time are the least likely to be dissatisfied whilst those who are economically inactive or unemployed are the most likely to be dissatisfied.

- Patterns of dissatisfaction are also strongly related to age. Younger householders are significantly more likely to be dissatisfied than are older ones.
- Patterns of area dissatisfaction are also associated with ethnicity. Those who identify themselves as Pakistani or Bangladeshi are more likely than are those who identify themselves as white, black or Indian to be dissatisfied with their areas.
- Finally, there is clear variation across household type. In particular lone parents are significantly more likely than other household types to be dissatisfied, and the highest of all the different groups examined.

Disentangling the Socio-Demographics of Neighbourhood Dissatisfaction

In order to disentangle which combination of variables gives us the greatest purchase on explaining variations in high levels of area dissatisfaction we use a method known as *segmentation modelling* - a statistical technique that is useful in any situation in which the overall goal is to divide a population into segments that differ with respect to some designated criteria - in this case whether a householder is highly dissatisfied with their area or not. The technique divides a population into two or more groups based on categories of the 'best' predictor of a dependent variable. It then splits each of these groups into smaller subgroups based on other predictor variables. This splitting process continues until no more statistically significant predictor variables can be found. The technique displays the final subgroups, or segments, in the form of a conceptually tidy and analytically useful *tree diagram*.

The analysis carried out on our SEH data on patterns of area dissatisfaction is shown in Figure 9.2. The analysis begins with the total sample at the top of the diagram. As we have already seen, overall some 9.7 per cent of householders are classified as being highly dissatisfied with their area on our measure. The procedure first considers which variable is the most strongly correlated with variations in the proportions of those who are highly dissatisfied. This turns out to be housing tenure. As there is no significant variation in area dissatisfaction amongst those who are outright owners and those who are mortgagors these two categories are collapsed leaving just three categories. The next line of the diagram thus shows that the 9.7 per cent of the total population who were dissatisfied can be split into three main sub-groups: amongst outright owners and mortgagors 6.8 per cent were dissatisfied;

amongst those living in the PRS 10.4 per cent were dissatisfied; and amongst those living in social housing 18.0 per cent were dissatisfied. The procedure next considers which of the remaining variables best predicts significant differences in area dissatisfaction within each of these different housing tenure sub-groups.

Table 9.3   Percentage of different types of household who express high levels of area dissatisfaction

Socio-demographic characteristics	Proportion scoring 4 or more	Number of households in England (000s)
All	9.7	19,198
Region		
London	14.0	2,699
South East	5.9	2,898
South West	5.8	1,995
Eastern	5.3	2,309
East Midlands	7.9	1,540
West Midlands	10.4	2,017
Yorks & Humber	10.8	2,038
North East	18.1	980
North West	12.9	2,764
Urban/rural		
Rural	6.6	996
Semi-Rural	6.1	2,320
Urban	10.4	15,930
Type of accommodation		
Detached house		
Semi detached house	4.1	3,904
Terraced house	7.8	6,114
Flat etc.	12.4	5,453
	15.0	3,727

Table 9.3 (continued/-1)

Socio-demographic characteristics	Proportion scoring 4 or more	Number of households in England (000s)
Tenure		
Outright owner	6.2	4,626
Mortgagor	7.1	8,280
PRS	10.4	4,407
Social housing	18.0	1,932
Social class of head of household		
I	4.5	1,351
II	7.1	5,048
IIIN	10.1	2,780
IIIM	10.9	5,295
IV	12.5	2,800
V	14.0	1,063
Other	10.3	909
Age of head of household		
16-44	11.4	8,235
45-64	10.2	6,053
65+	6.3	4,958
Current economic status of head of household		
Employed full-time	8.3	9,964
Employed part-time	12.0	887
Unemployed	20.8	1,189
Retired	6.1	5,226
Other inactive	18.6	1,967

Table 9.3 (continued/-2)

Socio-demographic characteristics	Proportion scoring 4 or more	Number of households in England (000s)
Ethnicity of head of household	9.7	18,319
White	9.5	329
Black	9.3	242
Indian	13.0	136
Pakistani/Bangladeshi	10.4	216
Other		
Household structure		
Couple, no dep. children	8.5	7,002
Couple, with dep. children	9.1	4,694
Lone parent	22.2	1,101
Large adult household	8.8	1,183
Single male	11.1	2,241
Single female	8.3	3,024

Source: Survey of English Housing, 1994/95; Analysis by authors

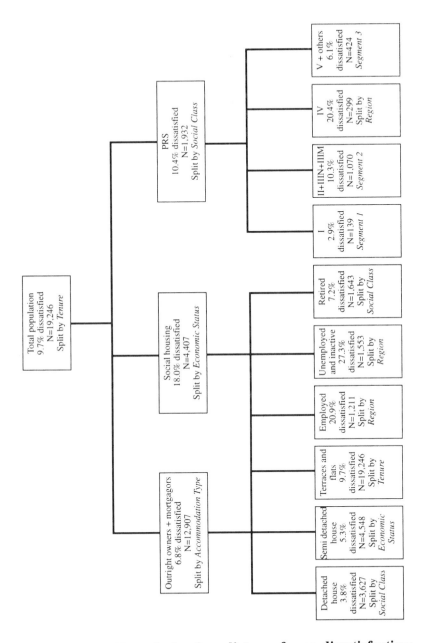

Figure 9.2a CHAID analysis of predictors of area dissatisfaction: first split by housing tenure

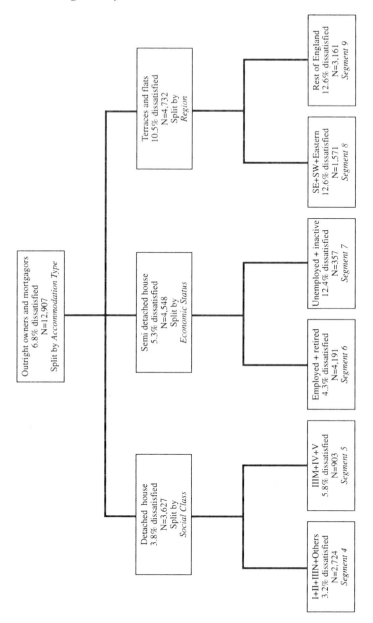

Figure 9.2b   CHAID analysis of predictors of area dissatisfaction among outright owners and mortgagors: Detached houses split by social class; semi-detached houses split by economic status; and terraced houses and flats split by region

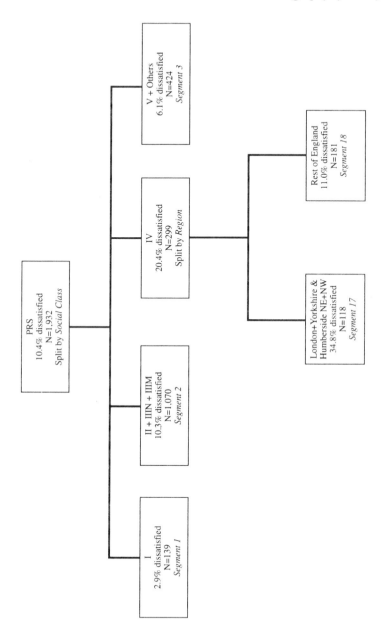

Figure 9.2c   CHAID analysis of predictors of area dissatisfaction: first split by housing tenure

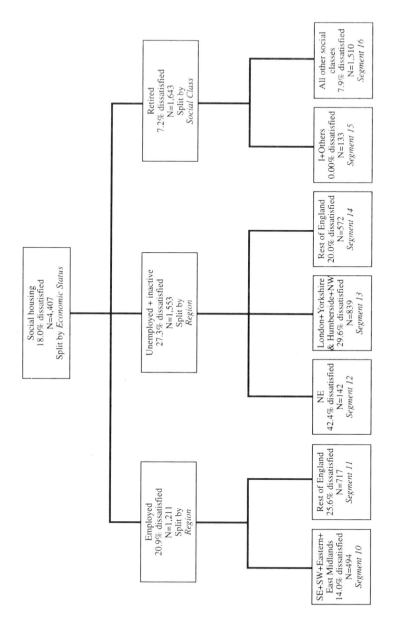

Figure 9.2d CHAID analysis of predictors of area dissatisfaction among those living in social housing: employed split by region; unemployed and inactive split by region, and retired split by social class

Home Owners

Amongst outright owners and mortgagors, the variable which best differentiates variations in area satisfaction is the type of accommodation the household lives in. Owners living in detached houses were the least likely to be dissatisfied with their neighbourhoods, in total just 3.8 per cent were dissatisfied. However, the analysis shows that this proportion varies significantly across *social class*. Amongst those in non-manual occupations the proportion is just 3.2 per cent whilst amongst those in manual occupations it is significantly higher at 5.8 per cent. No other variables significantly differentiate these proportions.

Amongst households living in semi-detached houses, 5.3 per cent were dissatisfied with their neighbourhoods. However, the analysis shows that this proportion varies significantly not across social classes, as was the case above, but by *current economic status*. Amongst those currently employed (full-time or part-time) or retired the level of area dissatisfaction runs at just 4.3 per cent. However, amongst those currently unemployed or otherwise economically inactive the proportion is almost three times greater than this at 12.4 per cent. No other variables significantly differentiate these proportions.

Amongst households living in terraced houses or in flats there were no significant differences in levels of area dissatisfaction, with 10.5 per cent being dissatisfied with their neighbourhood. However, the analysis shows that this proportion differs significantly across the *regions* of England. In the south of England outside of Greater London the proportion of householders who were outright owners or mortgagors living in terraces or flats dissatisfied with their areas is just 6.1 per cent. However, in the rest of England the figure for householders with the same combination of attributes is over double this at 12.6 per cent.

Thus, the analysis reveals that although those in the owner occupied sector were likely to be the least dissatisfied with their neighbourhoods overall, this masks very wide patterns of variation within the tenure. Within this tenure those from non-manual social classes living in detached houses were, not surprisingly, the households which were the least likely to express high levels of dissatisfaction with their locality. Outright owners and mortgagors living in terraced houses or flats in London or outside of the South East, the South West and the Eastern region, were the most likely to express dissatisfaction. This pattern illustrates the extent to which owner occupation has become a tenure which is increasingly socially differentiated (Ford and Burrows, 1999).

Private Rented Sector

Amongst those living in the PRS the variable which gives the greatest purchase on variations in area dissatisfaction within the tenure is social class. The PRS is known to be a highly differentiated tenure with huge disparities in both rent levels and in the quality of accommodation - ranging from the luxurious down to the pitifully inadequate. We might expect this variation in the sector to be reflected in some quite stark variations in levels of area dissatisfaction amongst PRS tenants, and this proves to be the case. Amongst those living in the PRS and located in social class I, levels of dissatisfaction were very low at just 2.9 per cent. It is likely that these households live, for the most part, in high rent high quality accommodation in pleasant neighbourhoods. No other variables significantly differentiate these proportions.

Households in the PRS located in social classes II, IIIN and IIIM show much higher levels of area dissatisfaction. Amongst this sub-group 10.3 per cent express high levels of dissatisfaction with their neighbourhood. No other variables significantly differentiate between these subgroups. Households in the PRS located in social class IV were even more likely to be dissatisfied with their neighbourhoods. Amongst this sub-group 20.4 per cent express high levels of dissatisfaction - a proportion almost twice as great as amongst those in social classes II, IIIN and IIIM. Further, this level of dissatisfaction can be shown to vary significantly across different *regions* of England. In London, Yorkshire and Humberside, the North East and the North West the proportion expressing high levels of dissatisfaction is over one-third whilst in the rest of the England the proportion is less than half of this at 11.0 per cent. No other variables significantly differentiate between these subgroups. Amongst households in the PRS located in social class V or who could not be classified within the class schema used here the proportion expressing high levels of dissatisfaction with their area was lower at 6.1 per cent.

Thus, the analysis reveals that although those in the PRS were, in general, more likely (10.4 per cent) to be dissatisfied with their neighbourhoods than were those living in the owner occupied sector (6.8 per cent) and, as we shall see below, less likely to be dissatisfied with their neighbourhoods than households living in social housing (18.0 per cent), this masks very wide patterns of variation within the tenure. Some sub-groups in the PRS express levels of dissatisfaction lower than those found anywhere in the owner occupied sector, whilst other sub-groups express levels of dissatisfaction as high as those found amongst those living in social housing.

Social Housing

Amongst those living in social housing the variable which gives the greatest purchase on variations in area dissatisfaction is current economic status. Amongst employed (full-time and part-time) householders levels of area dissatisfaction run at 20.9 per cent. However, this proportion varies significantly across the *regions* of the country. In the South East, the South West, the Eastern region and the East Midlands the proportion is significantly lower at 14.0 per cent than it is for the rest of the country. Outside of these regions, levels of area dissatisfaction amongst those living in social housing who were employed is over one-quarter.

Levels of area dissatisfaction amongst householders living in social housing where the Head of Household is either unemployed or economically inactive under retirement age were significantly greater than for those households where the head is employed. Overall 27.3 per cent express high levels of area dissatisfaction. This already high proportion is also revealed to vary significantly across the *regions* of England. In the North East the figure is the highest for any of the sub-groups identified in the analysis. Amongst households living in social housing where the head is either unemployed or economically inactive under retirement age over 42 per cent express high levels of dissatisfaction with their neighbourhoods. Levels of dissatisfaction were also higher than they were nationally for such households living in London, Yorkshire and Humberside and the North West. Amongst this sub-group just under 30 per cent express high levels of dissatisfaction with their areas. In the other regions of England exactly one-fifth of households in this sub-group express high levels of dissatisfaction with their areas.

Levels of area dissatisfaction amongst households living in social housing where the Head of Household has retired were significantly lower than for other groups in the tenure. In general just 7.2 per cent of such households express high levels of dissatisfaction. This figure is also significantly associated with differences in the *social class* backgrounds of such household heads. For the great majority of the sub-group, levels of area dissatisfaction run at 7.9 per cent. However, for a very small sub-group of retired households headed by someone who could not be classified using the social class schema or from a social class I background, levels of area dissatisfaction were so low that they were practically non-existent. Close examination of this group reveals that it is predominantly made up of single women aged over 65 who have lived in the local authority sector for many years and who were either widowed or have never married. In general this group tends to possess positive views about both the quality of both their accommodation and their neighbourhoods.

The Geography of Misery

We have applied the probabilities of area dissatisfaction for each of our 18 sub-groups to population data at ward level from the 1991 Census. In order to do this we commissioned a special cross tabulation from the Office for National Statistics (ONS) showing the *social class of the head of household* by the *current economic status of the head of household* by the *type of accommodation the household lived in* by the *tenure of the accommodation*. It has been possible to estimate the levels of area dissatisfaction amongst Householders for all but 93 of the 8619 wards in England. A full listing of our estimates of levels of area dissatisfaction by ward is not feasible here but is available on the world wide web as an SPSS portable file at http://www.york.ac.uk/inst/chp/misery.htm.

Perhaps the most insightful way of describing the distribution of high levels of area dissatisfaction at the ward level is by making use of an ONS system of area classification which clusters wards together into a set of exhaustive and mutually exclusive set of categories differentiating between *groups* and *clusters* of different types. Table 9.4 shows the estimated levels of area dissatisfaction for each group and cluster. The highest levels of area dissatisfaction are estimated to occur in Inner City Estates - those in London in particular - Liddle in Southwark and Evelyn in Lewisham are prime examples. Next come Deprived Industrial Areas, especially those marked by heavy industry - Pallister and Thorntree in Middlesbrough are examples. Third, come Wards characterised as Deprived City Areas - those in Inner London in particular. Fourth come industrial areas, those involved in primary production in particular. Fifth come lower status owner occupied wards - those dominated by Miners Terraces in particular. Sixth come wards dominated by Metropolitan Professionals - especially those with large numbers of young single people.

This geography of misery is of course *synthetic* rather than real. By this we mean that the probabilities of area dissatisfaction estimated for each ward in England are not based upon data collected from real people in those wards. Rather, the estimate is based on national level patterns of area dissatisfaction and the data on population characteristics in each ward is used to estimate what the level of dissatisfaction would be in that particular locality *if* the national level figures operate uniformly. This method of estimation means that no allowance has been made for cultural factors. We have been forced to assume that differences in attitude are primarily a function of economic forces. In reality of course this is a dangerous assumption to make. We know from both contemporary cultural studies in general (Featherstone, 1995) and from the new cultural geography in particular (Urry, 1995; Westwood and Williams, 1997) that the cultural sphere has always possessed a powerful efficacy in the determination of individual attitudes and beliefs and also in the formation and 'feel' of places. Our geography of misery is then best thought of as (what sociologists would call) an 'ideal typical' construct. Our estimates are for the pattern of area dissatisfaction which would pertain if spatial variations in attitude were simply a function of demographic and socio-economic variations over space and if any cultural differences over and above those related to demographic and socio-economic variations did not exist. The 'accuracy' (or otherwise) of our estimates are however something which can be explored empirically in the future.

Table 9.4   Estimated mean levels of the proportion of head of households who are dissatisfied with their areas by the ONS classification of wards - groups and clusters

	Groups %	Clusters %
1 Inner city estates	**17.96**	
London public housing		18.09
High rise housing		17.38
2 Deprived industrial areas	**15.57**	
Heavy industry		17.04
Ethnic groups in industry		13.68
3 Deprived city areas	**14.55**	
Inner London		15.59
Low amenity housing		14.79
Cosmopolitan London		13.90
4 Industrial areas	**12.07**	
Better off manufacturing		11.54
Growth points		11.70
Traditional manufacturing		10.87
Primary production		13.48

	Groups %	Clusters %
5 Lower status owner occupation	**10.58**	
Declining resorts		9.51
Industrial towns		9.91
Textile towns terraces		10.71
Margins of deprivation		11.57
Miners terraces		13.65
6 Metropolitan professional	**10.16**	
Urban achievers		9.73
Young singles		11.17
7 Middling Britain	**8.90**	
Small towns		8.36
West Midlands manufacturing		8.49
Expanding towns		9.19
Mixed economies		9.26
8 Suburbia	**7.63**	
Leafier suburbs		7.05
Classic commuters		8.35
9 Mature populations	**6.84**	
Coastal very elderly		5.61
Remoter retirement areas		6.65
Better off retired		7.06
Retirement areas		8.12
10 Rural fringe	**6.80**	
Edge of town		6.67
Industrial margins		6.68
Town and country		7.09
11 Rural areas	**6.72**	
Agricultural heartland		6.68
Accessible countryside		6.64
Remoter coast and country		7.06
12 Transient populations	**6.56**	
Transient populations		6.56
13 Established owner-occupied	**5.96**	
Green belt		5.74
Other suburbs		6.12
14 Prosperous areas	**5.68**	
Concentrations of affluence		5.07
Established prosperity		5.68
Affluent villages		5.95

Source: Survey of English Housing, 1994/95; 1991 Census data; Analysis by authors

The Geography of Misery and the Geography of Area Disadvantage:
A Comparison

We are now in a position to be able to take our estimates of levels of area dissatisfaction at ward level and compare them with some of the more common scales of area disadvantage: the DoE 1991 *Index of Local Conditions;* the *Townsend* Index; and the *Breadline Britain* index. Both Spearmans Rank correlation coefficient and Pearsons correlation coefficient lead to the conclusion that it is *the Breadline Britain index which is most strongly associated with our measure of area dissatisfaction* and the *DoE Local Conditions Index which is the least strongly associated with our measure.* These results are confirmed by fitting simple regression models. Variations in the DoE Index can - at best - account for only about 54 per cent of the ward based variation in levels of area dissatisfaction. The strength of the association is stronger if one uses the Townsend Index - it is possible to account for 68 per cent of the variation using this measure. However, it is the Breadline Britain which is most clearly associated with variations in levels of area dissatisfaction - it is possible to 'explain' over 73 per cent of the variation in ward level differences in area dissatisfaction by regressing on the Breadline Britain index. It follows then that *if one is interested in identifying areas where there are likely to be high levels of area dissatisfaction amongst residents then, of the available indices, it is the Breadline Britain measure which does the best job and the DoE Local Conditions Measure which is the least adequate for this purpose.*

Although the *Breadline Britain* Index appears to be the most appropriate for identifying areas of high levels of area dissatisfaction an inspection of scatterplots shows that some wards are estimated to have significantly higher levels of area dissatisfaction than would be expected from their Breadline Britain scores, and some have significantly lower levels of area dissatisfaction than would be expected from their Breadline Britain scores. Given this, it becomes important to ask what sort of wards are the most likely not to 'fit' the model? An inspection of the wards which possess the largest positive and the largest negative residuals shows that the *Breadline Britain* Index tends to underestimate the proportion of householders who are dissatisfied with their areas in some very unpopular areas in the North East of England and to overestimate the proportion of householders who are dissatisfied with their areas in some wards located outside of Greater London and the North with levels of estimated area dissatisfaction close to the national average.

Concluding Comments

The concept of neighbourhood dissatisfaction which has been the focus of our work is, of course, a problematic construct, not least because it will always be a function of both objective realities and sometimes highly variable subjective evaluations of these realities. However, we are not overly concerned about this mixing of objective and subjective spheres because, as Wilkinson (1996) has recently demonstrated, our health and well-being is as strongly influenced by our perceptions of material phenomena as by the material phenomena itself. For instance, *feelings* of insecurity and/or *fear* of crime can be just as damaging to us as their actuality. Nevertheless, even if our measure of neighbourhood dissatisfaction is a complex amalgam of objective and subjective elements we have shown that it is profoundly and starkly socially and spatially patterned - it has a decipherable epidemiology (relating to a range of socio-economic and demographic variables) and, correspondingly, we suggest that it has a clear geography. What though are the substantive implications of our analysis?

First, it is clear that householders experiencing the deprivations associated with high levels of dissatisfaction with their neighbourhoods are not only located within the social rented sector - problematic neighbourhoods are also experienced by home owners and households living in the PRS. Consequently any policy targeting of the 'worst estates' will miss a significant proportion of households living in what they perceive to be squalid neighbourhoods - on this point our analysis strongly concurs with the conclusions of Lee and Murie (1997).

Second, although we did not set out to contribute yet another measure of area disadvantage to what is already an overcrowded and confusing market, as a byproduct of our analysis, we have done so. Initial work (by ourselves and others) using our measure of high levels of neighbourhood dissatisfaction suggest that it is a powerful tool in explaining area based variations in mortality and morbidity and, possibly, variation in a range of other factors associated with poverty and social exclusion.

Third, our analysis suggests that the geography of misery in England most clearly corresponds to the map of poverty generated by the *Breadline Britain* index and is most weakly associated with the perception of the spatial distribution of poverty one gains when using the *DoE Index of Local Conditions*. The policy implications of this are clear - if one were to be guided by our geography of misery rather by any of the existing indices of area disadvantage (but especially the *DoE Index of Local Conditions*) when targeting social resources then the North East of England - Teesside in particular - would fare much better than it currently does.

References

Burrows, R. and Rhodes, D. (1998), *Unpopular Places?: Area Disadvantage and the Geography of Misery*, Policy Press, Bristol.

Featherstone, M. (1995), *Undoing Culture: Globalization, Postmodernism and Identity*, Sage, London.

Ford, J. and Burrows, R. (1999), 'The Costs of Unsustainable Home Ownership', *Journal of Social Policy*, vol. 28, no. 2, pp. 1305-330.

Gordon, D. and Pantazis, C. (1985), *Breadline Britain in the 1990s*, Avebury.

Green, H., Thomas, M., Iles, N. and Down, D. (1996), *Housing in England 1994/5: A Report of the 1994/5 Survey of English Housing*, HMSO, London.

Jarman, B. (1983), 'Identification of Underprivileged Areas', *British Medical Journal*, vol. 286, pp. 1705-9.

Lee, P. and Murie, A. (1997), *Poverty, Housing Tenure and Social Exclusion*, Policy Press, Bristol.

Lee, P., Murie, A. and Gordon, D. (1995), *Area Measures of Deprivation: A Study of Current Methods and Best Practices in the Identification of Poor Areas in Great Britain*, Centre for Urban and Regional Studies, Birmingham.

Townsend, P. (1979), *Poverty in the UK: A Survey of Household Resources and Standards of Living*, Allen and Unwin, London.

Urry, J. (1995), *Consuming Places*, Routledge, London.

Westwood, S. and Williams, J. (eds) (1997), *Imagining Cities: Scripts, Signs, Memory*, Routledge, London.

Wilkinson, R. (1996), *Unhealthy Societies*, Routledge, London.

10 From Poverty to Social Exclusion? The Legacy of London Overspill in Haverhill

LINDA HARVEY and DAVID BACKWITH

Introduction

Haverhill is an anomaly: a manufacturing town in the rural heartland of East Anglia. It is also a prisoner of its own history. As a London overspill town Haverhill experienced a social transformation in the post-war period. Today the legacy of that expansion, in combination with other social and economic factors, sets the town apart from its more prosperous neighbours. This paper addresses the existence and nature of this primary exclusion or segregation 30 years on and how it overlays and compounds other forms of exclusion and has generated spatial exclusion and spatial stress.

The analysis here follows Berghman (1995, p.15) who in discussing social exclusion in Europe, focuses on spatial exclusion:

> referring not so much to spaces where there are poor persons but to the 'poor spaces' themselves ... such a space may be a poor region, [or] a poor 'island' surrounded by a developed region.

The argument here is that Haverhill, experiencing spatial exclusion within a Suffolk borough, can be seen as 'a poor island' in a more developed region. It is also suggested that one estate in Haverhill, Clements, experiences this exclusion most intensely.

In highlighting the difference between poverty and social exclusion Commins (cited Berghman, 1995: 18-9) says, 'the former concept has to do with a lack of resources, whereas the latter is more comprehensive'. He suggests that social exclusion can be defined with reference to, 'the failure of one or more of the following four systems:
- the democratic and legal system, which promotes civic integration;
- the labour market which promotes economic integration;
- the welfare state system, promoting what may be called social integration;

214

- the family and community system, which promotes interpersonal integration.

Commins' framework is utilised here to delineate the processes at work in Haverhill which have generated a form of spatial exclusion and stress. In particular, Kristensen (1995, p.148) has used the concept of spatial stress in relation to social exclusion on Danish housing estates, describing a 'slumming process' whereby 'spatial stress sets in'. It is argued here that similar processes have occurred in Haverhill, particularly on the Clements estate.

Methods

The core of the research was a survey of 'key actors' in local service provision. This was complemented by analysis of secondary data on the social characteristics of the Haverhill area. For the semi-structured interviews with service providers we prepared a questionnaire which addressed four main themes:

- general social needs and provision;
- the functioning of respondents' particular service;
- the impact of London overspill;
- current efforts to improve provision.

Twenty-three service providers were interviewed (selected from contacts made in previous research); the sample being constructed to include people involved in all the main areas of service provision and at different levels within services. Two councillors were included for specific reasons: one as leader of the borough council, the other had been in local government throughout the overspill period.[1] Selection of the sample was intended to facilitate investigation of the cultural aspects of social exclusion, to see whether attitudes to the town varied between service providers, for example, by sector or role.

Overspill: The Roots of Exclusion

In 1957 Haverhill Urban District Council became the first local authority to sign an expansion agreement with London County Council (LCC) under the 1952 Town Development Act (*Haverhill Echo*, 1974). The social issues now confronting the town are to a large extent derived from the implementation of this agreement. Thus an outline of town's recent history is required for an understanding of contemporary social exclusion in Haverhill.

Of the ten East Anglian towns which entered into Town Development Agreements with the LCC, relative to the size of existing population, the planned expansion of Haverhill was greatest (East Anglia Economic Planning Council, EAEPC, 1968). This ensured that the overspill transformed the town. In the 1950s Haverhill was a town of little over 4,000 people whose prospects were not bright. More than other Suffolk country towns Haverhill relied heavily on industry and while there were jobs for women in the local textile factories, by 1956 one-seventh of economically active males travelled to Cambridge for work, nearly 20 miles away. As there were also 'limited opportunities' for school leavers, the fear was that it was only the post-war housing shortage that was keeping many families in Haverhill (West Suffolk, 1956).

In the ten years to 1966 the population more than doubled to approximately 9,000 people (Young, 1992). By the 1970s Haverhill was an apparently thriving industrial town. Nearly 60 per cent of the male labour force and 72 per cent of the men who had migrated from London worked in manufacturing (Gorst, 1966). But the extent to which expansion was underwritten by the state was critical. Under the Town Development Agreement (Stage 1) 3,000 council houses were built in Haverhill under an 'Agency' scheme by which the LCC built the houses and handed them over to the Urban District Council which then let them to LCC nominees (EAEPC, 1968). Much of the new factory development was also subsidised by the LCC. Employment and housing were linked: firms relocating to Haverhill were assured of council housing for their employees. This was the basis for the development of Haverhill's council estates, by 1967 two-thirds of all housing in the town was council housing, most of it occupied by migrants, 'newly marrieds and the younger men and women with children'. The expansion created Haverhill's own 'demographic time-bomb'. Not only was the population very young but the migrant population had a 'natural rate of increase some five times that of England and Wales' (Gorst, 1966; Haverhill, 1968; Haverhill Echo, 1974).

If by the 1970s Haverhill was a 'young, affluent and working class' town (*Haverhill Echo*, 1974: 2) the conditions which made it so were changing. With the end of the post-war economic boom the vulnerability of British industry could not but be felt in a town so dependent on manufacturing. In transport, a factor in Haverhill's selection for expansion (West Suffolk, 1956) change was also to the town's detriment. In 1967 the Sudbury to Cambridge railway, via Haverhill, was closed and the A604 (a main road link between the Midlands and the east coast) was not included in the development of the region's trunk road network. The significance these changes was probably not realised at the time but Haverhill was being cut-off, its geographic isolation exacerbated.

Democratic and Legal Exclusion

If in the analysis of social exclusion civic integration implies 'being an equal citizen in a democratic system' (Commins, 1993, quoted Berghman, 1995, p.19) it is arguable that for much of its recent history the people of Haverhill have not been so integrated, formal democracy notwithstanding. With a population of 19,715 in 1991, Haverhill is a medium sized Suffolk town. For local government services it has been the second town in a borough with a total population of 92,700 (1991) 57 per cent of whom live in rural areas (St Edmundsbury, 1993a). By weight of population the people of Haverhill are a small, atypical minority in the borough.

In 1974 the Urban District Council dissolved itself into the Borough; a decision which one of the parties now recognises as mistaken (Interview 23). Six years later the development agreements which had secured LCC support were terminated. This marginalisation in the formal structures of local government was compounded by other factors. Having only 20 per cent of the borough's population it follows that Haverhill's elected representatives are a numerical minority on the Council. A situation compounded by the fact that politically, until 1994, the Borough was Conservative controlled whereas Haverhill returned mostly Labour members. The combined effect of these factors has been that Haverhill has been perceived by service providers as not receiving the (political and financial) support that its needs warranted. This also applies to the County Council, where again the town's geographic location on the borders of three counties is seen as serving to marginalise the town. One respondent summarised these views: '... it has always been non-conformist socialist compared to the borough. There is a lack of voice, it is seen as [being] on the margins of Suffolk.' (Interview 9)

Whatever the legacy of the overspill on the political integration of Haverhill, the situation is now improving. In formal structures the reconstitution of the Town Council in 1989 was a harbinger of what was to come. For the past four or five years the Borough Council has become much more positively involved in the town: the Council offices have been refurbished; the old Town Hall re-opened as an Arts Centre and the High Street shopping precinct pedestrianised. There have also been positive developments in community involvement and development. At the more formal level the Haverhill Regeneration Project (HRP) has brought together prominent people in the town, from the public, private and voluntary sectors, which has generally been seen as having a positive effect. This is despite the HRP's two bids for funding from the Single Regeneration Budget having failed. The consensus among service providers is that the HRP has brought people together and/or raised the profile of Haverhill; although in interviews reservations were expressed about the 'bitter-sweet' experience of bringing key players together but failing to secure funding and, for example, the need to involve the wider community.

In local government the prime mover behind the HRP is a senior executive at the borough council whose involvement in Haverhill seems to have dispelled some of the scepticism of local service providers towards the local authority. However, improvement is not all 'top down'. The initial momentum for the HRP came from local concern about the lack of provision for young people in the town. This has led to the election of a Youth Council and the Town Mayor is cited as a driving force in these initiatives (Interviews 14 and 19).

The borough's recent interest in Haverhill, although predating the return of a Labour council in 1994 has been sustained by it; for example, the Council Leader is a Haverhill councillor. With the Labour majority came a new emphasis on providing access to services and community consultation. Under the slogan of *'Putting Community First'* the council has encouraged the development of a range of forums (organised by area and interest). There is a definite local motivation here, articulated in one councillor's determination that Labour will 'Never again allow [the borough's] total neglect of Haverhill' (Interview 12). In relation to Haverhill's past political exclusion these changes are comparable to the processes Anne Power describes which have challenged the decline of residualised council estates:

> Localisation of key services is possible and effective in improving conditions; resident involvement forms an important part of the approach; and area-based services work over time as long as stronger bridges to the wider urban community are created as a result.
> (Power, 1996, p.1562)

Examples of each element of Power's summary can be found in recent developments in Haverhill. And there is evidence to suggest that efforts to integrate Haverhill are working. Although the causes are not certain, there has for instance, been a recent improvement from Haverhill having had some of the worst crime rates in Suffolk to the point that the HRP has recently debated adopting a target of the lowest crime statistics in the country (*Haverhill Echo*, 15/1/98). While these developments have had a positive impact it is too early to assume that political exclusion has been overcome.

As regards user empowerment and participation, for instance, only one third of the respondents in our survey (a quarter of the entire sample) could give an unqualified yes in reply to the question whether their service had provision for user participation. Although, on the other hand, only 20 per cent said there were no such facilities, this does at least suggest that political participation is as yet a relatively new, unproven, phenomenon in Haverhill. The available evidence can be read both ways. For example, it is clear that in housing the greater emphasis the borough is giving to tenant participation is bearing fruit. The south of the borough (that is, Haverhill and surrounding villages) now has its own Tenant Liaison Officer servicing five tenants' and residents' associations and has a tenants' rep on the Housing Committee (Interview 10; St Edmundsbury, 1996b and 1997). In other areas while some service providers felt there was, for example, a 'lack of infrastructure for empowerment'; others had very negative perceptions about empowerment: 'No, none at all, resources are better spent doing other things' and 'users do not have much power I actually think they are very oppressed' (Interviews 22, 7 and 9). More generally, that only one of the nine managers in our sample lived in Haverhill lends credence to the view that strategic decision making is largely in the hands of people who do not live in the town.

Employment and Economic Integration

Haverhill has an economically active population of some 10,000 people (1991 Census). In the 1990s the unemployment rate for the Haverhill Travel To Work Area has fluctuated at slightly below the national average (Figure 10.1). There are two noticeable aspects of Haverhill's unemployment rate. First, for the most of the 1990s unemployment in the town has been higher than in either Bury St Edmunds or Suffolk, often by a considerable margin. Second, presumably because of the local preponderance of manufacturing, the labour market in Haverhill is much more vulnerable to recession than is the norm in

Suffolk. As Figure 10.1 shows, at the beginning of this decade there was little difference in the three local unemployment rates, all were well below the national average. As the recession of the early 1990s deepened unemployment rose much more quickly in Haverhill than in the surrounding areas, was significantly higher at the depth of the downturn but has since recovered to a rate slightly below the county average. The long-term social implications of this fragility of the local labour market are hard to gauge; although debt enquiries to the Citizens Advice Bureau (CAB) have continued to rise even as unemployment has receded (Haverhill CAB, 1997).

That Clements suffers particularly acute exclusion within Haverhill, is borne out by the unemployment statistics. The ward had the largest proportion of people out of work in 1991, the biggest increase in unemployment to April 1994 and, in January 1996, unemployment had fallen only slightly: Clements still had a far higher level of unemployment than the average for the town, the county and the country. In contrast to the volatility of unemployment rates for Haverhill, in Clements the picture that emerges is of chronically high levels of unemployment (Table 10.1).

Table 10.1   Unemployment rates (%) in Haverhill wards, 1991 to 1996

	1991 (Census)	April 1994	January 1996
Clements	9.6	13.211	11.371
Cangle	5.2	8.605	6.142
St Mary's and Helions	9.2	9.101	5.760
Chalkstone	5.7	7.523	5.595
Castle	5.5	6.063	5.130

Source: Suffolk County Council, 1995 and 1996

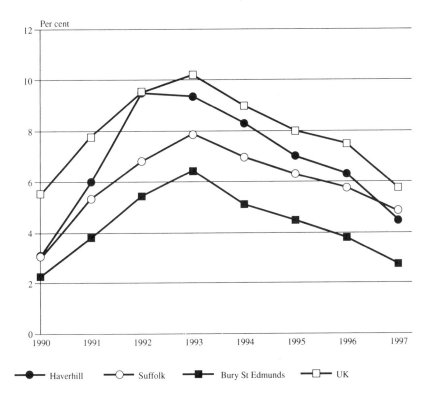

Figure 10.1   Unemployment rates (%), 1990-97

Projections of future trends in the Suffolk labour market generally correspond to the national picture: women's employment is expected to grow much more than men's; various forms of precarious employment (part-time, self-employment, etc.) will expand and (by 2000) 'there will [still] be more people in the labour force than in employment' (Suffolk TEC, 1997, p.1). Given that Haverhill's economic structure is significantly different from that of the county, how these trends will work out locally is not clear, although manufacturing employment in Suffolk is predicted to remain at its present level.

Haverhill's economic well being is bound up with its political integration. Economic development is among the priorities of the borough Labour Group. In general terms this seems to mean encouraging investment into the area through partnerships with private sector employers and with subsidies. One aim of this strategy is to encourage 'good quality' employment (skilled and well paid) as a counter to the relatively low skilled, poorly paid work which seems to have been characteristic of industrialisation during the overspill period (Interviews 12, 23). It is through the partnerships created in the HRP that the local authority is confident of being able to find jobs for the approximately 130 18-24 year olds in Haverhill who have been unemployed for six months or more (Interview 13). Visible evidence of this partnership approach is the conversion of the disused Cangle school into a foyer which will provide training and employment advice for residents and 'where appropriate the surrounding community'. The 52 bed project is scheduled to open in January 1999 (ECHG, 1996-97).

As there is a significant local 'skills gap' which particularly disadvantages school leavers seeking jobs in manufacturing (Cooper, 1996) the Cangle project will clearly not meet all the training needs of young people. Here again forms of social exclusion, economic, spatial and gender, interact. The nearest further education colleges are in Bury St Edmunds and Cambridge. Yet the expense and time spent travelling, given the infrequency of bus services, is known to prevent people from completing courses. The problem (single) young mothers had in finding child care effectively deny them access to these colleges altogether (Interview 18). This lack of training opportunities can be seen as compounding the general disadvantage women face in finding (secure) employment in a town whose economic development has focused so heavily on manufacturing; a common feature of overspill development which was intended to provide jobs for men, to the exclusion of women (Ungerson and Deakin, 1977).

The Welfare System

The importance of the welfare system in preventing social exclusion is summarised by Commins (cited by Berghman, 1995, p.19): 'Social Integration means being able to avail oneself of the social services provided by the state'. An analysis of the interviews revealed that a lack of welfare services and consequent lack of access was identified as the major social problem of Haverhill. Respondents from the voluntary sector, staff not working for the Borough and front-line staff were more likely to mention this lack of resources. The majority of respondents claimed that Haverhill has greater needs and fewer resources than other areas within the borough and county. A lack of facilities and resources for young people was one of the most frequently mentioned shortages. 'There are a lot more young people here than in Bury but we do not have their services' and local demographics show that Haverhill has a young population with 47.2 per cent of the population under 30 years old compared to 40.7 and 39.8 per cent in the borough and county respectively (OPCS, 1992; St Edmundsbury, 1993b).

National policies were seen as barriers to obtaining resources: 'There is a lack of recognition of how much is needed in Haverhill. The regeneration group applied for £2.5 million for Haverhill and failed, yet others got the same for one estate', and: 'It is difficult to argue for a health action zone when there are pockets of inequality in an affluent county'.

A lack of public transport combined with the distance to hospitals and welfare services in Bury and Ipswich, the county town, was the other most frequently mentioned barrier to people accessing the welfare system. Car ownership in Haverhill is low and this has left significant groups faced with large transport costs and long bus journeys are a barrier to accessing services. As there is no hospital in Haverhill vulnerable groups experience forms of exclusion, for example, people with mental health problems depend on inpatient treatment in Bury which undermines their continued participation in their local community and family life. A day hospital, an employment project for people with mental health problems and specialist mental health housing were also based in Bury (Suffolk Social Services, 1996) so that when discharged from hospital people have difficulty in accessing services which promote their social participation.

It was also emphasised that there is a shortage of support services for parents and children, a recent bid for a family befriender service had failed and there is no state funded nursery provision in the town. This is in a town with a higher than average number of households with dependent children: 62.8 per cent in Haverhill and 50.6 and 49.7 per cent in the borough and county respectively (OPCS, 1992; St Edmundsbury, 1993b) In addition Haverhill had the second highest number of referrals by Social Services Area Team in Suffolk of children in need (Suffolk Area Child Protection Committee, 1998).

The respondents reported a shortage and lack of access to housing for young or elderly single people. Backwith and Walentowicz (1997, p.38) reported a 'crude housing shortage' which in addition to the small rented sector and the rapid rate of household formation contributed to homelessness. There is no direct access hostel or Women's Aid refuge which have to be accessed in Bury. The CAB have proposed a Housing Advice Centre as 'There is no question that there is a need for such a centre' (Haverhill CAB, 1997).

A lack of good quality housing was reported and attributed to design faults, although these properties are now being 'upgraded'. The estates had their own schools and with inadequate town centre facilities a fragmented community was described where people identified with specific estates and were reluctant to access resources elsewhere in the town.

Cultural factors including attitudes and behaviours of the service users such as 'a lack of self esteem and self-confidence', 'disbelief of young people that they can change anything' and a 'lack of health behaviour' were reported as a barrier to their access of services. Services were also identified as being unresponsive to users 'agencies have their own culture, there is very little investment into reaching the client group as it is'.

Difficulties in ensuring that services are used by older people, people with mental health problems and particularly young people were reported 'a handful of people will not use the services'. There was concern that, 'Two-thirds of young people are not accessible they do not go to the youth club and they are not on the streets, so we are failing.' and 'building design is not attractive to young people'. Some respondents suggested specific changes to increase responsiveness and access. 'We need to create secret places or sanctums for young people, in the design of the building'. It was emphasised that problems of access and unresponsive services were due to the need for more public participation to 'Find out more what people want'. Examples of public participation in services were mainly specialist support groups in social care and policies for inclusion in policy forums and committees was a very recent though positive development in a few services such as the housing department.

Respondents from the state sector, staff working for the Borough and managers and politicians were less likely to mention a lack of resources. Smaller group of respondents said that services adequately met needs and compared well with other towns 'The difference in Haverhill is that we have multi-agency links and share responsibility in developing an holistic approach.'

The Family and Community System Which Promotes Interpersonal Integration

According to Commins (cited in Room 1995, p.19)

> Interpersonal integration means having family and friends, neighbours and social networks to provide care and companionship and moral support when these are needed.

Paugam (1995) develops the model of a 'spiral of precariousness' where he demonstrates that factors such as weak support networks, weak family relationships, no social life and single status after the breakdown of a relationship contribute to a fragility and retreat from the labour market.

Analysis of the qualitative data showed that respondents who live in Haverhill and also those who were front line workers were more likely to report the existence of specific social supports and people who do not live in Haverhill, who are service managers, who are not employed by the Borough, and who work in the voluntary sector are more likely to report a lack of specific social supports.

The respondents elaborated on the effect of Haverhill's history as an overspill town some describing how 'families were torn apart and lost their support system' and how 'people are isolated as they have no extended family here' this was linked to problematic social relationships by some respondents. There were reports of a lack of 'neighbourliness' and a report that 'some young people do not know how to form a friendship with a neighbour'. Some reported how their services had developed social networks by organising support groups.

Some supported the view that the overspill history had hindered community development as the town expansion created centres and schools based on different estates which fragments the town leading to a territorialism so that 'each estate is a distinct entity and people are isolated'. This territorialism was linked to the existence of 'gangs' who whilst offering protection to some excluded others.

Others were positive about the effects of the town development. 'The overspill enriched life , there is no local resentment here' and, 'Now there is a change, in the 1970s people used to go to London at weekends and never saw this as truly home. Now the children were born here, Haverhill has moved on', and 'There is a change in people's identity 'they were seen as "outsiders" but now they are more assimilated politically and have their own identity'. Reports of informal support included tenants associations, over 200 local groups and football clubs.

Supportive and regular contacts with elderly relatives in London were reported although the point was made that 'those who keep in contact have the money and the time'. There were reports that people still identified with London and of a kind of social insularity in Haverhill 'Londoners bond with each other' and 'Haverhill people think of themselves as different'. Reports also contradicted the existence of social insularity, 'It [overspill] was a long time ago and now the 2nd and 3rd generation have been to school together.

There were also reports that people were not in contact with family and social networks in London or that only 1st generation 'overspill' visit London. Finally there was an emphasis on the new private estates whose residents commute to London and Cambridge and whose social networks are elsewhere, 'There is a potential split between the commuters with cars who use Haverhill as a dormitory and people whose whole focus is Haverhill and who are not being given the skills to move out'. However these newer residents were also experiencing social isolation.

Respondents who live in Haverhill largely reported that the overspill history promoted community development whilst those not living in Haverhill largely thought it hindered community development. Those respondents not employed by the Borough were more likely to report social insularity.

Spatial Exclusion and Stress and the Urban Rural Dilemma

Haverhill can be seen as suffering spatial exclusion at two levels. First, Haverhill, although located in a rural setting, has the social conditions usually associated with urban areas. Haverhill can be seen as one of the 'pockets of relatively intense deprivation' identified in the County Council's recent survey (Suffolk County Council, 1995, p.5). Second, within Haverhill one council estate suffers particularly marked levels of deprivation and other disadvantages such that it can be seen as an area of more acute exclusion.

Yet the full extent of social exclusion can go unrecognised as the first edition of Suffolk's (1995) poverty report uses four indicators from the 1991 census as one way of showing levels of poverty between wards in Suffolk and Haverhill's scoring by these indicators (Table 10.2) suggest that, relative to both the county and the borough poverty in Haverhill is low. However, Haverhill's distinct social profile mean that the nature and extent of deprivation in the town is masked by indicators mainly intended to focus on rural areas. For instance, a low proportion of people working over 40 hours in Haverhill is probably a reflection of the dominance of manufacturing in the local economy as long hours are a characteristic of agricultural employment. Equally Haverhill's low scores on two of the other indicators, long term illness and lack of central heating, are partly attributable to, respectively, the very young population and the high proportion of council housing. Thus three of these four indicators do not correspond to the nature of poverty in Haverhill and so do not reveal its extent. In fact the relatively high levels of unemployment (discussed above) suggest that there is considerable poverty in Haverhill.

Table 10.2 Poverty indicators (%) in Haverhill wards 1991

	Households with no car	Households with no central heating	Persons with long term illness	Persons working over 40 hours per week
Clements	29.77	6.51	9.52	13.17
Castle	21.56	2.90	8.79	12.23
St Mary's and Helions	21.17	11.88	11.49	7.59
Chalkstone	18.65	2.58	8.33	11.31
Cangle	16.72	3.38	9.41	10.53
St Edmundsbury	15.91	6.75	10.80	17.09
Suffolk	18.20	15.37	9.78	19.57

Source: Suffolk County Council, *Poverty in Suffolk: a Profile*, 1995, Appendix 2

A further dimension of this urban-rural dilemma can be found in the use of lack of car ownership as an indicator of poverty. In the 1995 report Haverhill has four wards among the 60 with the highest proportions of households without cars in Suffolk. The County Council point out, however, that 'in rural areas car ownership may reflect isolation more than affluence' (Suffolk County Council, 1996a, p.14). But the relatively low levels of car ownership in Haverhill, with its lack of facilities and transport links, mean that it suffers the worst of both worlds, rural and urban.

Within the town Clements suffers acute levels of deprivation, for instance, 'Clements [ward] has the highest standardised mortality ratio and the second worse position on the Townsend Index for deprivation' in Suffolk (St Edmundsbury, 1996a: 3.2). While social conditions are not as severe as on the council estates discussed by Power (1996) relative to its regional context Clements has many of the socio-economic disadvantages which 'overlap to make area segregation extreme'. Perhaps the sharpest expression of this is in educational disadvantage. Castle Hill Middle School, which serves the Clements estate, recently returned the second worst primary school test results in Suffolk (Table 10.3). Even allowing that to some extent this is because the school has a special need unit, to score so far below other schools in the town would seem to indicate effects of spatial exclusion.

Table 10.3   Haverhill primary school (age 11) test results 1997

	English % Level 4 or above	Maths % Level 4 or above	Science % Level 4 or above	Average % for school
Castle Hill Mid.	41	35	43	39.7
Chalkstone Mid.	63	70	68	67.0
Parkway Mid.	59	58	80	65.7
Suffolk	66.8	65.0	73.9	68.6
England	62.5	61.3	68.1	63.9

Source: *Guardian Education*, 27/1/98

Local demographics are one dimension of this exclusion as there is a difference in the pattern of household formation in Clements compared to the average for the town. For women especially there is a tendency to get married earlier (before age 24) in the ward. Yet at a later age, between 25 and 39, there is a much higher proportion, over ten per cent, (Figure 10.2) of women who are not married compared to the average for Haverhill. This indicates a high rate of marriage breakdown and consequently a high proportion of female headed households. While the causes of are currently being investigated, it seems likely that with the generally high level of deprivation in the ward, this contributes to a Standardised Mortality Ratio of 151.55 for women in Clements, easily the highest in Suffolk (Suffolk County Council, 1996a).

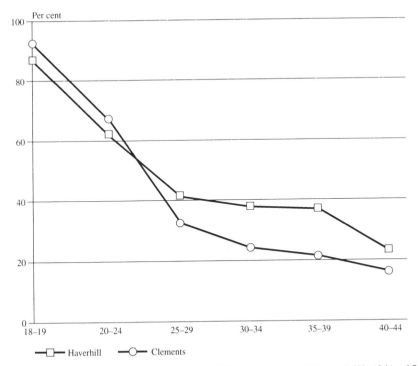

Figure 10.2 Female single adults, Clements and Haverhill (%), 1991

The social implications of this are manifold, one example is that domestic disputes and family break-up have been found to be major causes of youth homelessness in Haverhill. So it is not surprising that the numbers of both lone parent families and young people from Haverhill on the (West Suffolk) housing register are much higher than those from the more populous northern part of the borough (Backwith and Walentowicz, 1997). And it seems likely that a disproportionate amount of these come from the Clements estate.

Kristensen (1995) argues that the connection between physical appearance and perceptions is a causal factor in the 'slumming process' leading to 'spatial stress' and that different dimensions of this process impact on each other in a way which is mutually reinforcing. The planning of the estates was emphasised as a main social problem, particularly the 'Radburn idea' of separating housing from traffic flows, as used on the Clements (Swaby, 1996). This was perceived as having an effect on crime rates and creating a stressful environment and 'A depressing environment on Clements' was reported. Thus the design of the estate (which has a higher population density than other estates in the town) was widely criticised, most succinctly by a youth worker: 'The pillock who designed the Clements deserves to be lynched' (Interview 14). As Kristensen argues 'Poor appearance ...was a signal to the tenants as well as to the outside world that there was no future. This gradual branding and bad reputation ... perpetually reinforces itself' (Kristensen, 1995, p.149). In total there were 16 responses citing Clements' negative reputation, some of which saw the process as self-perpetuating: 'People live up to the reputation, it is internalised, 'Clements Kids' is like a badge of office' (Interview 15). However, evidence from the interviews was contradictory, some saying they had no knowledge of the estate having a negative reputation, others focusing on positive aspects of the area. Nonetheless, both aspects of Kristensen's slumming process were cited.

Hence, with a lack of resources and (access to) services, the respondents described the main social problems in Haverhill as cultural and behavioural issues linked to the negative reputation of Haverhill and Clements. These are both internal and external, for instance one respondent said Haverhill's 'crap self-esteem' had the effect of a 'self-fulfilling prophecy'. Another believed Haverhill was seen as rough, 'very London, not very Suffolk; a place where folk wouldn't like to live'; and that the town served as 'a scapegoat' for the area; together this created: 'a vicious circle, [the reputation] tends to rub off on people here. Then they find it really difficult to lift themselves to challenge it' (Interviews 19 and 15).

Conclusion

This account has sought to emphasise both the cumulative effects of exclusion over time and the interaction of the different processes of exclusion: political, economic, in welfare provision and in the community. As a response to this, the development of a multi-agency strategy, such as the HRP, is to be welcomed; although whether this will be sufficient to overcome Haverhill's multiple disadvantage remains to be seen.

The frameworks of social exclusion discussed here have been useful in identifying forms of deprivation which focus on two groups:

•   Key actors' different perceptions of social exclusion may influence policy responses to it. For instance, service providers who live in Haverhill seem generally to have more positive attitudes to local people and their needs than those who live elsewhere, and the latter tend to be those who have strategic influence over service provision.

- Children, young people, the elderly, people with disabilities and, especially, single parents all experience particularly intense social exclusion and deprivation. In different ways, and to various degrees these groups all suffer the cumulative impact of the four areas of social exclusion examined here. They are caught on the horns of Haverhill's urban-rural dilemma.

Finally, this paper does not claim to be definitive. One weakness revealed in the application of Commin's framework of social exclusion is that it does not adequately address gender divisions. As is most starkly illustrated by the death rates on Clements, the evidence suggests women bear the greater part of the costs of deprivation in Haverhill. Second, a glaring omission from the picture presented here is the perspectives of the people who use, or have restricted access to, local services. Thus further research is clearly required: to examine the experiences of those who suffer the consequences of Haverhill's spatial stress.

Note

1   To preserve respondents' anonymity numbered references are given where interviews are cited in the text.

References

Backwith, D. and Walentowicz, P. (1997), *Haverhill: Homelessness in a Suffolk Town*, Population and Housing Research Group, Anglia Polytechnic University, Chelmsford.

Berghman, J. (1995), 'Social Exclusion in Europe: Policy Context and Analytical Framework' in G. Room (ed), *Beyond the Threshold: The Measurement and Analysis of Social Exclusion*, The Policy Press, Bristol, pp. 10-28.

CAB (1997), *Annual Report 1996/97*, Citizen's Advice Bureau, Haverhill.

Cooper, V. (1996), 'Skills Shortage Areas', unpublished report, Employment Service, Haverhill.

East Anglia Economic Planning Council (1968), *East Anglia: A Study*, HMSO, London.

ECHG (1996-97), *Vision on Cangle* (newsletter, various editions), English Churches Housing Group, Madingley.

Gorst, J.M. (1966), *People in Haverhill: A Report on the Population in 1966*, West Suffolk County Council.

Guardian Education (1998), 1 January.

Haverhill CAB (1997), *Annual Report, 1996/1997*, Haverhill and District Citizens Advice Bureau.

Haverhill (1968), *Haverhill Official Guide and Industrial Review*, Haverhill Urban District Council.

Haverhill Echo (1974), *Haverhill: A Survey*, Haverhill.

Haverhill Echo (1998), 15 January.

Kristensen, H. (1995), 'Social Exclusion and Spatial Stress: The Connections', in G. Room (ed), *Beyond the Threshold: The Measurement and Analysis of Social Exclusion*, The Policy Press, Bristol, pp. 146-57.

Office of Population Censuses and Surveys (OPCS) (1992), *1991 Census*, HMSO, London.

Paugam, S. (1995), 'The Spiral of Precariousness: A Multidimensional Approach to the Process of Social Disqualification in France', in G. Room (ed), *Beyond the Threshold: The Measurement and Analysis of Social Exclusion*, The Policy Press, Bristol, pp. 49-79.

Power, A. (1996), 'Area-based Poverty and Resident Empowerment', *Urban Studies*, vol. 33, no. 9, pp. 1535-64.

Room, G. *et al.* (1991), *National Policies to Combat Social Exclusion* (First Annual Report of the EC Observatory on Policies to Combat Social Exclusion) European Commission, Brussels.

St. Edmundsbury (1993a), *St. Edmundsbury Borough Local Plan, Topic Paper No. 8, Economic and Social Profile of St. Edmundsbury*, St. Edmundsbury Borough Council, Bury St. Edmunds.

St. Edmundsbury, Research Section, Department of Technical Services (1993b), *Profile of the Borough*, St. Edmundsbury Borough Council, Bury St. Edmunds.

St. Edmundsbury (1996a), 'Haverhill Regeneration: Haverhill's bid for resources from the Government's Single Regeneration Budget Challenge Fund', (unpublished draft), St. Edmundsbury Borough Council, Bury St. Edmunds.

St. Edmundsbury (1996b), Environmental Health and Housing, *Strategic Statement and Service Plan*, St. Edmundsbury Borough Council, Bury St. Edmunds.

St. Edmundsbury (1997), Environmental Health and Housing, *Housing Strategy 1997-2000*, St. Edmundsbury Borough Council, Bury St. Edmunds.

Suffolk County Council (1995 and 1996a, 2nd edn.), *Poverty in Suffolk: A Profile*, Suffolk County Council, Ipswich.

Suffolk County Council (1996b), *Anti-Poverty Strategy and Action Plan*, Suffolk County Council, Ipswich.

Suffolk Area Child Protection Committee (1998), *Child Abuse Statistics,* Suffolk County Council Social Services, Ipswich.

Suffolk Social Services (1996), *A Joint Strategy for Adult Mental Health Services in Suffolk, 1997-2002*, Suffolk County Council Social Services & Suffolk Health, Ipswich.

Suffolk TEC (1997), *Employment Forecasts: 1996 to the Year 2006*, Suffolk Training and Enterprise Council/Partners for Prosperity, Ipswich.

Swaby, S. (1996), 'Haverhill: A Microcosm of Post-War Planning Policy', (unpublished dissertation) Hull School of Architecture, University of Humberside.

Ungerson, C. and Deakin, N. (1977), *Leaving London: Planned Mobility and the Inner City*, Heinemann (for Centre for Environmental Studies), London.

West Suffolk (1956), *The Factual Survey and Outline Plan for the Urban District of Haverhill (including Town Expansion proposals under the Town Development Act 1952)* County of West Suffolk.

Young, J. (1992), 'Haverhill's Expansion of the 1950s and 1960s', *Haverhill Historian*, vol. 3.10, Haverhill and District Local History Group, Haverhill, pp. 3-21.

11 Patterns of Exclusion in the Electronic Economy

JAN PAHL and LOU OPIT

We are currently in the midst of a revolution in the ways in which ordinary people receive, hold and spend their money. Far more people than ever before now have bank and building society accounts, use cheque cards, debit cards and credit cards, and pay their bills by direct debit or standing order. At the same time new financial systems are developing, such as banking by telephone, or through the Internet. All these developments, which we include within the term 'new forms of money', are creating a fast-growing electronic economy, in which money is increasingly abstract and invisible.

The development of new forms of money raises many questions for anyone who is interested in financial arrangements within families. Until recently many men handed over a wage packet to their wives each week, social security payments came as cash, and cash was used for much bill-paying and most shopping. How have the financial arrangements of individuals and households adapted to the development of the electronic economy? What items are bought with credit cards, rather than with cash? What are the implications for the control and allocation of money within the household? And what is the position of those individuals and households who do not, or cannot, use new forms of money?

Employment status is a crucial variable, since credit card companies use income and employment as measures of credit worthiness. Are some groups, such as unemployed people or pensioners, being excluded from the credit based economy? And what is the position for married women, whose right to a credit card may be derived from their own employment, or may be dependent on the employment status and income of their husbands? The main aim of this article is to present some tentative answers to these and other questions, using results from new analyses of the Family Expenditure Survey (FES). The paper focuses on households containing a married couple, on patterns of spending within these households, and in particular on their use of credit cards.

The hypothesis which underpins the research is that new forms of money are creating a set of filters which enhance or constrain the access which

234

individuals have to the market. Those who are credit-card-rich must not only be credit-worthy, but they must also be confident of their ability to manage the technology and to repay the debts which will be incurred. Some wives may have gained the right to a credit card through the credit worthiness of their husbands, but with the constraint that their spending will be subjected to the scrutiny of the main card holder. Individuals who are credit-card-poor may have failed to pass the scrutiny of the credit assessors, or they may simply lack the confidence to use the new forms of money. Thus spending money is no longer a simple cash transaction, but an electronic process which is shaped by fundamental social and economic forces. The effect is to create a global, electronic economy in which some individuals are privileged and from which others are excluded.

Background

Research on the intra-household economy has shown that spending patterns depend, not just on the total income of the household, but on the relative incomes of husband and wife and on the control and allocation of money within the household (see, for example, Brannen and Wilson, 1987; Buck *et al.*, 1994; Morris and Ruane, 1989; Pahl, 1989 and 1995; Vogler and Pahl, 1993 and 1994; Wilson, 1987). Financial arrangements within households tend to reflect other characteristics of the individuals involved and of the household as a whole. Important individual characteristics include educational level, employment status and income. So wives who are in employment, and who contribute a relatively high proportion of the household income, tend to have more power in purchasing decisions. In general women have rather different expenditure priorities than men, spending relatively more of their income on goods for the family and household, and relatively less on their own leisure interests and social life.

Patterns of employment within households have been shown to have important implications for the access which individuals have to financial resources. For example, work on the Social Change and Economic Life Initiative suggested that greater financial power for women came from *full time* employment, not from employment *per se* (Vogler and Pahl, 1993). Other research has suggested that there is a growing gap between 'work rich' households, where two or more adults are in full time employment, and 'work poor' households where no one has paid work (Pahl, 1984). A number of studies have shown that in low income households women tend to have responsibility for making ends meet (Kempson *et al.*, 1994; Kempson, 1996; Morris and Ritchie, 1994).

However, most previous research on financial arrangements within marriage has implicitly conceptualised money as cash, while acknowledging that in many cases the cash is actually held in a joint or individual bank account. It is important that debates about family financial arrangements move forward to take account of the fast-changing reality of new forms of money.

Research on the ways in which couples use bank accounts has suggested that the development of more complex forms of money management is leading to a lessening of collective financial arrangements (Cheal, 1992; Treas, 1993). Even though opening a joint account is often a symbol of togetherness, many individuals within couples also maintain their own separate accounts, and these are legally available only to those whose names are specified as having access to them. Qualitative work carried out for the British Household Panel Study has shown that setting up banking systems, such as standing orders, feeder accounts and transfers between current and deposit accounts, tends to be a male activity, and can have the effect of reducing the access which women have to the financial resources of the couple (Laurie, 1996).

Most previous research on credit cards has been carried out by economists, who have not traditionally been concerned with financial arrangements within households. Their research has focused on the individual credit card user, on the development of user profiles, and on the exploration of broader economic issues (see, for example, Brito and Hartley, 1995; Burton, 1994; Crook *et al.*, 1994; Duca and Whitesell, 1995; Feinberg *et al.*, 1992). Among mainstream economists interest has focused on the implications for the money supply of the increased use of credit cards (Begg *et al.*, 1994; Laidler, 1993). Psychologists have focused on the ways in which financial services are perceived by consumers (Lewis, Betts and Webley, 1997).

In the field of social policy, research on new forms of money has been concerned in particular with issues related to access to credit and credit card default. For example, research at the Policy Studies Institute has documented the increase in the use of credit cards since the first Barclaycard was issued in 1966. It has shown that the use of credit cards rises with income, so that in 1989 only one in seven of the poorest households had a credit card, compared with three quarters of the most affluent. Credit card default was often the result of job loss, small business failure or changes in family circumstances (Ford, 1991; Kempson, 1994; Rowlingson and Kempson, 1994).

The Credit Card Research Group produces information about the use of different types of credit and debit cards. In 1994 there were 27 million credit cards and 26 million debit cards in the United Kingdom. About 40 per cent of adults held a credit card and 60 per cent a debit card. About 12 per cent of retail expenditure involved the use of a credit card, and 11 per cent a debit card (Credit Card Research Group, 1995, 7). However, since then all these figures have increased, with the rise in the numbers and the use of debit cards being particularly striking. Credit cards are particularly likely to be used for spending on hotels and travel, which is one reason why this paper includes a section on expenditure on holidays.

There is also a more general issue about the relationship between information technology and society. Do technological developments alter social structures, or do social structures influence the ways in which people use technological developments? The growing literature on this topic has underlined the complexity of the inter-relationships between technology and the social order, pointing to the 'real differences of power, access and control in relation to technology along gender, class, racial and other lines' (Gill and Grint, 1995, 26; see also Webster, 1995, and Green *et al.*, 1993). However, most of this literature has been concerned with the impact of new technologies on the workplace, and little attention has been paid to their implications for people's private lives.

Research on the use of new forms of money within households is taking place at the Centre for International Research on Communication and Information Technologies (CIRCIT) in Melbourne by Singh (1997). This has shown how developments in banking technology are altering the ways in which couples manage their money. Different forms of money can be used for different kinds of payments, in a way which expresses not only what is being bought but also who is making the purchase. Singh concludes:

> The connections between banking and marriage are so critical that electronic banking technologies are altering the way in which money is managed and controlled within marriage.
> (Singh, 1997, p.166)

This brief review of the existing literature suggests that most research on the control and allocation of money within marriage has paid little attention to the implications of new forms of money. Most research on new forms of money has focused on credit cards, and has been concerned with either individuals or households, but not with the complex social and economic processes which shape financial arrangements between individuals within households. The work reported here is part of a study entitled 'New Forms of Money and Financial Arrangements within Families', which aims to explore the ways in which credit cards, debit cards, telephone and computer banking are changing the access which individuals and couples have to financial resources.

Methods

The Family Expenditure Survey (FES) is a long-running continuous survey, carried out by the Office for National Statistics (ONS), using a random sample of households drawn from every country in the United Kingdom. Interviews take place in about 7,000 households every year, and involve all 'spenders' over the age of 16. The overall response rate is 70 per cent. The survey collects information about the income and out-goings of the household as a whole, and in addition each spender is asked to complete an expenditure diary over a two week period. Respondents are asked to note in the diary every single item which they have bought, and to record if a credit card was used to make the purchase.

The FES offers an opportunity for exploring some of the issues which we have outlined, using a large, nationally representative data set. We used the data set which was collected in 1993/94; the data from the year following this was complicated by changes in the poll tax/community charge and more recent data was not available when the study began. Other work on new forms of money is involving qualitative methods, such as focus groups and interviews. However, this article is concerned with the findings which have come from the new analyses of the FES. A secondary aim of the article is to demonstrate the wealth of information which is available within this data set.

Since the study was concerned with the control and allocation of money within marriage, the re-analysis began by selecting households containing a married couple. The FES does not identify stable cohabiting households, so these could not be included in the analysis; also excluded were households where the 'head of household' was under 20. This gave us a total of 3,691 couples, or 7,382 individuals. However, there were a few cases in which crucial data was missing, so the total sample on which we based the analysis numbered 3,676.

The data derived from the expenditure diaries were re-coded in order to make the analysis more manageable. There were some 315,633 entries in the diaries kept by the couples who were the focus of the analysis, and in the raw data set they had been classified by FES into several hundred expenditure categories. We re-coded these to produce a total of 37 major categories, ranging from food, motor vehicles and household goods, which were the largest items in the diaries in terms of amounts spent, to clothes, holidays, gambling and alcohol. The re-coding involved grouping linked items together. So the category 'motor vehicles' included, not simply the purchase of cars and motor bicycles, but also petrol, vehicle insurance, tax, repairs and other running costs; the category 'household goods' included purchases of bedding, furniture, carpets, kitchen appliances, lamps and clocks.

It is important to remember that many items of household expenditure were not recorded in the diaries because they were paid by direct debits or standing orders out of bank accounts; these included payments for mortgage or rent, for council tax and for utilities such as water and electricity. Some people paid these by cash or cheque, and noted them in their diaries, but since many did not these items were excluded from the analysis.

The analysis also made use of the wealth of socio-economic information contained in the FES, and especially the information about age, employment, household composition and social class. In some cases these data too were re-coded in order to produce new variables.

The Gendering of Spending

The new analysis began by examining the different expenditure responsibilities of men and women within households. Table 11.1 is based on the whole sample, that is all 3,676 couples. The expenditure categories in the table were chosen because they represented significant elements in most household budgets, with the two largest categories being spending on food and motor vehicles, which represented on average 16 per cent and 11 per cent of the total amount recorded in the expenditure diaries. The items were also chosen because they were unlikely to have been paid by direct debit or standing order; in other words all spending was likely to have appeared in the expenditure diaries.

Table 11.1 presents women's expenditure on particular items as a percentage of total expenditure by the couple on that item, and also gives information about credit card spending.

Table 11.1   Women's expenditure as a percentage of total expenditure and of credit card expenditure

Items	Total expenditure on item		Women's % of credit card spend
	% of total spent by women	% of total spent by credit card	
Women's clothes	90	28	89
Children's clothes	85	17	84
Food	80	9	76
Course fees	79	2	74
Child care/school expenses	78	9	68
Medical/dental	59	12	44
Household goods	51	24	45
Tobacco	43	2	40
Recreation	42	17	30
Men's clothes	40	32	34
Holidays	36	29	31
Gambling	35	-	-
Meals out	34	7	21
Repairs to house	33	1	81
Motor vehicles	31	15	28
Alcohol	27	9	35

N= 3,676

Source: Family Expenditure Survey, 1993/94

Table 11.1 suggests that patterns of spending were highly gendered. Women spent more than men on food, women's and children's clothes, child care and educational courses. Men spent more than women on alcohol, motor vehicles, repairs to the house, meals out, gambling and holidays. The balance between men and women in spending was more even when it came to household goods, medical and dental expenses, tobacco and recreation. Rather surprisingly, perhaps, women were responsible for two fifths of the amount spent on men's clothes. More detailed analyses of patterns of spending are available in another paper (Pahl and Opit, 1997).

The table also shows that credit cards were used quite selectively. The expenditure categories for which credit cards were most often used were men's clothes (32 per cent bought with a credit card), holidays (29 per cent), women's clothes (28 per cent) and household goods (24 per cent). By contrast, credit cards were rarely used for paying course fees and bills for household repairs, for gambling or buying tobacco.

Table 11.1 also shows that women are, in general, less likely than men to use a credit card to make a purchase. For nearly every item the percentage of credit card spending made by women was less than their percentage of the total spending on that item. The only real exception to this was spending on alcohol, perhaps because women were more likely to buy alcohol from supermarkets and off licence shops, where credit cards were acceptable, while men bought more alcohol in pubs, where cards were less welcome.

However, Table 11.1 leaves many questions unanswered. For example, do women buy men's clothes because they are not in employment, and so are more likely to be free when the shops are open, or is it something that wives are expected to do, even when they have a job? Do men spend more on meals out because they tend to pay when the couple go out, or is their larger expenditure a reflection of the fact that being in employment involves eating away from home?

Table 11.2 suggests some tentative answers to these questions, and also illustrates some of the complexities which lie behind Table 11.1. It shows selected items of expenditure, chosen because relatively large sums of money were involved and because there was a range in terms of whether men or women were the main spenders. Some items, such as food and motor vehicles, appeared in the expenditure diaries of most couples; other items, such as holidays and repairs to the house, were purchased by a minority of couples but were quite costly when they did appear.

Table 11.2   Impact of women's employment on expenditure patterns within households, mean spending shown as £ per two weeks   (N = number of couples recording some expenditure)

	Both in full time employment			Man full time employment woman no paid work				
	Men's mean spending	Women's mean spending	N	Men's mean spending	Women's mean spending	N	Sig. of difference for men	Sig. of difference for women
Food	24.76	78.49	856	17.36	88.05	688	ns	<0.005
Household goods	25.94	38.38	609	23.57	25.11	492	ns	ns
Holidays	74.06	71.59	192	133.48	35.09	132	<0.05	<0.005
Men's clothes	22.73	17.24	298	21.73	12.89	239	ns	<0.01
Repairs to house	121.90	91.57	120	39.38	48.42	91	<0.05	ns
Meals out	21.41	13.00	822	18.49	5.91	611	<0.05	<0.001
Motor vehicles	61.29	38.39	769	50.22	31.29	606	ns	ns
Gambling	6.22	3.65	424	5.94	2.38	296	ns	<0.005

Source: Family Expenditure Survey, 1993/94

The figures for mean spending are based only on those individuals who recorded expenditure on the item in question during the two weeks when the diaries were being kept. The table presents the differences between 857 couples where both partners were in full time employment and 688 couples where the man was in full time employment, while the woman was defined as 'economically inactive' or 'unoccupied', in the disparaging words of the ONS. The significance of the differences in mean spending for the two employment categories was tested separately for men and for women, using a t test and pooled variance.

Table 11.2 suggests that women's employment status made a significant difference to patterns of spending within households, but that many other different variables were relevant. Women spent significantly more on food when they were not in paid work. Men with wives in full time employment spent a little more on food than those whose wives were not in paid work, but the difference was not significant, suggesting that the employment status of their wives did not cause these men to alter their behaviour. Women's continuing responsibility for buying the food was underlined by the fact that even when both partners were in full time employment women were still responsible for three quarters of spending. By contrast employment status did not affect spending on household goods and on motor vehicles

Spending on holidays underlined the effects of women's employment status on the expenditure patterns of both partners. Compared with couples where both were in full time work, men who were the sole earners spent significantly more on holidays, nearly doubling their expenditure; by contrast, women who were not in paid work spent half as much on holidays as women in full time employment. Men's spending on their own clothes did not reflect their wives' employment status. However, women in paid work spent significantly more on this item, suggesting that women were responsible for buying men's clothes, not because they were free when the shops were open, but because for some couples buying her husband's clothes was part of a wife's domestic work.

Spending on repairs to the house reflected employment status in quite complicated ways, though here only the male difference was statistically significant. Couples where both were in full time employment spent much more on this item than couples with only one earner, suggesting that they were paying for repairs to be done rather than doing repairs themselves. The fact that the difference was statistically significant for men but not for women was puzzling, but it may be that women without paid work were taking responsibility for painting and decorating, while men whose wives were in full time employment recognised that they would have to pay a professional to do this work.

Differences in other areas of spending seemed to reflect the greater spending power and increased autonomy of women who were earning. Spending on meals out was greater for both men and women when both were in full time employment, but the difference was particularly marked for women. There are many possible explanations for this finding. It may be that the additional spending of women represents eating lunch at work or going out for drinks with workmates; it may be that couples in full time employment have less time and energy for cooking and more money for eating out; or it may be that they are more likely to share the bill when they go out. Women who were in full time work were significantly more likely to spend money on gambling, though they still spent less than men.

Up to this point the focus has been on the ways in which spending is gendered, with men and women tending to take responsibility for different items of expenditure. The next step was to look for patterns in the use of credit cards.

Patterns of Credit Card Spending

Previous research has suggested that people prefer to use different forms of payment for purchases of different cost, with a trend away from cash towards credit cards as cost increases, except for very expensive items which tend to be paid by cheque. There is also a trend over time away from cash and towards credit cards as a means of payment. Thus a survey of 2,000 adults, carried out for Girobank, showed that cash was the preferred means of paying for items costing under £10. For purchases of £100, cash was preferred by 25 per cent of those surveyed, down from 28 per cent a year earlier, while cards were preferred by 43 per cent, compared with 39 per cent a year earlier. For purchases costing £1,000 cheques remained the first choice for 46 per cent, compared with 33 per cent who said they would use a card and ten per cent who would use cash (Graham, 1997).

The new analyses of the FES data produced a similar pattern, with credit cards being used less often for items costing under £10 or over £1,000, as Table 11.3 shows. Credit cards were most likely to be used for goods costing between £100 and £1,000, where 15 per cent of payments were made in this way. More detailed analyses, not shown in the table, revealed that the peak of credit card use came in the price range of £250 and £500, where 38 per cent of payments involved credit cards.

Table 11.3   Expenditure on items of different cost by use of credit cards and gender of purchaser

Cost of item purchased in £

Under 10	10-100	100-1000	Over 1000
6	12	15	8
71	52	39	38
72	47	37	38
281,811	31,492	2,330	105

Source: Family Expenditure Survey, 1993/94

Table 11.3 also underlines the enormous differences between men and women in the number and costs of the items which they buy. Women make many more low cost purchases than men, and many fewer high cost purchases: so nearly three-quarters of items under £10 were bought by women compared with under two-fifths of items over £1,000. In general women's share of credit card expenditure was similar to their share of total expenditure, though men were slightly more likely than women to use a credit card. The greatest gender difference came in the price range of £500 and £1,000, where only 33 per cent of all the credit card purchases were made by women.

Treating the sample as a whole, however, obscures variations between different sub-groups: as we have seen, women's full time employment made a significant difference to their expenditure patterns. However this does not take account of the divide between full time and part time employment for women; nor does it explore the effects of unemployment and retirement. The next stage in this exploration of spending and of the use of credit cards was to sub-divide all the couples in the sample according to employment status.

Employment Patterns within Households

Previous research had suggested that two aspects of employment were particularly relevant. These were, first, the employment status of women, with a distinction being made between full time, part time and no employment, and, secondly, household employment status, with distinctions being made between 'work rich' and 'work poor' households in particular. In order to examine the effects of these two aspects of employment, a variable was created which combined the employment situations of both the man and the woman. This involved re-coding the employment variables given by the FES to make six broad *household employment categories*.[1]

Table 11.4 shows the six employment categories, giving the mean gross income for each partner in £ per week. The table also gives the mean expenditure by each partner in £ per week, as given in the FES expenditure diaries.[2] It is important to remember that some expenditure, such as direct debits and standing orders, did not appear in the diaries and that couples differed in the extent to which they made use of these forms of payment. However, payments by cash, by cheque and by credit and debit card all appeared in the diaries. All the differences between men's income and women's income were highly significant, except in the 'Woman main earner' category. The expenditure differences would have been significant in some categories if outliers had been removed, particularly from men's expenditure. As it was, the differences between male expenditure and female expenditure were only significant in the case of 'Both full time' employed couples ($p<0.001$) and 'Both retired' couples ($p<0.01$).

Table 11.4 **Income and expenditure for household employment categories, mean gross income £ per week, mean expenditure from FES diary £ per week (= standard error of means)**

Household employment categories	No. of couples	Men's income	Women's income	Men's expenditure	Women's expenditure
Both full time	857	352 =8.0	243 =5.6	179 =8.8	201 =7.7
Full time/ part time	858	371 =9.6	118 =3.0	145 =16.2	184 =6.64
Full time/no paid work	688	412 =16.6	44 =2.3	152 =11.9	161 =7.9
Woman main earner	274	164 =9.1	180 =8.0	201 =76.6	134 =5.4
Both retired	848	164 =4.7	60 =2.3	135 =13.0	99 =3.9
Both unemployed	151	130 =11.6	34 =3.2	101 =38.4	100 =7.0

Source: Family Expenditure Survey, 1993/94

The first category contained 857 couples where *both partners were in full time employment or self employed*; in a very few cases one or both worked part time. These were the households with the largest mean household incomes, and their expenditure was correspondingly high. Despite the fact that both partners were in full time work, the men had substantially higher incomes than the women, with mean gross incomes of £352 per week, compared with £243. However, despite their lower incomes, women spent more than men, with a mean expenditure of £201 compared to £179. The differences between income and expenditure shows that some financial transfers had taken place within these households between men and women. These are the 'work rich' couples, and only two fifths of them had dependent children.

The second category contained 858 couples where the *man was in full time employment or self employed, while the woman in part time employment.* As might be expected, there was a greater disparity between mean male and female incomes in this group, with mean male earnings of £371, compared with mean female earnings of £118 per week. Women continued to take a larger part in shopping, spending on average £184 per week compared with the men's average of £145. It seemed as if women in part time employment had more time for doing the family shopping and less excuse for not doing it, compared with women in full-time employment. Over two-thirds of these couples had dependent children.

The pattern is even clearer among the third category, which contained 688 couples where the *man was in full time employment or self employed, while the woman was 'unoccupied' or 'unemployed'*. Men in this category had the highest incomes of all at £412 per week. This may have reflected their responsibility as the sole breadwinner in a family with young children; it may be that having a full time housewife at home enabled them to work longer and harder; or it may simply be that the high earnings of the man freed the woman from the need to take paid work. The women in this category had an average income of just £44 per week, coming partly from child benefit and benefits for disabled people, but also from interest on savings and investments. A few of these women were very wealthy indeed. Over three-fifths of the couples in this category had dependent children

The fourth category consisted of 274 couples where the *woman was the main earner*. This was the most heterogeneous of all the household employment categories, with some women employed full time, some part time and some self employed, while some of the men worked part time, but most had retired from paid work, or were unemployed or disabled. As Table 11.4 shows, male incomes were not so much less than female incomes in this category, but in general the woman was the only person in the labour market. Here men spent much more than women, which was probably a reflection of the extra time at their disposal. Many of these couples were approaching retirement and only a third had dependent children.

The fifth category contained 848 couples where *both partners were retired*. Here again mean incomes were low, especially for women, a consequence of the financial difference between the married man's retirement pension and that of his 'dependent' wife. Men's greater than average share of the expenditure in this group surely reflects the fact that going shopping is an activity which many elderly men enjoy? In addition, this is an age cohort in which men traditionally expected to control finances and in which many still give their wives a housekeeping allowance. As might be expected, very few of these couples had dependent children.

Finally, the sixth category consisted of 151 couples where *both partners were 'unemployed' and/or 'unoccupied'*. These were the poorest couples in the sample, as well as the poorest men and women on an individual basis: they might be described as the 'work poor'. Mean expenditure in this group was larger than mean income. However, further analysis showed that this discrepancy only applied to 15 per cent of the group, and typically was the result of buying one expensive consumer good during the two weeks when they were keeping the expenditure diary (for further discussion of this issue see Pahl and Opit, 1998). Here men spent as much as women. This may be because when money was tight women cut back on spending in a way that men did not. On the other hand it may be that some unemployed men had taken on the job of doing the family shopping. Whatever the explanation, this finding casts doubt on the idea that in low income households women carry sole responsibility for the family budget. Two-thirds of these couples had dependent children.

In referring to Table 11.4 it is important to remember that the figures for income are gross, with net take home pay at a lower level, except among unemployed people. The figures for expenditure represent only expenditure recorded in the diaries; household bills paid by direct debit or standing order, which are likely to include mortgage repayments and some utility bills, will not appear here. So real household expenditure will usually be greater than the table suggests. Nevertheless Table 11.4 does underline the part which households play in the re-allocation of financial resources. In general women appeared to spend more than they earned, except where they were in full time paid work or were the main earner for the household, partly because their spending was more likely to appear in the expenditure diaries. By contrast men appeared to earn more than they spent, partly because some large items of household expenditure, such as mortgage repayments, did not appear in this table.

Table 11.4 highlights some of the differences which flow from employment status, both on a household and on an individual basis; it also underlines the rather different market experience of men and women. How are these differences translated into differences in spending patterns, and more specifically into spending involving credit cards?

Employment Status, Credit Cards and Spending

We have seen that employment status, both at an individual and at a household level, affects patterns of spending. Does the same apply to the use of credit cards?

Table 11.5 Percentages of individuals using a credit card for making a purchase over a two week period by household employment categories

Household employment categories	Credit card used for a purchase				
	Men %	N	Women %	N	Significance p <
Both full time	42	350	41	349	ns
Full time/part time	42	356	35	304	0.085
Full time/no paid work	37	256	25	170	0.001
Woman main earner	24	66	23	63	ns
Both retired	21	174	14	119	0.003
Both unemployed	6	9	7	12	ns
All	33	1221	28	1017	

Source: Family Expenditure Survey, 1993/94

Table 11.5 suggests that gender, employment and age all have an impact on the use of credit cards. The table gives the percentage of men and women, in each employment category, who used a credit card to make a purchase over the two week period during which they kept the diary for the FES. Significance was tested by chi squared test, N being the number of households with expenditure on the item in the two week period.

The results suggest that between a quarter and a third of all those who took part in the survey used a credit card over this period, with men being slightly more likely than women to use cards. Differences in employment status were associated with differences in the use of credit cards. When the man and the woman were both in full time employment they were equally likely to have used a credit card. However, women in part time employment were less likely, and women without employment very significantly less likely to have used a credit card, by comparison with their employed husbands.

The table highlights the exclusion of unemployed people from the credit card economy, with only a very few individuals in this category using a credit card during the two weeks. This is consonant with research on access to credit more generally, which shows that low income households find it hard to obtain credit; if they are forced to borrow they tend to be forced to contact more expensive money lenders than the typical credit card company (Ford, 1988 and 1991; Kempson *et al.*, 1994).

Retired people are the other group which appeared to be relatively excluded from the credit card economy. This may partly be a result of low income and lack of credit worthiness. But it may also be a consequence of a lack of financial confidence in new forms of money and of a general mistrust of getting into debt. There was a significant difference between men and women in this group, which may reflect the income differences revealed in Table 11.4.

In order to examine the interacting effects of different variables, we carried out a linear multiple regression analysis, with the dependent variables being total household expenditure, as recorded in the diaries, or total credit card expenditure. The independent variables were the man's gross income, the woman's gross income, the age of each partner, each partner's age at the end of full time education, and dummy variables representing being economically active and the presence of children in the household. The regression was carried out stepwise and significant results are shown in Tables 11.6 and 11.7.

Table 11.6   Regression analyses on total household expenditure and total credit card expenditure

	Standardised coefficients Beta	t.	Significance p <
Household expenditure			
Man's income	0.21	12.49	0.000
Woman's income	0.11	6.82	0.000
Man's age at end of full time education	0.04	2.55	0.000
$r^2 = 0.08$			
Credit card expenditure			
Constant		-6.80	0.000
Man's income	0.33	20.10	0.000
Woman's income	0.12	7.82	0.000
Man's age at end of full time education	0.09	5.33	0.000
Man's age	0.06	3.85	0.000
$r^2 = 0.17$			

Source: Family Expenditure Survey, 1993/94

Table 11.6 shows that the total household expenditure was correlated strongly with the man's gross income and the woman's gross income, and less strongly with the age at which the man ended full time education, with men who spent longer in full time education having higher household expenditure. The pattern for credit card expenditure was similar, but with one interesting difference. The beta values suggested that the relative effect of the man's income was only twice that of the woman's in estimating the overall expenditure, but three times that of the wife's income in estimating credit card expenditure. In other words, compared with total expenditure, credit card spending was more strongly influenced by male than female incomes.

We have already shown that employment patterns within the household had significant effects on spending. What could regression analyses tell us about the interactions between all the relevant variables? In order to answer this question we repeated the procedure, first, with households where both partners were in full time employment and, secondly, with those where only the man was in employment, while the woman was not in paid work.

Table 11.7 Regression analyses on total household expenditure and total credit card expenditure for households with two and one earners

	Standardised coefficients Beta	t.	Significance p <
Both FT: household expenditure			
Constant		5.19	0.000
Woman's income	0.26	8.00	0.000
Man's income	0.24	7.27	0.000
$r^2 = 0.17$			
Both FT: credit card expenditure			
Constant		-4.42	
Man's income	0.23	6.22	0.000
Woman's income	0.14	4.25	0.000
Man's age at end FT education	0.12	3.55	0.011
Man's age	0.08	2.43	0.015
$r^2 = 0.13$			
FT/no paid work: household expenditure			
Man's income	0.45	12.45	0.000
Man's age at end FT education	0.08	2.35	0.019
Woman's income	0.07	1.97	0.050
$r^2 = 0.25$			
FT/no paid work: credit card expenditure			
Constant		-3.73	0.000
Man's income	0.47	13.56	0.000
Man's age at end full time education	0.12	3.33	0.001
$r^2 = 0.27$			

Source: Family Expenditure Survey, 1993/94

The results are shown in Table 11.7. When both partners were in full time employment, only the two income variables proved to be relevant in explaining total household expenditure, with the income of the wife having marginally more impact than that of the husband. However, the pattern was different for credit card expenditure. Here the man's income was the more significant of the two income variables, with his age at the end of full time education and his current age also being important: households in which the man was older when he ended full time education tended to spend more by credit card.

When only the man was in employment, as might be expected, his income was by far the most significant variable in terms of the total household expenditure, though once again his age at the end of full time education was also important. It was perhaps surprising to find that the wife's income also appeared in the regression results, since the average income for this group of women was quite small: this finding may represent the high spending of a few affluent women who did not have paid work because they had independent incomes of their own. However, when the regression analysis was repeated for credit card expenditure only the man's income and his age at the end of full time education were significant. Once again there was a contrast between total expenditure and credit card expenditure, with the latter being more closely related to men's than women's incomes. The association between credit card expenditure and the man's age at the end of full time education may reflect the greater confidence which better educated men have in using new forms of money.

Up to this point we have been concerned with credit card use in general, and have shown that credit cards are used more for purchasing some items than others. The next step was to take an area where credit cards were widely used. We focused on holidays, partly because nearly one third of all payments were made by credit card, and partly because spending on holidays was relatively discretionary, so it might be expected to show significant variations between employment categories. We have already seen in Table 11.2 that women's employment status affected the ways in which spending was divided between men and women. When both partners were in full time employment women spent very much the same amounts as men on holidays; however, when only the man was in full time employment, the woman spent less absolutely, and much less proportionately compared with her husband, on holidays. In the next section we examine spending on holidays in more detail.

Expenditure on Holidays

The expenditure category described as 'holidays' included payments for holidays in the United Kingdom and abroad, cash withdrawn to be spent on holiday, payments for other people's holidays, and spending on luggage and travel goods. Some of these payments would have included paying instalments on holidays yet to come.

Table 11.8   Expenditure on holidays by household employment categories, mean expenditure in £ over two weeks (= standard error of means)

Household employment categories	% of couples spending on holidays	No. of couples	Mean total expenditure of couple	% of total spent by women	Significance of gender difference $p <$
Both full time	22	192	146 =17.8	49	ns
Full time/ part time	22	191	126 =19.9	35	0.06
Full time/no paid work	19	132	169 =31.4	21	0.004
Woman main earner	18	48	126 =31.9	33	ns
Both retired	12	102	140 =32.8	21	0.02
Both unemployed	9	14	24 =14	42	ns

Source: Family Expenditure Survey, 1993/94

Table 11.8 presents information for the 754 couples, about 21 per cent of the whole sample, who spent money on holidays during the two weeks when the diaries were being kept. The table divides the sample into the six different household employment categories, and information is presented about those couples who included some expenditure on holidays in their two week diaries.

The table shows the percentage of couples in each employment category who spent anything on holidays, the number of couples involved, the mean expenditure of each group and the proportion of the total which was spent by the woman. The standard deviation of the proportion spent by women was calculated and was used to test the significance of the gender difference.

Table 11.8 suggests that there were significant differences between occupational groups, between those below and above retirement age and between men and women in spending on holidays. For example, couples where both partners were in full time employment had a relatively high mean expenditure, but their most marked characteristic was that these were the couples in which women made the greatest contribution to spending on holidays, paying very nearly half the cost. When women were the main earners they were also likely to contribute relatively more to expenditure on holidays: both in this category, and in the previous category of couples, the difference in spending between men and women was not statistically significant.

The largest sums were spent in households where the man was in full time employment, while the woman was not in paid work: 20 per cent of this group spent something under the heading of holiday, and the average sum involved was £158. This was the employment category where the difference between male and female spending was greatest, with women on average being responsible for only one-fifth of the total holiday spending, a highly significant difference. Retired couples, and couples where the woman was in part time employment, spent relatively little on holidays, with a significant tendency for the man to spend more than the woman. Unemployed people, as might be expected, spent very little on holidays: only 11 per cent of this group had any expenditure at all under this heading and the mean amount spent was £24 over the two weeks. Differences between men and women were slight, mainly because so little was spent.

Table 11.9   Credit card expenditure on holidays by household employment categories

Household employment categories	% of total spent by credit card	Women's % of total credit card spending	Significance of gender difference $p <$
Both full time	31	44	ns
Full time/part time	35	26	ns
Full time/no paid work	23	17	0.005
Woman main earner	35	38	ns
Both retired	20	7	0.005
Both unemployed	-	-	-

Source: Family Expenditure Survey, 1993/94

Table 11.9 is concerned with the proportion of the total expenditure on holidays which involved the use of a credit card and with the gender divide in the use of credit cards. The table is based only on the 754 couples who actually spent money on holidays during the two weeks. It shows the percentage of the total which involved the use of a credit card and the percentage of credit card spending for which women were responsible. The standard deviation of the proportion spent by women was calculated and was used to test the significance of the gender difference.

The table suggests that couples, and individuals, varied greatly in the extent to which they used credit cards for spending on holidays. Unemployed people appeared to be completely outside the credit card economy, in that none of their holiday spending involved cards. Households where someone was in employment were more likely to use credit cards than households where both partners were retired. Women's use of credit cards reflected their individual employment status, in that those in full time jobs were more likely to use cards than women in part time jobs or those outside the labour market.

Conclusions

The results presented here make a contribution to debates in a number of different fields. Previous work on the intra-household economy has been able to offer little detail about spending, but the Family Expenditure Survey contains a wealth of information about individuals, households and their spending patterns. Our analyses showed that household spending patterns reflected, not only total household income, but also the relative economic status of individuals within the household. The gendered nature of spending, and the different positions of men and women in the labour market, both had an effect on the expenditure patterns of married couples. In particular, we demonstrated that whether women were in full time employment, in part time employment, or without paid work had significant implications for spending on a wide variety of items.

The Family Expenditure Survey has proved to be a very fruitful source of information about a wide range of issues in sociology and social policy. In future articles we shall be examining some of these in more detail (see for example, Pahl and Opit, 1997). However, there are also limits to the questions which can be answered using this data set. At various points in the article we have speculated about the reasons for the patterns we were describing, but we were always aware of the limitations of quantitative data. Further qualitative research is now in progress, using focus groups and individual interviews, which will enable us to say more about the feelings, attitudes and beliefs which underlie the patterns which we have documented.

Future research on the control and allocation of money within the household will have to take account of the growth of the electronic economy. We showed that patterns in the use of credit cards did not precisely match patterns of total expenditure. In the longer term credit cards are likely to appear as a first stage, to be followed by increasingly sophisticated smart cards, and the extension of telephone and Internet banking. Previous research has underlined the importance of power relations within households in understanding financial arrangements. From this point of view, access to the electronic economy can be seen as another source of power, and one which will advantage some members of households and disadvantage others. It was interesting that the regression analyses highlighted the man's age at the end of full time education in explaining the use of credit cards, since longer education may create more confidence in dealing with new technologies.

Previous research on credit cards has focused on the individual credit card holder. However, understanding the use of credit cards by married people must involve taking into account both individual and household variables. People can be issued with a credit card on the basis of their own or their partner's income, but our results suggested that women whose credit worthiness depended on their husband's income used cards less often and spent less with them. It may be that even invisible money can feel like 'his money' as opposed to 'my money'. Certainly women in full time employment used credit cards more, and spent more with them, than any other group of women. The regression analyses showed that income was crucial in explaining patterns of spending by credit cards, and this point was underlined by our more detailed analyses of spending on holidays.

We have also been able to extend the scope of previous research on access to credit and on exclusion. The main barriers to the electronic economy are credit status and confidence: those who are not considered credit worthy by the gate keepers to the system, or who lack confidence in their ability to use the new technologies, are likely to be excluded from this fast-growing phenomenon. The analyses presented here suggested that patterns of exclusion were complicated, but that key variables were income, employment status, gender and age. Unemployed people typically remained in the cash economy, making little use of credit cards. Elderly people, and especially elderly women, were also unlikely to use a credit card to make a purchase, either because of low income or because of lack of confidence.

Finally, the study could make a contribution to debates about the relationship between technological developments and social relations. Increasingly debit cards are overtaking credit cards in terms of the numbers of holders, supermarkets are moving into banking, and many people now obtain cash, not from the high street bank, but from the 'cashback' facility at the supermarket check out. As we have shown, compared with men, women do far more of the sort of shopping which takes place in supermarkets. Older and poorer women may continue to be disadvantaged, but younger women, with their own earnings and an easy familiarity with new forms of money, could be at a distinct advantage in the electronic economy of the future.

Acknowledgements

The work reported in this article is part of a study on 'New Forms of Money and Family Financial Arrangements', which is being funded by the Joseph Rowntree Foundation and the University of Kent at Canterbury. We are grateful to the funders, and also to the ESRC Data Archive, at the University of Essex, and to the Office for National Statistics, for making the Family Expenditure Survey available to researchers. We should also like to acknowledge very helpful comments by the Advisory Group for the project.

Table 11.10 Composition of household employment categories

Household employment categories		Employment status of individuals					
		Employed full time	Employed part time	Self employed	Unemployed	Unoccupied (below retirement age)	Unoccupied (retired)
Both full time N=857	M	653	33	171	-	-	-
	W	683	33	141	-	-	-
Full time/part time N=858	M	701	-	157	-	-	-
	W	-	858	-	-	-	-
Full time/no paid work N=688	M	512	45	131	-	-	-
	W	-	-	-	75	536	77
Woman main earner N=274	M	-	28	-	69	131	46
	W	139	132	13	-	-	-
Both retired N=848	M	-	-	-	-	202	646
	W	-	-	-	-	163	685
Both unemployed N=151	M	-	-	-	142	7	2
	W	-	-	-	35	101	15

N = 3676

Source: Office for National Statistics, 1998

Notes

1   The *household employment categories* were derived from the standard employment status categories recorded by the FES, which divided individuals according to whether they were employed full time, employed part time, self employed, unemployed, or unoccupied (Office for National Statistics, 1998). The composition of each of the categories is set out in Table 11.10.

2   In the analysis income and expenditure were calculated separately in terms of the mean and the median. Each way of calculating produced rather different figures, but in general similar overall patterns. The differences between the mean and the median reflected the fact that for many items the distribution approximated a negative exponential. Most expenditures were in the lower range, but the small number of much larger expenditures could have considerable influence on both mean and median. It seemed more appropriate to present the results in terms of means.

References

Begg. D., Fischer, S. and Dombusch, R. (1994), *Economics*, McGraw Hill, London.

Brannen, J. and Wilson, G. (1987), *Give and Take in Families: Studies in Resource Distribution*, Allen and Unwin, London.

Brito, D.L. and Hartley, P.R. (1995), 'Consumer Rationality and Credit Cards', *Journal of Political Economy*, vol. 103, no. 2, pp. 400-33.

Buck, N., Gershuny, J., Rose, D. and Scott, J. (1994), *Changing Households: The British Household Panel Survey 1990-1992*, University of Essex, Colchester.

Burton, D. (1994), *Financial Services and the Consumer*, Routledge, London.

Cheal, D. (1992), 'Changing Household Financial Strategies', *Human Ecology*, vol. 21, pp. 197-213.

Credit Card Research Group (1995), *Understanding Credit and Debit Cards*, Credit Card Research Group, London.

Crook, J.N., Thomas, L.C. and Hamilton, R. (1994), 'Credit Cards - Haves, Have-nots and Cannot-haves', *Service Industries Journal*, vol. 14, no. 2, pp. 204-15.

Duca, J.V. and Whitesell, W.C. (1995), 'Credit Cards and Money Demand - A Cross-sectional Study', *Journal of Money, Credit and Banking*, vol. 27, no. 2, pp. 604-23.

Feinberg, R.A., Wesgate, L.S. and Burroughs, W.J. (1992), 'Credit Cards and Social Identity', *Semiotica*, vol. 91, no. 1-2, pp. 99-108.

Ford, J. (1988), *The Indebted Society: Credit and Default in the 1980s*, Routledge, London.

Ford, J. (1991), *Consuming Credit: Debt and Poverty in the UK*, CPAG, London.

Graham, G. (1997), 'Cash Still Preferred for Small Payments', *Financial Times*, 9th June.

Green, E., Owen, J. and Pain, D. (1993), *Gendered by Design? Information Technology and Office Systems*, Taylor and Francis, London.

Gill, R. and Grint, K. (1995), *The Gender-Technology Relation: Contemporary Theory and Research*, Taylor and Francis, London.

Kempson, E. (1994), *Outside the Banking System: A Review of Households without a Current Account*, HMSO, London.

Kempson, E. (1996), *Life on a Low Income*, Joseph Rowntree Foundation, York.

Kempson, E., Bryson, A. and Rowlingson, K. (1994), *Hard Times: How Poor Families Make Ends Meet*, Policy Studies Institute, London.

Laidler, D. (1993), *The Demand for Money*, Harper Collins, London.

Laurie, H. (1996), *Women's Employment Decisions and Financial Arrangements within the Household*, PhD Thesis, University of Essex.

Lewis, A., Betts, H. and Webley, P. (1997), *Financial Services: A Literature Review of Consumer Attitudes, Preferences and Perceptions*, University of Bath School of Social Sciences, Bath.

Morris, L and Ruane, S. (1989), *Household Finance Management and the Labour Market*, Avebury, Aldershot.

Morris, L. and Ritchie, J. (1994), *Income Maintenance and Living Standards*, Social and Community Planning Research, London.

Pahl, J. (1989), *Money and Marriage*, Macmillan, London.

Pahl, J. (1995), 'His Money, Her Money: Recent Research on Financial Organisation in Marriage', *Journal of Economic Psychology*, vol. 163.

Pahl, J. and Opit, L. (1997), 'Patterns of Spending Within Households', *Paper presented at the Royal Statistical Society*, April.

Pahl, R. (1984), *Divisions of Labour*, Blackwell, Oxford.

Rowlingson, K. (1994), *Moneylenders and their Customers*, Policy Studies Institute, London.

Rowlingson, K. and Kempson, E. (1994), *Paying with Plastic: A Study of Credit Card Debt*, Policy Studies Institute, London.

Singh, S. (1997), *Marriage Money: The Social Shaping of Money in Marriage and Banking*, Allen and Unwin, St Leonards, NSW, Australia.

Treas, J. (1993), 'Money in the Bank', *American Sociological Review*, vol. 58, pp. 723-34.

Vogler, C. and Pahl, J. (1993), 'Social and Economic Change and the Organisation of Money in Marriage', *Work, Employment and Society*, vol. 7, no. 1, pp. 71-95.

Vogler, C. and Pahl, J. (1994), 'Money, Power and Inequality Within Marriage', *Sociological Review*, vol. 42, no. 2, pp. 263-88.

Webster, J. (1995), 'The Difficult Relationship Between Technology and Society', *Work, Employment and Society*, vol. 9, no. 4, pp. 797-810.

Wilson, G. (1987), *Money in the Family*, Avebury, Aldershot.

12 Poverty Studies in Europe and the Evolution of the Concept of Social Exclusion

JOHN WASHINGTON, IAN PAYLOR and JENNIFER HARRIS

The European Union currently faces a major challenge to its status as a political structure. It is poised to move towards a stronger federal organisation. The establishment of Economic and Monetary Union will involve the creation of supra-national processes operating above the interests of individual Member States. The challenge this poses is marked by the uncertain reaction of these Member States to the increasing loss of sovereignty. Whilst this issue is fundamental for most Member States, the issue of sovereignty itself needs to be placed in the context of the wider international environment (Henig, 1997). The impulse to relinquish sovereignty does not come easy for European political parties whose very presence depends on the existence of the modern form of the 'nation state'. The economic challenge of the world market system is the strongest motivation for these European states to move towards closer integration. To be able to compete as a strong contender in this global market place the European Union has not only to be economically fit but it is essential that its social structures are sound and do not pose problems of internal disorder. The condition of poverty and the process of social exclusion could be considered the most serious of these threats to the social order of Europe with the process of deprivation poised to destroy the fabric of modern European society.[1]

This concern with social disorganisation and the realisation that the marketplace was not capable of rectifying social disadvantage impelled the European Council to propose intervention in the social area of Europe. This realisation first crystallised in the early 1970s but in the late 1990s became of crucial significance for the continuation of the European association - both within Europe and in the context of the global economic and political situation.

The European Union, legally established in 1993, inherited from its predecessor organisations a primary focus on the economic management of its Member States. In particular the Treaty of Maastricht (1992) strengthened the structure of an internal market as the central plinth of the Union's organisation. However, a key component of that Treaty recognised that the existence of the Union was also contingent on it having an interest in non economic aspects of European society. The Union's concern in the area of social policy was legitimised in the 'Agreements and Protocol on Social Policy - The Social Chapter' which was an annexe to that Treaty. The importance of this was solidified in 1997 through the Treaty of Amsterdam (1997) which secured both the acceptance of the United Kingdom to the social policy agreement but also the incorporation of that agreement into the main framework of the Union.

The provenance of The Social Chapter was established in 1989 when the European Council, meeting at Strasbourg adopted the Community Charter of the Fundamental Rights of Workers (Council of the European Communities, 1989a). This for the first time in a basic Treaty formally recognised that the European Community had a social dimension to its activities (Hantrais, 1995). The Community Charter was a solemn declaration from Member States binding them to take action in the area of social provision. The Community Charter did not have the force of law and individual Member States were left at their discretion to introduce individual measures related to concerns of the Charter. The Social Chapter of the Treaty of Maastricht three years later constructed a means by which the Union itself as an organisation could take decisions in the social area. This social area was focused upon the work place - on conditions for workers in the workplace and on the integration of those excluded from the workplace. Whilst there was a primary focus on the workplace the Social Chapter did move the Union into activities associated with social security and social protection. It provided legitimation for the Commission to become active in the promotion of actions in the social area. The crystallisation of this came in the Green and White Papers on European Social Policy (Commission of the European Communities, 1993,1994a). Both Papers opened up the possibility that the Union could intervene itself or direct Member States themselves to intervene in the social area - a shift from the Union's concern with European workers to a wider concern for the welfare of European citizens.

In parallel with these developments in European Union policy there has been a significant change in the way of perceiving those individuals and groups who are not in employment and who are on the margin of society. In particular, the concept of social exclusion has increasingly been used as an analytical tool in relation to marginalised individuals. The developing usage of social exclusion (and the linked concept of social integration) can be seen in the increased references the Community/Union has made to social exclusion from the period 1989 onwards. This can be directly related to work of the Commission following the European Council adoption of the Community Charter. It is articulated in an elaborate form in the in the Work Programmes of the European Commission's Science Research Development Directorate towards 'Targeted Socio-Economic Research' (European Commission, 1995). Other European Union agencies have also taken the concept as central to their work. In the first three years of the decade the Directorate of the Commission for Employment, Industrial Relations and Social Affairs published reports on the results of the National Observatories on Social Exclusion (Commission of the European Communities, 1994b). These National Observatories were instituted by the Commission in 1989 to promote an analysis of poverty in each Member State. The reports from the Observatories are indicative of the central importance the Commission gave to the concept in its initiatives to combat the social process creating marginalisation and social deprivation in Member States.

Although this interest is now marked, it is not new. In 1974 the then European Economic Community began a sustained European endeavour in the social area of activity. The focus of this concern was on poverty. Since that time there have been Three Poverty Programmes organised at a European level and established to combat poverty and social exclusion, both being recognised as major social problems in European society. Whilst during the 1970s and 1980s there was growing evidence of the marginalisation and deprivation of both individuals and groups in Europe, only the Third Poverty Programme was given a clear mandate to bring the dimension of social exclusion into the analysis. This raises key problem issues which this chapter will seek to address. Is the concept of social exclusion distinctly different from that of poverty? Does it provide a strictly separate type analysis to that of poverty studies? Is the phenomena of poverty different from that of social exclusion? Tangential to this, but no less important, we explore the proposal that, over the past two decades within Europe, there have developed markedly new forms of marginalisation and social deprivation.[2]

Silver (1994) suggests that economic and social upheavals gives rise to new conceptualisations of social disadvantage and that the evolution of the concept of social exclusion has emerged following the profound economic restructuring in Europe from the mid 1970s. Her analysis offers three paradigms of exclusion based on different notions of social integration - solidarity, specialisation and monopoly. This chapter will take the paradigm of solidarity as the nearest to that implied by the European Community/Union use of social exclusion. In examining the three Poverty Programmes undertaken in Europe this chapter will seek to trace the development of the concept of social exclusion and discuss how its use may differ from the concept of poverty.

The establishment of the European Economic Community, through the Treaty of Rome (1957) made limited provision for action at a social level. The basic foundation of the Economic Community was to establish a common market and to promote harmonious development of economic activities. Although the motivation for the creation of the EEC was political, the European structure which emerged from discussions in the early 1950's was essentially a bureaucratic organisation for harmonising the economic activities of member states (Henig, 1997). At this stage in the development of the Community it was felt that the economic market within Europe would generate a situation of ever increasing resources which would result in an enhanced social development and rising standards of living in all Member States (Hantrais, 1995). The Treaty of Rome which laid the basic legal framework of the Community did have provision for minor activity in the social area. This was set within the articles 123 to 128 of the Treaty and provided for a Social Fund to assist vocational training and occupational mobility within the Community. In essence although the Treaty had a social dimension, the focus for European activity was on the workplace.[3]

During the late 1950s and the 1960s the concerns of Europe were not on poverty but on the perceived threat from communism and on a drive to maximise economic productivity. Within the European Economic Community there were no important initiatives in social affairs but rather a steady progress to harmonise trading relationships both within the Community and with those countries outside the Community.

The First Poverty Programme

The first major European endeavour in social policy developed from a meeting of the European Council in Paris in October 1972. The Heads of State of the original six Member States (Belgium, France, Germany, Italy, Luxembourg and the Netherlands) met with their counterparts in the three countries about to join (Denmark, Eire and the United Kingdom), to consider the future of the European Economic Community (Dennett *et al.*, 1982). The communiqué which followed the meeting emphasised that the Council now attached as much importance to vigorous action in the social field as to the achievement of

Economic and Monetary Union. Consequently, the Commission were instructed to develop with Member States, a Social Action Plan. The focus of this Plan was on obtaining full and better employment, the improvement of living and working conditions and the increased involvement of management and labour in economic and social decisions (Hantrais, 1995). The European Council adopted this Plan in 1974. The First Poverty Programme from 1975 to 1980 derived from this (Council of the European Communities, 1975). It was funded by Structural Funds of the European Social Funds and thus required specific authorisation by the Council of Ministers.

The Programme had two phases - from 1975 to 1977 and an extension from 1977 to 1980. The types of activities conducted in the Programme were set by the Commission; area-based community action programmes; projects for special categories of poor people; specific interventions for poor people and improving service delivery and organisation. The latter two activities were deemed by the Commission to be within the remit of social services. The overall Programme comprised over 60 Individual Projects in Member States, six Cross-National Studies and eight National Reports on poverty and policies to combat it. Each Project was intended to have a research component that permitted a clear evaluation to be drawn from work undertaken. However, the Commission engaged a research group ESPOIR (European Social Policy Observation, Information and Research) to report on the overall Project during its final three years.

Specific examples of Individual Projects included; activities with young people and children in the Champagne area of France; provision of a housing scheme for elderly people in Brittany; evaluation of social assistance in Cologne; work with battered women in Dublin; health and social services work with women and children in Naples and provision of a nursery and a day care project in Croydon, UK (Dennett *et al.*, 1982).

The central focus on poverty was defined by the Council as:

> persons beset by poverty: individuals or families whose resources are so small
> as to exclude them from the minimum way of acceptable way of life of the
> member States in which they live.
> (Council of the European Communities, 1975)

In this definition resources were taken to include goods, cash income, plus services from public and private sources. It was a significant move away from the budget standards approach to measuring poverty that had dominated research methodology up to the 1960s. The condition of poverty was placed in the context of the society in which it was located and considered in terms of the relative deprivation approach developed in the late 1960s. The Programme itself was significant in that it involved action research and intended not solely to analyse the causes of poverty situation but to devise means to reduce the condition.

Room (1982) in evaluating both the research component of the Programme and the Council's definition acknowledges that it moves some way from the United Kingdom tradition of social enquiry using mainly a budgetary standards approach established by Booth and Rowntree. The Council definition has similarity to that of Townsend's shift to a consideration of poverty in terms of relative deprivation. This was articulated in 1967 at an international conference on poverty (Townsend, 1970) sponsored by the Joseph Rowntree Memorial Trust. Its more focused presentation on the United Kingdom was published in 1979 and established his distinct orientation which was a shift in the United Kingdom tradition to poverty studies. Room (1982) in his critique of the Council definition draws on the Programme's cross - national studies. Two of these studies conducted in the first phase of the Programme established that there was a valid way of viewing poverty using criteria other than budget standards. This conceptualisation of poverty in terms of 'relative deprivation' although contested was gaining increasing usage from key politicians and bureaucrats in the European Community.

Room concluded that the Council's definition required reconsideration. In particular the focus on 'individuals and families' tended to cast both the cause and experience of poverty away from the social processes involved in establishing their condition. A European definition, he felt ought to take into account the structural factors that many researchers now viewed as being central to their explanations of poverty. The inclusion of 'the minimal acceptable way of life' as a phrase did not adequately take into account the differences in standards of living considered as acceptable within one country. This was further compounded by the variation in 'acceptable standards of living' across the Member States in the Community. 'Resources' within the definition tended to imply that both the condition of poverty and its remedy could be interpreted primarily in terms of the lack of these resources, which thus tended to ignore the relationship between poverty and participation in society.

James (1982) draws specific conclusions for social services practice from the study of both individual projects and cross national projects, in particular the inadequacy of the income maintenance/means testing approach to reducing poverty. The complexity of the claiming systems and the stigma associated with depending on them mitigates against the participation and integration of the receivers into mainstream society. The evidence from the Programme relevant for Personal Social Services was that a community development approach was favoured by most individual projects. For the United Kingdom the implications of this were not followed through, at local or central government level, despite the findings of the Barclay Report in 1972 (NISW, 1972), and the legitimation the Report could have given to community social service practice.

James (1982b) indicates that the types of activities and strategies of community development used during the Programme could be seen as an antidote to the 'top down' large scale bureaucratic planning that formed the main thrust of the European Community's economic activity. The community development activities were, he considered, a means of replacing a communal neighbourhood association that was a former basis of social and economic life in European society.

The First Poverty Programme did have impact on the study of poverty. For the first time it introduced a wide scale European dimension through a number of individual projects in Member States. These had both an action and a research component. To this extent, the combination of action and research in all projects gave the Programme a unique approach. This was the first occasion that poverty studies had been undertaken on such a scale and the cross national studies added to the importance of the individual projects. Although no particular generic proposals emerged in the area of social policy, the cross national studies did highlight the varying perceptions of poverty in Europe. Both the activities and the findings of the projects indicated a broadening of the methodology of study to include a relative dimension. Increasingly the project work indicated that poverty could be viewed as being more than lack of income. The deprivation from the 'normal' social processes and 'marginalisation' from the mainstream social structure were seen as a key indicators of a 'new poverty'. Whether or not this poverty was 'new' is now open to debate. However the Poverty Programme at least confirmed that poverty and its associated conditions were not diminishing. On the contrary they were increasing and in some circumstances manifesting themselves in areas and groups not previously associated with poverty, at least in post Second World War Europe.

The Second Poverty Programme

The period between the end of the First Poverty Programme and the commencement of the Second indicates the problematic aspect of managing the European Economic Communities activities in the non economic area. The First Programme took three years from acceptance by the Council of Ministers in 1972 to implementation by the Commission in 1975. The Second Programme was being planned from the time of the concluding report on the First Programme in 1982 to the adoption by the Council in 1984. The Commission commenced implementation in 1985 and completed in 1988. Again the Programme was funded by the Structural Funds of the Community. However by the end of the Programme the structure of the European Community had notably changed. This change made possible an increased involvement of the Community in the social area.

In the early 1980s the commitment of the French President, Franscoise Mitterand to the concept of 'l'espace social' gave the European Economic Community a new perspective on social policy (Hantrais, 1995; Cannan *et al.*, 1992). This was later adopted by Jaques Delors when he became President of the Commission in 1985. The concept of a social space is intricately associated with the French concern with social solidarity. This particular articulation of the relationship between the individual and society is one that is markedly Gallic. Its origins can be seen in Rousseau's philosophy on the social contract (Russell, 1946) and in it's modern context in the work of Durkheim (1947). Delors and Mitterand used the idea of social space to create a concept of society that was not dominated by the market. Basic to the idea of the social space is the tenet that both workers and employers have commitments and obligations above wages and profits. These commitments are to aspects of social living beyond the workplace. This view holds that social cohesion is a function of social processes other than the market place. Solidarity in society is based on the acceptance that there are commitments and obligations to social and economic mores that are binding on all members of society. Durkheim's concept of solidarity was organic. He saw it as an aspect of progressive social development through the process of the increasing division of labour in society. For Delors, the idea of solidarity was political. It was a means to develop the European association, a conviction that social as well as economic interests were at the heart of the Community. In the 1980s a view also began to develop in the Commission that before meaningful economic integration could take place the Community should have the mechanism for securing social integration. Part of this concern for social integration focused on those individuals and groups who were not integrated but who were excluded from social and economic living. The Second Poverty Programme developed in parallel with changes in the structure of the Community intended to strengthen the integration of Member States. The growing interest and influence of the Commission in the processes of social exclusion and integration in Europe was affected by these changes.

The objectives of the Programme were established by the European Council as being to:

> combat poverty more effectively and carry out positive measures to help the underprivileged and identify the best means of attacking the causes of poverty and alleviating its effects in the European Community.

and the definition of poverty as:

> 'the poor' shall be taken to mean persons, families and groups of persons whose resources (material, cultural and social) are so limited as to exclude them from the minimal acceptable way of life in the Member States in which they live.
> (Council of the European Communities, 1984)

Room (1993) notes the emphasis on action and considers that the research component was very much secondary to the implementation of the poverty projects. The main research element was undertaken outside the individual projects and conducted by the Centre for the Analysis of Social Policy (CASP) at the University of Bath. They were commissioned to evaluate the Programme. An important component of this evaluation derived from national reports from all the participating Member States and self evaluation built into the objectives of all the projects involved. The three criteria used in evaluating the projects were innovation, participation and cost effectiveness.

In total 91 individual projects were accepted in the Programme. They were grouped into eight themes; integrated action in urban areas; integrated action in rural areas; long-term unemployed; young unemployed; older people; single-parent families; migrants and marginals.

Room (1993) indicates that all the projects worked at a micro level. They were diverse and small scale but they did contribute to developing a new understanding of poverty, in particular the relationship between unemployment and poverty. Structural unemployment and industrial decline, cyclical unemployment, structural unemployment and underdevelopment, precarious employment and hidden unemployment were identified as the main labour market problems creating and reinforcing poverty. Common with the First Poverty Programme the information received from the projects indicated that the social protection and social assistance systems of the Member States did not adequately help either the 'traditional' or the 'newly emerging poor'. The 'new poor' were by the Second Poverty Programme more evident and more particularly associated with homelessness. The processes of marginalisation and exclusion were also manifestly more evident. Room's analysis of the Second Poverty Programme consciously used the terminology of exclusion and marginalisation. They were used to both describe and explain the condition of sections of the European Community on whom the projects focused. The main thrust of his analysis was that the social policy of the European Union should be framed around national policies to both prevent and combat social exclusion. This marks a shift from the First Programme which was conducted using the discourse of poverty. The social policy recommendations had implications for social protection and social assistance as well as for the personal social services. However, the recommendations were set with the framework of action at the level of individual Member States. Marginalisation and deprivation were acknowledged as problems but taken as an aspect of poverty viewed essentially as a budgetary deficiency. The implications for social policy were seen at that time as requirements for the improvements of existing welfare systems. The Second Poverty Programme recognised the need for much more than this and that the nature of the problem was set much deeper in social processes than had hitherto been conceived. The change is neatly stated by Jaques Delors at a Conference on 'Social Exclusion and Social Integration' in 1993:

> we will in the future continue to distinguish between poverty and social exclusion - although exclusion includes poverty, poverty does not cover exclusion.
> (Delors, 1993)

The Third Poverty Programme realised this change and acknowledged the European dimension of the problem.

The Third Poverty Programme

Hantrais (1995) contended that by the end of the 1980s the relative and multifaceted nature of poverty necessitated a new approach, one that ostensibly was accepted by the European Council adopting the Third Poverty Programme immediately following the termination of the Second Programme (Council of the European Communities, 1989b). The terminology used in both the title and the action programme itself reflected the move to a focus on the relative deprivation and marginalisation of 'least privileged groups in society' and a concern that the focal point of action should be on their economic and social integration. In tandem with the Third Poverty Programme the Council gave the Commission authority to establish an 'Observatory on National Policies to Combat Social Exclusion' which was to report annually (Council of the European Communities, 1989c). In 1989 the Council had a specific concern with 'social affairs'. An indication of this was a move to give some identity to the increasingly important concept of 'social exclusion':

> social exclusion is not simply a matter of inadequate[resources], and that combating exclusion also involves access by individuals and families to decent living conditions by means of measures of social integration and integration into the labour market; accordingly request Member States to implement or promote measures to enable everyone to have access to: education, by acquiring proficiency in basic skills, training, employment, housing, community services, medical care.
> (Council of the European Communities, 1989c)

Whilst still lacking in specificity this attempt to give 'social exclusion' identity mirrors a tendency within the Community to shift the language relating to individual members of the Community from being viewed in economic terms as 'workers' to being viewed more socially as 'citizens' of the Community. The Observatory on social exclusion running parallel with the action plan tended to inform the interpretation of social exclusion; in particular the definition by Room who was the first co-ordinator of national reports of the Observatories:

> Individuals suffer social exclusion where: a) they suffer generalised disadvantage in terms of education, training, employment, housing, financial resources and so on; b) their chances of gaining access to the major social institutions which distribute these chances are substantially less than those of the rest of the population; c) these disadvantages persist over time.
> (Room, 1990)

The Poverty Three Programme itself constituted 42 local projects (Commission of the European Communities, 1995). Some 30 of these were pilot projects designed to have a well defined area of operation related to economically and socially disadvantaged groups. Examples of these included low cost renovation of buildings involving participation of tenants in Munich; the development of new social work practices to integrate families in poverty in Gerona; urban renewal, socio-cultural organisation and co-operation with local institutions in Porto; anti racist initiatives between the black community and local institutions in Liverpool.

In addition there were 12 projects designed as innovative. The innovative nature was typified in a project based in Dublin to provide a reception centre for travellers to promote their rights and recognition and identity. Similarly, in Bologna project work was undertaken to find a response to problems of social integration of people leaving prison whilst in Paris there was a project to offer loans and advice to people without resources.

The specific objectives of the Third Poverty Programme were seen as essentially different from the first two Programmes. The latter were conducted as exploratory, local micro projects. Diverse in nature and only loosely integrated into national and transnational activities. In contrast, the Third Poverty Programme was designed to operate in a more focused and co-ordinated manner. Three principles formed the basis of the Programme. First, a multi dimensional approach requiring a coherent strategy that accepted both poverty and exclusion as multi faceted phenomena - not solely the result of the lack of financial resources. As such the projects were to be linked to local and national strategies to combat social exclusion in all participating Member States.

Second, the principle of partnership was to complement the multi dimensional approach. This involved a range of key players from different organisations accepting collective responsibility for the projects. Irrespective of the separate interests, the organisations were to work to develop a common and consensus approach to defining and managing the project.

Finally, in order to counter the dependency or passivity considered as an aspect of social exclusion the active involvement of the groups concerned in the integration project was viewed as essential. Citizenship and democracy were to be accorded a pre-requisite for success of the projects.

Just like the Second Poverty Programme research was considered secondary to the action component. Local projects undertook some individual work as part of their objectives. There were, however, two research initiatives which were undertaken at a European level.

First, in co-operation with Eurostat, statistical work was commissioned to refine the measurement of poverty; the intention being to devise a harmonised system of analysing family budgets in all Member States that would allow reliable comparison. Up to the Third Poverty Programme, the Commission had used an income based criteria for measuring poverty. That is, those persons whose personal disposal income being less than half of the average equivalent per capita income in the Member State in which they resided. The Programme in seeking to elaborate on this, used data on household income that had been collected up to 1988. The data collected was problematic in that there was some uncertainty regarding its reliability. The researchers in reviewing their work considered that there are limitations in an approach to poverty based solely on the criterion of financial resources. Irrespective of this, most of the statistical work of the Poverty Three Programme sought to harmonise this method. The Programme did however also endeavoured to develop the analysis of poverty using a multi-dimensional approach. In the Final Report on the Poverty Three Programme (Commission of the European Communities, 1995) the Annexe on statistical work accepts that the latter approach is still at a preliminary stage. It expected that work would continue to examine the multi-dimensional and dynamic aspects of exclusion through the Commission establishing a panel to conduct at regular intervals a longitudinal analysis of households being surveyed.

Second, economic and social research was undertaken on a transnational basis. A number of research teams were selected to work on several themes: the process of disengagement from the labour market; the role of regional development policy; the links between poverty and migration; the involvement of management and labour in the fight against social exclusion; moves to bring poverty into the province of social policy and the effects of active employment policy in the fight against social exclusion (Commission of the European Communities, 1995).The work of the research teams was presented at a Seminar in London and formed the basis of a text on the measurement and analysis of social exclusion (Room, 1995).

The research themes selected by the Third Poverty Programme were echoed in the work programmes of the Science Research Development Directorate of the European Commission (European Commission 1995, 1996) - developing new knowledge about social exclusion through defining the forms and processes of social exclusion; analysing the causes of social exclusion, particularly the changing structure of European employment and employment policies relating to this; migration and multi cultural society; evaluating the impact of social integration policies; inequality and economic growth; criminal behaviour and informal economies; the spatial dimensions of social exclusion and the implications of European integration; welfare states and inter-generational solidarity. The spill over from the Third Programme into research thus continued after the Programmes as a new aspect of the Commission's work despite the hiatus over the implementation of the Fourth Poverty Programme.

The overall Programme was reported as a success in terms of its principles (Commission of the European Communities, 1995). Particularly the partnership approach, was viewed as being one of the strengths of the Programme. New organisational structures were created which it was considered would enable the projects to continue after the Programme ceased. Whilst the Programme took the multi-dimensional focus on social exclusion there was diversity in the way this was both interpreted and implemented. Whilst the validity of multi-dimensionality was accepted in the Report, it was considered that more thought was needed here and more knowledge of the aspects of multi-dimensionality at a local level (urban/rural) and at a national level (northern/southern countries) was required. The approach to participation was seen as a challenge to the projects but one with which most projects made progress. The success of the Programme led to the Commission proposing to the Council a Fourth Poverty Programme for the period 1994 to 1999. This Programme has not been accepted as planned and has been replaced by a Medium Term Action Plan for 1995-97. The Commission moved its emphasis to the promotion of social protection policies. The Social Action Programme 1995-97 (European Commission, 1997) now places action against social exclusion and the promotion of social integration as a component of work in the area of 'social protection, equal rights and civil dialogue'.

Social Exclusion, Social Policy and Social Work

To date this chapter has traced the three Poverty Programmes of the European Community/Union in relation to the growing use of the concept of social exclusion. It has examined these in the context of the development of this European Union. Part of any analysis of this development must give attention to the use by the Commission of the concept of social exclusion as a means of promoting a strong social policy component within the Union. Irrespective of any discussion regarding social exclusion as a heuristically valid sociological concept we must acknowledge its power as a concept in the practical world of political and social policy. Indeed, an acceptance of the reality of the influence of the concept in social affairs contrasts with its lack of respectability in the domain of academic discourse (Levitas, 1996; Byrne, 1997). Room (1995) has argued that the three Poverty Programmes conducted under the auspices of the Commission have been isolated from the major theoretical debates on European social policy. In particular, he cites the resurgence of recent literature on welfare regimes as having important contributions to the analysis of poverty but which have been ignored by the Commission whose perspective is constructed around concepts of harmonisation and convergence. The analysis of poverty in the Union is in effect undertaken on the terms of the Commission and in the language of the Commission.[4]

This corresponds with an interpretation of the European poverty initiatives as essentially political. In essence concepts are developed and used heuristically to promote the policies of European integration (Henig, 1997). In the period 1989 to 1995 the concept of social exclusion was used politically by the Commission bureaucracy. When it was challenged, it was by a Member State citing the principle of subsidiarity as a means of preventing the Commission acting in its own right in the area of poverty and social exclusion. The response of the Commission has been both to face that challenge through the fairly slow process of the European Court of Justice and also by substituting the concept of social protection as a focus of its initiatives in the area of poverty. It could be argued that the potency of social exclusion as a concept is now being tested. Interestingly it is currently being used in by organisations not directly managed by the Commission. Both the European Anti-Poverty Network (EAPN, 1996) and the International Federation of Social Workers (IFSW, 1997) are utilising social exclusion as a means of changing the policy of the Union. The IFSW in accepting that social exclusion is a valid concept for interpreting the threats to social stability in Europe has also proposed activities aimed at integrating excluded people into society. These actions include proposals for individual care plans for excluded people; out reach work; user participation and developing an holistic social work approach which will assist practitioners to develop interventions to prevent social exclusion.

Whilst it is still too early to make an appraisal of the effectiveness of these initiatives in preventing social exclusion, it is clear at this stage that the identification of groups and individuals at risk of social exclusion and initial analyses of the underlying problems faced by these people will be far easier than the task of identifying strategies to effect integration or reintegration. Social work as a profession will inevitably play a key role in both exercises but in many crucial respects, the success of the latter rests upon the rigour and integrity of the former. Social work as an activity practised in a multitude of settings and organisations throughout Europe, is united in its focus upon assisting individuals and groups marginalised by modern societal processes. Despite the huge variety of forms and guises that social work can take, this uniting feature is essential in understanding and ameliorating social exclusion throughout the European Union. It is therefore most highly probable, that in the years to come, social work practice will be pivotal in the processes of the identification of social exclusion and eventually, in effecting social inclusion. In accepting this it is vital that the value of social work practice to effect change within the lives of socially excluded individuals is recognised, supported and encouraged by the EU as it is only through this recognition and support that the findings of the Poverty Programmes can be rendered useful.

For practitioners in the disciplines of social work and social policy, a fundamental issue raised here is the extent to which a concept that has been used essentially to promote political integration can be validly adopted for use in their domain of academic and professional activity. As stated earlier in this chapter the concept of social exclusion derived from a Gallic concern with social solidarity and a belief in holistic nature of society. One aspect of this, which has influenced all the Poverty Programmes, has been the primacy of action over research. This has tended to deny any conceptual exploration of the nature of European Society at both the level of the European Union and of the constituent Member States. Social work and social policy are interrelated disciplines. Neither can afford to refrain from a critical analysis of the societies in which they practice. It is therefore paramount that the values that underpin these disciplines are explicitly stated. Only in this way can politically developed concepts be used with integrity. Much work still needs to be undertaken in this area. But this is not an area that has been ignored and research and practice has been undertaken outside the specific framework of the European Union.

Papers presented at the Seebohm Rowntree Centenary Conference at the University of York in 1998 suggest that there has been a limited but noticeable change in the way in which poverty is conceived by academics in the United Kingdom. Poverty remains the key conceptual focus but the perception of poverty as a social condition has changed (Gordon, 1998; Miller, 1998). This reflects a change not only in the study of poverty but a developing change in the way welfare is researched (Williams and Popay, 1998). It is increasingly less set in a confining framework of the academic discipline until very recently named as social administration, but is informed by other contributions in the broader knowledge area of social living, an area of knowledge that itself is experiencing an epistemological move. As Lorenz (1994) has noted, social movements initiated by women, people with disabilities and members of minority ethnic groups of disabled people have influenced both research and practice in welfare. This change has paralleled the growth of the idea of social exclusion.

Social exclusion, we are claiming is a recently developed concept which has been used politically. But has it heuristic value in those disciplines and practices whose domain is in the area of social living? The Poverty Programmes have evidenced that there are sections of European society whose deprived condition cannot be solely explained in terms of lack of income resources. Conversely, the lack of income resources can primarily be related to the deprived and marginalised condition in which these sections of society are located. Social exclusion as a concept begins to develop an understanding of this deprived human condition and place it within a social context. In this century most interpretations of this condition have either been influenced by Marxist class structured exploitative perspectives or by neo liberal interpretations of the primacy of individual self help as a means of human betterment. Social exclusion has the potential to be a concept that can be used to develop an understanding of deprivation and marginalisation that avoids a deterministic structural or philosophical individualist a priori analysis.

For the social professions the problem lies not with the concept of social exclusion but with that of social integration. The process of integration requires an examination of the nature of society into which people are to be integrated. Societies that have excluded, deprived and marginalised large numbers of people must have serious faults in their social structures. It is a matter for both politicians and the social professions to have concern not only for the integration of marginalised people into society but also to establish a decent and civilised society into which they can be integrated.

Notes

1   The underclass debate continues, despite Novak's (1997) and others (Mann, 1994) protestations. The emphasis on the wider structural processes behind the creation of a marginalised group in society seems a more plausible view than one which sees it as the product of its own fecklessness and criminality - but certain conceptual problems are evident. The concept of an underclass is of course a controversial one which is often

used in an emotive rather than analytical manner by other commentators (Murray, 1990). As a sociological concept, class implies some reproduction over time and some degree of common identity for its members (Marshall *et al.*, 1988). The self-proclaimed school of Left Realism in particular, has sought to explain the recent changes in crime rate and the growth of urban disorder in the context of the changing nature of class structuration over the last 200 years. However, the underclass thesis undoubtedly raises important questions with regard to recent developments in class structuration across Europe, but it is not clear whether such a distinct grouping can be said to empirically exist. This point leads Robinson and Gregson (1992) to ponder on whether 'the best thing to do is to avoid it altogether and abandon any use of the term'(p.47). But they do not, not least because the term is now widely used and to pretend otherwise would be foolish and also they argue, because we have a responsibility to enter the debate and not leave the right and the tabloid press to go unchallenged because of 'our discomfort over terminology'. There is no doubt that a discriminating use of the term or concept underclass can be very compelling. It can serve to accentuate key problems areas such as the increasing polarisation; the entrapment of the poorest, the most disadvantaged and the lack of routes for upward social mobility; and the increasing concentration of the poorest, the most disadvantaged, in a residualised rented housing sector. (Robinson and Gregson, pp. 48-9)

2   But it is not only within the European Union that the concept has increased in currency. Abrahamson (1996) has charted the increased usage in European social sciences. Taking entries in the Social Sciences Citation Index he demonstrates that for period 1986 to 1993 an average of 2.6 articles appeared referencing social exclusion - rising to an average of 25 articles over the years 1994 and 1995. Despite this dramatic rise in the number of articles on social exclusion, in comparison with other related concepts, the use of the social exclusion concept is low. In 1994, 469 articles were entered on poverty; 224 entries on deprivation; 25 on marginalisation and 62 on underclass. Abrahamson's review of the concept of social exclusion concludes that it is correct to consider social exclusion as a concept being different from that of poverty; the latter being about structural, material and 'objective' phenomena, whilst social exclusion is a concept for analysing individual, subjective and psychological phenomena.

3   Social affairs at this time were within the remit of the Council of Europe, established in 1949 as a forum for dealing with concerns of 'human rights and freedoms'. The adoption by the Council's 26 members of a 'Social Charter' in 1961 laid the foundation for the 1989 Economic Community 'Community Charter of the Fundamental Social Rights of Workers' which became the blueprint for the 'Social Chapter' of the Treaty of Maastricht.

4   The Maastricht Treaty's convergence criteria also imposes cuts in public expenditure which require fiscal retrenchment which could affect the level of economic activity, subsequently undermining welfare provision in Member States. This leads Burkitt and Baimbridge (1995) to argue that the provisions of the treaty 'constitute the most serious attack on the welfare state during the post-war period' (p. 110).

References

Abrahamson, P. (1996), *Social Exclusion: New Wine in Old Bottles*, Roskilde University and Consejo Superior de Investgaciones Cientificas, Roskilde.
Burkitt, B. and Baimbridge, M. (1995), 'The Maastricht Treaty's Impact on the Welfare State', *Critical Social Policy*, Issue 42, Winter, pp. 100-11.
Byrne, D. (1997), 'Social Exclusion and Capitalism', *Critical Social Policy*, vol. 17, no. 1, February.
Cannan, C., Berry, L. and Lyons, K. (1992), *Social Work and Europe,* MacMillan, Basingstoke.
Commission of the European Communities (1993), *Green Paper on European Social Policy. Options for the Union*, (COM(93) 551, 17 November 1993).
Commission of the European Communities (1994a), *White Paper on European Social Policy - A Way Forward for the Union,* (COM(94) 333, 27 July 1994).
Commission of the European Communities (1994b), *Observatory Report on National Policies to Combat Social Exclusion*, EEIG 'Animation and Research'.
Commission of the European Communities (1995), *Final Report on the Implementation of the Community Programme Concerning the Economic and Social Integration of the Economically and Socially Less Privileged Groups in Society*, COM(95) final Brussels 27.03.1995.l.
Council of the European Communities (1975), *Concerning a Programme of Pilot Schemes and Studies to Combat Poverty*, 75/458/EEC of 22nd July 1975 (OLJ 199/34 30.7.75).
Council of the European Communities (1984), *Council Decision on Specific Action to Combat Poverty*, 85, EEC, Brussels.
Council of the European Communities (1989a), *Community Charter of the Fundamental Rights of Workers*, European Council Meeting, Strasbourg, 9 December 1989.
Council of the European Communities (1989b), *Council Decision of 18th July 1989 Establishing a 2 Medium Term Combine Action Programme Concerning the Economic and Social Integration of the Economic and Socially Less Privileged Groups in Society*, OJ L 224 of 2.8.1989.
Council of the European Communities (1989c), *Council Resolution of 29 September 1989 on Combating Social Exclusion*, OJ No C227 of 31.10. 1989.
Delors, J. (1993), 'Giving a New Dimension to the Fight Against Exclusion', *Copenhagen Conference June 1993*, EEIG Animation and Research, Lille.
Dennett, J., James, E., Room, G. and Watson, P. (1982), *Europe Against Poverty*, Bedford Square Press, London.
Durkheim, E. (1947), *The Division of Labour in Society*, The Free Press, New York.
European Anti-Poverty Network - EAPN (1996), *Proposals for the Revision of Treaties*, http://europa.eu.poverty.
European Commission (1995), *Targeted Socio-Economic Research (TSER)*, Science Research Development.
European Commission (1996), *Targeted Socio-Economic Research (TSER)*, Science Research Development.
European Commission (1997b), *Social Europe: Progress Report on the Implementation of the Social Action Programme 1995-97*, Social Europe- Supplement 4/96.
Gordon, D. (1998), 'The Scientific Measurement of Poverty: Recent Theoretical Advances',

Paper presented at the Conference to Mark the Centenary of Seebohm Rowntree's First Study of Poverty, University of York, March 1998.

Hantrais, L. (1995), *Social Policy in the European Union*, Macmillan, Basingstoke.

Henig, S. (1997), *The Uniting of Europe*, Routledge, London.

International Federation of Social Workers (1997), *Social Work and Social Exclusion in Europe*, International Federation of Social Workers, Oslo.

James, E. (1982a), 'Policy Implications', in Dennett, J., James, E., Room, G. and Watson, P. (eds), *Europe Against Poverty*, Bedford Square Press, London.

James, E. (1982b), 'Combating Poverty', in Dennett, J., James, E., Room, G. and Watson, P. (eds), *Europe Against Poverty*, Bedford Square Press, London.

Levitas, R. (1996), 'The Concept of Social Exclusion and the New Durkheimian Hegemony', *Critical Social Policy*, vol. 16, no. 1, February.

Lorenz, W. (1994), *Social Work in a Changing Europe*, Routledge, London.

Mann, K. (1994), 'Watching the Defectives: Observers of the Underclass in the USA, Britain and Australia', *Critical Social Policy*, Issue 41, Autumn, pp.79-99

Marshall, G., Newby, H., Rose, D. and Vogler, C. (1988), *Social Class in Modern Britain*, Hutchinson, London.

Miller, C. (1998), 'Poverty and Social Exclusion: The Poor Will Participate!', Paper presented at the Conference to Mark the Centenary of Seebohm Rowntree's First Study of Poverty, University of York, March 1998.

Murray, C. *et al.* (1990), *The Emerging British Underclass*, Institute of Economic Affairs, London.

NISW - National Institute for Social Work (1982), *Social Workers: Their Role and Tasks*, (The Barclay Report), Bedford Square Press, London.

Novak, T. (1997), 'Poverty and the "Underclass"', in Lavalette, M. and Pratt, A. (eds), *Social Policy: A Conceptual and Theoretical Introduction*, Sage, London.

Robinson, F. and Gregson, N. (1992), 'The "Underclass": A Class Apart?', *Critical Social Policy*, Issue 34, Summer, pp.38-51.

Room, G. (1982), 'Definition and Measurement of Poverty', in Dennett, J., James, E., Room, G. and Watson, P. (eds), *Europe Against Poverty*, Bedford Square Press, London.

Room, G. (1990), *Observatory on National Policies to Combat Social Exclusion. Synthesis Report*, University of Bath, Bath.

Room, G. (1993), *Anti-Poverty Action Research in Europe*, SAUS, Bristol.

Room, G. (1995a), *Beyond the Threshold*, The Policy Press, Cambridge.

Room, G. (1995b), 'Poverty in Europe', *Policy and Politics*, vol. 23, no. 2.

Russell, B. (1946), *A History of Western Philosophy*, George Allen and Unwin, London.

Silver, H. (1994), 'Social Exclusion and Social Solidarity: Three Paradigms', *International Labour Review*, vol. 133, 1994/5-6.

Townsend, P. (1970), *The Concept of Poverty*, Heineman, London.

Townsend, P. (1979), *Poverty in the United Kingdom*, Penguin, Harmondsworth.

Williams, F. and Popay, J. (1998), 'Developing a New Framwork for Welfare Research', Paper presented at the Conference to Mark the Centenary of Seebohm Rowntree's First Study of Poverty, University of York, March 1998.

Treaties of the European Union

Treaty of Amsterdam (1997), Amending the Treaty on European Union, the Treaties Establishing the European Communities and Certain Related Acts, July 1997

Treaty of Maastricht (1992), Treaty on European Union. Office for Official Publications of the European Communities,1992.-m6557755.

Treaty of Rome (1957), Treaty establishing the European Economic Community: Act of Accession. Inde- London: Commission of the European Communities. m 6951268.

13 Where are 'the Poor' in the Future of Poverty Research?

RUTH LISTER and PETER BERESFORD (with DAVID GREEN and KIRSTY WOODWARD)[1]

Introduction

Poverty research has traditionally been preoccupied with measuring poverty and its impact, deploying increasingly sophisticated techniques to do so. This tradition has recently come under criticism on two counts. First, it has been argued that it has encouraged 'a cramped and atheoretical empiricism' (Novak, 1995, p.58), producing no real theory of poverty (Jordan, 1996). Second, it has excluded and objectified those who are its subjects.[2] This criticism has been spelt out by Peter Beresford and Suzy Croft who argue that people with experience of poverty are effectively excluded from discussions about and campaigns against poverty as well as from its conceptualisation and analysis. Poverty, they claim, 'is a last bastion of people's exclusion from discussions of which they are the subjects' (1995, p.77).

This paper begins by setting out the arguments in favour of a more inclusive approach to researching poverty and explores some of the difficulties. It then reports on the 'Poverty First Hand' project which has attempted to build on developments in both poverty research and anti-poverty action that are enabling the voice of people in poverty to be heard more clearly than hitherto.

The Case for a More Inclusive Approach

Before spelling out the arguments in favour or a more inclusive approach to poverty research, we need to stand back and ask ourselves, why do we research poverty? Most would probably answer because we want to do something about it. As Kirk Mann observes, 'much of the history of social policy has been tied up with a belief in the ability of the researcher to, at the very least, improve things for the poor. From Rowntree to Townsend, that belief has inspired some of the most significant social research of the century' (Mann, 1996, pp.67-8).

David Piachaud warns that:

If the term 'poverty' carries with it the implication and moral imperative that something should be done about it, then the study of poverty is only ultimately justifiable if it influences individual and social attitudes and actions. This must be borne in mind constantly if discussion on the definition of poverty is to avoid becoming an academic debate worthy of Nero - a semantic and statistical squabble that is parasitic, voyeuristic and utterly unconstructive and which treats 'the poor' as passive objects for attention, whether benign or malevolent - a discussion that is part of the problem rather than part of the solution. (Piachaud, 1987, p. 161)

And, as Jo Roll observes, 'the moral imperative buried in the word has frequently been recognised even by those who have opposed, or wanted to limit, action' (Roll, 1992, p. 8; see also Desai, 1986; Alcock, 1997).

Researching poverty may thus be a scientific exercise, but it is not a politically or morally neutral one. In the same way, the arguments for involving 'the poor' in poverty research as more than just 'passive objects for attention' are in part political or moral. They are also methodological and epistemological. We will divide them into what might be called 'process' and 'outcome' arguments, paying particular attention to the former, while recognising the overlap between the two. While some of these arguments relate more widely to debates about and action against poverty, they are relevant too to how we approach research into poverty.

Process Arguments

Exclusion/Inclusion

The academic and political discourse on poverty is increasingly being couched in the language of social exclusion. Although poverty and social exclusion are not synonymous (see, for example, Room, 1995) and there is a tendency to define exclusion in narrow, economistic, terms (Levitas, 1996, 1998), part of the concern about poverty is a concern about exclusion from a range of social activities (Golding, 1986).

One of the advantages of the concept of social exclusion is that it encourages a focus on processes and not just outcomes. Poverty research that simply treats poor people as objects can serve to reinforce a process of exclusion rather than to challenge it, however valuable its insights about the exclusionary effects of poverty. As the UK Coalition Against Poverty puts it, 'being poor is about being excluded. Fighting poverty is about being inclusive' (1997, p.4). Thus, for instance, an inclusive analysis of poverty based on a piece of research would incorporate the views and perspectives of those interviewed and not simply their descriptions of the effects of poverty.

Being inclusive does not mean excluding those who are already part of the poverty debate or denying the role of 'experts'. In response to such an interpretation by Peter Golding (1996), Beresford and Croft reiterate the point that 'it has not been suggested that the discussion of poverty should be confined to people with direct experience of it, but that they specifically should not be *excluded* from poverty discussion' (1996, p.109).

Citizenship

Another dimension of the exclusion associated with poverty is restricted citizenship (Lister, 1990; Scott, 1994). Citizenship involves equality of status and respect. Research which accords with the principles of citizenship respects both sides of the research relationship as equals. It acknowledges the expertise that derives from the experience of poverty (alongside that from more traditional academic and professional perspectives) and that this experience can itself provide the basis for an analysis of the nature of poverty and of other people's reactions to it, a point which is developed further below. In this way, poor people cease to be 'different', 'the Other' lacking 'expert status on their own lives' (Wilkinson and Kitzinger, 1996, p.9; Becker, 1997). As Moraene Roberts, a lone parent and member of ATD Fourth World, puts it 'we are the real experts of our own hopes and aspirations' (Russell, 1996, p.4). During the National Poverty Hearing at which she spoke, the desire to be treated with respect and listened to was a recurrent theme among those with experience of poverty who spoke.

Agency and Voice

Exclusion and restricted citizenship are associated with a lack of political voice. This was demonstrated in the 1997 General Election when the concerns of poor voters hardly figured at all in the debates, so that it was not surprising that the evidence suggests that turnout was low in inner city areas. The United Nations Development Programme (UNDP, 1997, p.94), in its *Human Development*

Report 1997, places considerable emphasis on the 'political empowerment of poor people' as part of any strategy for poverty eradication: 'to advance their interests, their voices must be heard in the corridors of power'. Research into poverty is potentially one means of providing a space in which the voice of those in poverty can be heard. Yet, the traditional research relationship of the more powerful researching the powerless, means that, as Hartley Dean acknowledges, there is 'a growing concern that the research process can actually contribute to the disempowerment of such groups' (1996, p.4).

The inclusive approach that we are arguing for is consistent with developments in theorising about poverty, in which there has been a shift away from what could be interpreted as a structural determinism in which poor people are presented simply as powerless victims (Lister, 1996). Instead, there is an attempt to balance an understanding of the structural constraints that limit the opportunities of disadvantaged groups with recognition that members of these groups are also agents or actors in their own lives (see, for instance, Jordan, 1996). Fiona Williams (with Jane Pillinger) has spelt out the implications for poverty research of giving:

> more emphasis to issues of subjectivity, identity and agency. In methodological terms this implies a shift away from researching social groups simply as categories of researchers' or policy-makers', or the Registrar-General's own making - the poor, the working-class, the disabled, the elderly - towards integrating an acknowledgement of people's, or groups' own agency, experience and understanding of their position, and seeing them as creative, reflexive agents both constrained by and enabled by, as well as creating, the social conditions in which they exist....In other words we need to tease out the differences between people's subjectivity - their understanding of their own experiences, their identity - their own sense of belonging, their agency - their capacity to act individually or collectively, and their social position - and the objective interpretation of a person's position.
> (Williams, 1996, p.3)

She then incorporates this understanding of human agency into the framework of a new paradigm for poverty research.

Epistemology and Methodology

The issue is partly an epistemological one concerning the validity of different kinds of knowledge and analysis. Feminist researchers have challenged objective frameworks of knowledge which incorporate traditional gender power relationships and deny the validity of women's experience and the knowledge derived from it (Harding, 1987; Robinson, 1997). Writing about psychiatric system survivors, Croft and Beresford (1997) observe that 'different knowledges have different amounts of power' and that the powerful can edit out and dismiss as subjective or anecdotal the knowledge of the powerless. The history of social movements, they suggest, involves the development and increased visibility of the knowledge and analysis held by oppressed groups.

In the context of poverty research, recognition that people in poverty are able to apply their experience to develop their own knowledge and analysis of their situation suggests that this needs to be incorporated into the research process. Research subjects would then no longer simply be treated as a data source that informs the researcher's analytical and conceptual frameworks (Beresford and Wilson, 1997; Beresford, 1997). This is not to argue that *only* those in poverty can know what poverty means which, as Peter Golding says, would be 'both epistemological and political nonsense' (1996, p.122). But it is to recognise that 'people with experience of poverty ... have particular knowledge and understanding of and concern about their oppression, just as women, black people, lesbians and gay men, disabled people and others do of theirs' (Beresford and Croft, 1996, p.110). This extends to them being their own researchers, as is reflected in the emerging idea of user controlled research (Evans and Fisher, 1998). Drawing on the work of Mike Oliver, the disability activist and academic, Beresford and Croft (*ibid.*) suggest that intellectualising is an activity that describes any process of critical reflection. An inclusive poverty research epistemology and methodology would provide people in poverty with the opportunity to intellectualise about their own situation in relation to that of others in society and would acknowledge their expertise in relation to poverty. Some of the difficulties this raises are discussed later.

Methodologically such an approach draws on what has been called 'new paradigm research', a cluster of approaches including action-research and feminist research, which pays attention to the social relations of research (Reason, 1994). The aim is to promote a more equal research relationship between the researcher and the researched. Peter Reason calls participants 'co-researchers' and has promoted 'participatory action research' as a means of promoting 'research *with* people rather than research *on* people' (Reason, 1994, p.1). The research process thereby becomes more akin to a dialogue in which different voices are heard.

This approach is recommended by the UNDP under the rubric of 'participatory rural appraisals' (which are not exclusively rural). Their great value, it states:

> is in the way they empower communities and build their capacity for self-help, solidarity and collective action. Such appraisals can best be described as a family of approaches, methods and behaviours that enable people to express and analyse the realities of their lives and conditions, plan what action to take and monitor and evaluate results. They provide ways to give poor people a voice, enabling them to express and analyse their problems and priorities. (UNDP, 1997, p.104)

Mike Oliver (1996, p.141) talks about the 'empowering' transformation of respondents into participants through 'emancipatory' research. The two key fundamentals are, he states, 'empowerment and reciprocity'. These can be built in to the research process 'by encouraging self-reflection and a deeper understanding of the research situation by the research subjects themselves as well as enabling researchers to identify with their research subjects' (Oliver, 1996, p.141). The disabled people's movement has perhaps gone furthest in challenging traditional research paradigms and power relationships. They raise much wider questions about the funding and control of research (Barnes and Mercer, 1997). At a minimum, though, such a challenge problematises the traditional poverty research relationship in which poor respondents either simply provide the data for quantitative studies or are allowed to expand in greater depth on the effects of poverty but are rarely asked what they *think* about poverty and for their views on the issues that poverty researchers should be pursuing. Focusing on such questions facilitates the development of 'grounded theory' (Glaser and Strauss, 1967), in which theory is developed, at least in part, from research subjects' perspectives rather than simply being imposed upon them.

Outcome Arguments

Used well, such approaches can generate important (and surprising) insights into the nature of poverty that can, in turn, contribute to policies better fitted to serving the needs of poor people. Debates about poverty are likely to be better informed if the research upon which they draw is guided by and incorporates the views of people with experience of poverty themselves. Of course, different individuals and groups may hold conflicting views and have competing priorities. Nevertheless, research into user-involvement has demonstrated how the first hand knowledge and experience of service users provides an invaluable basis for developing policy and practice better attuned to service users' concerns and needs (Beresford and Croft, 1993). Members of the Citizens' Commission on the Future of the Welfare State, a research inquiry controlled by welfare state service users, believed that increasing the say of service users was 'an important way of ensuring that future welfare state services were of good quality, flexible, appropriate and accountable' (Beresford and Turner, 1997, p.xii).

Anti-poverty action is also likely to be stronger and more effective if it involves people in poverty themselves and if it can draw upon research that illuminates their views. The disabled people's movement provides a good example of the impact of more participatory campaigns supported by participatory research. It quickly moved from its members simply using opportunities to talk in public to bear witness to their individual experiences and difficulties to them offering their analyses and framing their demands (Beresford and Croft, 1996). The disabled people's movement has transformed thinking about disability. It has redefined disability, developed its own language and has generated its own sophisticated theory and praxis (Oliver, 1996). The speed with which it was able to respond to leaks about possible threats to disability benefits from the new Government in late 1997 and the responses to this action were a testimony to its effectiveness.

A Politics of Recognition as Well as Redistribution

The division between process and outcome is not a hard and fast one, as they interact with each other. Underlying both sets of arguments is an attempt to reconcile the traditional politics of poverty, which have been primarily a 'politics of redistribution' aimed at redressing socioeconomic injustice, with what a number of political theorists have termed a 'politics of recognition' which addresses what Nancy Fraser calls cultural or symbolic injustice (see, for instance, Honneth, 1995). According to Fraser, who has attempted such a reconciliation at a more general theoretical level,

> the 'struggle for recognition' is fast becoming the paradigmatic form of political conflict in the late twentieth century. Demands for 'recognition of difference' fuel struggles of groups mobilized under the banners of nationality, ethnicity, 'race', gender and sexuality [to which we would add disability]. (Fraser, 1995, p. 68; 1997a, p. 11)

She contrasts this with a traditional materialist 'imaginary centred on terms such as "interest", "exploitation", and "redistribution"' (*ibid.*, pp.69/11). The task, she argues, is to develop a '*critical* theory of recognition, one which identifies and defends only those versions of the cultural politics of difference that can be coherently combined with the social politics of equality'. Her underlying premise is that 'justice today requires both redistribution *and* recognition' (ibid., p.69/12). The dilemma, she suggests, is that recognition claims tend to promote 'group differentiation', whereas redistribution claims tend to do the opposite.

This is not the place to pursue Fraser's own argument or the debate that it has generated (see, Young, 1997; Fraser, 1997b; Phillips, 1997). Instead, the aim is to apply the idea of a 'politics of recognition' to people in poverty, a group not usually discussed within the discourses of difference, as Diana Coole (1996) observes. Likewise, identity issues tend not to figure in debates about economic inequality and exclusion (Pixley, 1997).

Fraser herself gives class exploitation as the paradigmatic example of the redistributive model, in which any cultural injustices derive from economic roots. The remedy lies in redistribution rather than recognition. Clearly, this applies to the more specific group of people in poverty also. However, if we focus on this group rather than the wider group of an exploited class, recognition claims have a greater saliency in their own right, even if they still ultimately derive from socioeconomic injustice. Among the examples of cultural or symbol injustice Fraser cites are:

> non recognition (being rendered invisible via the authoritative representational, communicative, and interpretative practices of one's culture); and disrespect (being routinely maligned or disparaged in stereotypic public cultural representations and/or in everyday life interactions).
> (Fraser, 1995, p.71; 1997a, p.14)

Non recognition and disrespect are the typical experience of those in poverty, especially when labelled pejoratively as an 'underclass' or as inhabiting a 'dependency culture' (for a critique, see Lister, 1996). As Fraser acknowledges, economic and cultural forms of injustice tend 'to reinforce each other dialectically' so that 'economic disadvantage impedes equal participation in the making of culture, in public spheres, and in everyday life' (Fraser, 1995, pp.72-3; 1997a, p.15). In her critique of Fraser, Iris Marion Young places greater emphasis on the interrelationship between the two forms of injustice and politics. She maintains that 'we should show how recognition is a means to, or an element in, economic and political equality and that 'so long as the cultural denigration (sic) of groups produces or reinforces structural economic oppressions, the two struggles are continuous' (Young, 1997, pp.156 and 159). Drawing on Fraser's own work on a 'politics of needs interpretation', she argues for a 'materialist culturalist approach [which] understands that needs are contextualised in political struggle over who gets to define whose needs for what purpose' (*ibid.*, p.155).

Such an approach is highly relevant to the politics of poverty and poverty research. Here a politics of recognition is not about the assertion of group difference, as in the case of women, black peoples, lesbians and gays, and disabled people (although it has to be remembered that we are not talking about discrete groups here). Indeed a successful politics of redistribution could remove the category altogether, as 'the poor' are a group that are the product of the distribution of resources. A politics of recognition in this context is, instead, about the assertion of recognition in the sense of equality of status and respect, together with the according of value to poor people's own interpretation of their rights and needs, which can be enhanced (or not) through the research process.

Thus, we would disagree with Diana Coole's assertion that respect for those at the bottom of the economic hierarchy is 'patronizing' (Coole, 1996, p.22). Coole makes the valid point that 'poverty robs groups of the economic and cultural capital needed for participation' (*ibid.*, p.20). But she seems to treat that as a given rather than asking how, alongside the struggle to eliminate poverty itself, the cultural and political capital of those in poverty can be strengthened and fostered so as to enable participation. The argument of this paper is that an inclusive research process can contribute to this task of strengthening the cultural and political capital of those in poverty and of promoting a politics of recognition as part and parcel of the more traditional politics of redistribution.

The 'P' Word and Other Difficulties

Negotiating the 'P' Word

Such an approach is, of course, beset with difficulties, not least that which derives from a politics of recognition, namely that poverty is not an identity that many want to embrace (Lister and Beresford, 1991). Referring to a study in which the majority of social security recipients interviewed resisted the ascription of 'poverty', Hartley Dean speaks of 'a certain crushing force behind the currency of the "p" word. ... "Poverty" evokes fear, resentment, guilt, confusion, mistrust and empowerment' (Dean, 1992, p.86). More recently, in the Social Policy Association volume, *Ethics and Social Policy Research*, he observes that 'to be identified or defined by research as "poor" or "vulnerable" can itself be stigmatising or damaging' and that 'some marginalised social groups, including "the poor", may prefer not to identify themselves in such terms, let alone mobilise in the name of their alleged "poverty"' (Dean, 1996, pp.4-5).

In the same volume, Ann Corden exemplifies this in her discussion of the ethical dilemmas raised in researching and writing about poverty. In a study designed to investigate poverty in a local area, demonstrating the usual indicators of poverty, the respondents were willing to discuss the difficulties of budgeting on a low income and the inadequacies of their environment. Yet, 'analysis of the discussions showed clearly ... that individually they did not wish to be associated with "poverty"' and the discourses they employed 'left no doubt in the mind of the researcher that these people did not want to be included among those who lived in "poverty"'. Moreover, they criticised the ways in which their locale was 'stigmatised and devalued by references to poverty', an outcome unwittingly created by the study itself (Corden, 1996, pp.11-12). Corden describes the dilemmas that this raises for her as a researcher and as a contributor to discussions about anti-poverty strategies, having 'learned from direct experience' about the harm that may be caused to poor people and local areas by association with "poverty"' *(ibid.*, p.18).

In the 'Poverty First Hand' study, the reluctance of some of those in poverty to wear that label created a methodological dilemma. The intention was to carry out a series of group discussions with people with current or past experience of poverty, using groups that already existed. This created something of a paradox: how should we select groups of people, as having direct experience of poverty, to take part in the project if our aim was to enable people in poverty to offer their own definitions of poverty and not pre-empt them? We sought to deal with this dilemma in the literature about the project that we circulated to potential participants by not taking the concept of 'poverty' as given and by making it clear that we recognised that many people do not like the term 'poverty' or necessarily define their experience in those terms.

Practical and Epistemological Difficulties

The project also illustrated some of the practical difficulties that a more inclusive approach faces. In particular, it is more expensive than more conventional forms of research and takes more time. The original intention was to involve people with research in poverty at every stage of the research process, including the formulation of the research schedule and the production of the final report. Unfortunately, the limited research funds available to us did not permit this more ambitious approach. Other financial implications of research which brings together people with experience of poverty on equal terms include the costs of: accessible meeting places; support for people to take part which can include travel expenses, child care and respite care, personal assistance, interpretation; payments for their time and expertise; and the provision of accessible information in appropriate formats including, for example, audio cassette, Braille, signed video and minority ethnic languages. Genuine involvement at each stage of the process also requires time: time that neither participants, for whom managing poverty can itself be a time-consuming process especially in the case of women, nor researchers required to work to tight deadlines, necessarily have.

For some people, not used to being asked for their opinions and views, engagement with a more participatory approach to research may initially be difficult. One of the lessons drawn by ATD Fourth World from a partnership project between families in poverty and professionals is that:

> After years of being on the receiving end of help, advice and directions [families in poverty] need to find ways of overcoming their long-held belief that they have no opinions, or that their opinions - even about their own lives - have no value in the eyes of others. The project showed us that as people gained self-esteem, self-confidence, and sometimes practical skills as well, they started to see that their views and opinions could be taken seriously.
> (ATD Fourth World, 1996, p.58)

Researchers themselves need to be able to demonstrate that respondents views will be taken seriously while acknowledging and respecting any difficulties that the latter might have with articulating them.

Analysis and presentation also present dilemmas. As Anne Corden observes, 'including participants' own views and experiences, or even using their own words, means that choices must be made about how to do this' involving not just methodological issues but also ethical and moral considerations regarding 'the way that people living in poverty are represented'. She suggests that the theoretical basis for selecting quotations from qualitative research is as yet poorly developed.   Furthermore, she speculates that 'presenting blocks of regional phraseology, with the interrupted sentence construction that characterises spoken language, alongside my own standard English grammatically organised written prose, might actually stereotype and stigmatise the speakers' (Corden, 1996, pp.9 and 17).   In his participatory research on a collaboratively-working social work team, Alan Stanton addressed this issue by offering participants the opportunity to correct and alter both their edited interview transcripts and drafts of the book based on them and to present their words as they wished.   Some then decided to remove regional variations (Stanton, 1989, pp.329-41).

In the report of our own study we have tried to resolve this issue by simply presenting extracts from the group discussions in the main body of the text adding only linking sentences and a summary at the end.   Our own analysis, which we have attempted to ground in those discussions, follows in the final section.   Responses from those readers used to more conventional accounts of qualitative research have raised questions about the readability of blocks of text taken directly from participants without intervening interpretation and analysis by the researchers.   On the other hand, readers familiar with the politics and process of putting together their own accounts, through their involvement in service user movements, have not found this a problem.

At the same time, the question arises as to whether even 'grounded theory' (discussed earlier) can escape the imbalance in the power relationship between researchers and participants and whether we, as researchers, can or should analyse participants' thoughts and views without reference to our own prior theoretical analysis of poverty.   This is a point made by Millen (1997) from the perspective of feminist research.   Arguing that it is illusory to suggest that the research relationship can involve genuine equality and that it is neither possible nor desirable for the researcher to disclaim her privilege in relation to participants, she cites Kelly *et al.*:

> It is we who have the time, resources and skills to conduct methodical work, to make sense of experience and locate individuals in historic and social contexts ... it is an illusion to think that, in anything short of a participatory research project, participants can have anything approaching 'equal' knowledge to the researcher.
> (Kelly *et al.*, 1994, p.37)

The question is whether ultimately, even in an attempt at a participatory research project, the inequalities of the research relationship have to be acknowledged and not hidden. Millen goes further and contends that:

> it is facile to assume that the analysis of experience necessarily means the exploitation of experience to the detriment of the participant' and that 'the *researcher* is the one who has been motivated to explore the theoretical ideas before conducting research, and to try to construct knowledge from experience. ... In addition, the individual herself may not necessarily be the best interpreter of her own experiences 'individuals do not necessarily possess sufficient knowledge to explain everything about their lives (Maynard and Purvis, 1994, p.6). Individuals may not have a full awareness of the systems which surround and constrain them, and as researchers, we have a responsibility to illuminate these systems using their experiences, and illuminate their experiences using these systems.
> (Millen, 1997, paras 3.4 and 3.5)

There is unlikely to be agreement about this. Indeed, the two of us, coming from different starting points, have different views. On the one hand, significantly, members of the disabled people's and psychiatric system survivors movement reject Millen's argument. They view interpretations of their ideas and experience by outside researchers over the years as damaging and exploitative (for example, Lawson, 1988; Oliver, 1990). They argue that they themselves *do* have a particular 'expertise in their own experience' and are quite capable of learning about and understanding structural as well as personal issues. One of the earliest and most trenchant critiques of traditional anti-poverty action and poverty research came from the disabled people's movement, which rejected its strategy of non-poor 'experts' collecting 'scientific evidence' to bring pressure on governments (UPIAS and Disability Alliance, 1976). These movements reject any suggestion that outside researchers 'know best'. They also challenge the traditional 'them' and 'us' of research relations, which has prevented groups like mental health service users, disabled people and people with experience of poverty from being actively involved in research or from becoming researchers themselves (Beresford, 1996).

> On the other hand, while researchers themselves cannot necessarily claim 'sufficient knowledge to explain everything' about the lives of participants, arguably it would be an abdication of responsibility if they did not attempt to deploy the knowledge and theories that they do have in order to try to

illuminate the experiences of those who have different forms of knowledge and who deploy different kinds of theories. By separating out participants' perceptions and our own interpretations in the report of the project, we have attempted to resolve these dilemmas without sacrificing either participants' interpretations of their own realities or our responsibility as researchers to set these in the context of existing poverty discourse and analysis. We have also sought not to attach different weight or value to one over the other; researchers do not necessarily know best and should not necessarily expect to have the last word. We cannot claim total success but hope that the attempt might stimulate debate as to how the presentation of research findings can best negotiate this difficult tightrope.
(Beresford, 1996)

The Poverty First Hand Study

The study itself was exploratory, reflecting the resources available to undertake it. A series of 20 discussions was conducted with groups that were sought on the basis of their likely current or past personal experience of poverty on conventional definitions. Contacts were used to identify a range of groups that reflected the diversity of people living in poverty and the different ways that they come together. Thus, we included groups which represented a particular age group, old and young; groups which came together around family type or concerns; groups relating to the provision of support including self-help and mutual aid groups; women's groups concerned with poverty issues; interest or identity groups such as disabled people and mental health service users; claimant groups including those of unemployed people; and community-based groups such as tenants and residents organisations. Overall there was a reasonable gender balance but an under representation of black and ethnic minority participants.

Prospective groups were sent information about the project to enable them to make an informed decision about participation. A semi-structured discussion schedule was used, designed to provide scope for groups to explore their own interests and concerns within a consistent framework developed by the researchers. The schedule was influenced by the views of people with experience of poverty at a meeting which brought them together with 'poverty professionals' in York and which was the inspiration for the project (Lister and Beresford, 1991). It covered participants' views on definitions of poverty, media and political images of poverty; causes of poverty and policies and action against poverty, as well as the more usual effects of poverty. The transcriptions of group discussions, and later the draft text, were returned to participants for comment.

The decision to use group discussions rather than the individual interviews more common in poverty research reflected a belief that this would make it possible for participants to have greater control over the research process and would provide a better opportunity for them to express and develop their ideas. Stuart Williams (1986), when at ATD Fourth World, emphasised, as a precondition of an inclusive approach, the importance of poor people being able to come together to clarify their ideas and share and make sense of their experiences.

The report contains a number of examples of how participants developed their responses in interaction with each other. The following one, from a women's educational project, was in response to an invitation to define poverty in their own terms:

> Well, I am insured, but the thing is the lawnmower was stolen and I've got a nice garden, I love my garden, and my luxury was a nice lawnmower and I had it stolen...

> You shouldn't be apologising for having a decent lawnmower. Put that down, that's poverty, apologising for having a decent lawnmower.

> ... apologising, yes, because that was my luxury. Having a decent lawnmower. Yes it was stolen, but the insurance company won't pay out until you've been and bought another one and actually got a receipt for it. Where the heck do you go and get the money to go and buy a decent lawnmower?

When asked to discuss definitions of poverty used in the British Social Attitudes Survey, participants were more likely to subscribe to an absolute than a relative definition, in line with the population as a whole. However, when asked to supply their own definition or when talking about their own experience, there was a greater tendency to see poverty in relative terms. The interaction of the two is illustrated by this exchange among a group of young people:

> I don't think any of us are in poverty and any of us have ever been in poverty.

> We're not in a third world country, we're just not well off.

I mean compared to them, we've got it rather cushy but compared to other people in this country, we're like we're the third world to them.

The use of phrases such as 'not well off' to describe their own position was fairly typical. While some did think that they were 'poor', others preferred to use terms like 'hard-up' or 'worse off' than some other people. With echoes of Runciman's relative deprivation thesis (1966), there was a tendency to point to others worse off than themselves to explain why they did not consider themselves to be poor. This frequently contrasted with their descriptions of their own harsh experience. As well as an expressed reluctance to wear the label of 'poverty', discussed earlier, this seemed to reflect also an unwillingness, born of altruism, to equate their own predicament with that of other people, both in the South and the UK, as if to do so was to belittle the even harsher situation faced by others. In contrast, some believed that it was necessary to use the word in order to render poverty visible:

I think it's an eye-opener.

Well, it's helpful isn't it?

I think the more people who accept that they're living in poverty and talk about it openly, I think more people would start admitting that they're living in poverty. All this crap about 'Oh, I can manage'.

Participants were invited to discuss four newspaper stories which focused on 'welfare mothers', 'professional begging', 'welfare queue jumping' especially by lone mothers (a report of Peter Lilley's 'I have a list' speech) and the 'underclass'. Many were critical of the images of poor people presented and, while they thought that some of the ideas expressed had a grain of truth in them, they felt that this had been distorted, magnified and taken out of context by the media and politicians. The stigma and negative identity attached to those in poverty was a central issue. While views differed as to the validity of the notion of an 'underclass', many believed it to be damaging and some that it could be counterproductive, as suggested by a participant in a group of disabled people:

But don't you think this could be part of a self-fulfilling prophecy as well that these kids are growing up being told by society, 'You are the dregs. We don't want anything to do with you.' And they think, 'Well, if that's how you are going to treat me, why should I be any different?' And that's creating a section of society that has nothing to lose which is a very dangerous thing to do.

Despite the limited opportunities many participants had previously had to discuss poverty in this way, they had clear views about its causes. Most thought it was caused by a combination of different social processes. They generally subscribed to a structural rather than an individualistic analysis, mentioning economic factors and government economic, social security and general social policies. At the same time, many talked at length about the efforts they and other people in poverty they knew made to improve their situation and to challenge these structural constraints.

Discussion of the effects of poverty placed particular emphasis on its psychological and physical effects, the ways in which it restricted opportunities and choices, and its destructive impact on children and young people and on family relationships. While not surprisingly the picture painted was an overwhelmingly negative one, a small minority did try to 'accentuate the positive', pointing to the skill it takes to survive on a low income and suggesting that it can make people more determined.

Ideas as to what should be done to tackle poverty reflected their analysis of causes, focusing on various aspects of government employment and social policy. At the same time, some also spoke of the efforts they themselves were making through various kinds of self-help initiatives and through efforts to find employment. There was strong support for greater involvement of people with experience of poverty in anti-poverty action. An example was a group of older people:

> We need a voice ... you're not a fool when you get old. Some people will deteriorate, but it's surprising how active a person's mind can be. And not only active but they have the knowledge and the experience. ...
>
> They should be allowed a voice even with, unfortunately the deterioration of old age, there's still an active, knowledgeable and powerful voice accessible to the public and never sought.

Many said that they were willing to be involved in local and national initiatives, but saw local action as the starting point. They recognised the difficulties involved, including overcoming people's lack of confidence and experience and the fact that many might not want to identify themselves as poor. There was also a feeling that if people in poverty made the effort to become involved, then politicians and policy makers should come and speak with 'people like us' and listen to what they had to say.

Conclusion

The project's findings combine new and familiar perspectives on poverty. While much of what was said can be found in conventional discussions of poverty, what is important and different is that the study begins to reveal the conceptualisations, interpretations and priorities held by people in poverty themselves. The approach builds on existing developments in poverty research which have given more space to people in poverty's own accounts of the effects of poverty (for instance, Cohen *et al.*, 1992; Middleton *et al.*, 1994: Kempson, 1996) and, less frequently, their views about changes needed (Shaw *et al.*, 1996). At the same time, it seeks to develop a different approach (as did Roger Green's poverty profile of the Kingsmead Estate in Hackney [Green, 1997]), by adopting a more participatory research process, in the emancipatory research tradition developed by the disabled people's movement.

In addition, by listening to the views of people in poverty, and not simply asking them about the effects of poverty on them personally, the research reflects developments in the theorising of poverty which emphasises the agency of poor people, while not ignoring the structural constraints they face. In turn, this contributes to developments in anti-poverty action which increasingly is emphasising the importance of the involvement of people with experience of poverty.[3] In this way, both poverty research and anti-poverty action can help to promote a politics of recognition as part of a politics of redistribution, in acknowledgement of the common citizenship of poor and non-poor.

Notes

1   Ruth Lister is Professor of Social Policy, Department of Social Sciences, Loughborough University. Peter Beresford is Professor of Social Policy [check], Brunel University, works with Open Services Project, is a member of Survivors Speak Out and spent eight years living on poverty level benefits. The authors would like to thank David Green and Kirsty Woodward for their contribution to the Poverty First Hand project upon which the paper draw (see Beresford *et al.*, 1998).
2   Sue Middleton's chapter in this volume, which bases the development of consensual budget standards on the views of a cross-section of the population, is an exception.
3   Examples include the work of: ATD Fourth World (see, ATD Fourth World, 1996 and *Fourth World Journal*); Church Action on Poverty (see Bennett, 1996; Russell, 1996); UK Coalition Against Poverty (see UK Coalition, 1997); Citizens' Commission on the Future of the Welfare State (see Beresford and Turner, 1997).

References

Alcock, P. (1997), *Understanding Poverty* (2nd ed.), Macmillan, Basingstoke.

ATD Fourth World (1996), *Talk with Us, Not at Us: How to Develop Partnerships Between Families in Poverty and Professionals*, ATD Fourth World. London.

Barnes, C. and Mercer, G. (1997), 'Breaking the Mould? An Introduction to Doing Disability Research', in C. Barnes and G. Mercer (eds), *Doing Disability Research*, The Disability Press, Leeds.

Becker, S. (1997), *Responding to Poverty: The Politics of Cash and Care*, Longman, Harlow.

Bennett, F. (1996), *Local People, National Voice: Speaking From Experience*, Church Action on Poverty, Manchester.

Beresford, P. and Croft, S. (1995), 'It's Our Problem Too! Challenging the Exclusion of Poor People From Poverty Discourse', *Critical Social Policy*, no. 44/45, pp.75-95.

Beresford, P. (1996), 'Challenging the 'Them' and 'Us' of Social Policy Research' in H. Dean, *op cit.*

Beresford, P. (1997), 'The Last Social Division? Revisiting the Relationship Between Social Policy, Its Producers and Consumers', in M. May, E. Brunsdon and G. Craig (eds), *Social Policy Review 9*, Social Policy Association, London.

Beresford, P. and Croft, S. (1993), *Citizen Involvement: A Practical Guide for Change*, Macmillan, Basingstoke.

Beresford, P. and Croft, S. (1996), 'Reply to "A response to Beresford & Croft's 'It's Our Problem Too'" by Peter Golding', *Critical Social Policy*, vol. 16, no. 3, pp.109-15.

Beresford, P. and Turner, M. (1997), *It's our Welfare: Report of the Citizens' Commission on the Future of the Welfare State*, National Institute for Social Work, London.

Beresford, P. and Wilson, A. (1997), 'Social Exclusion and Social Work: Challenging the Contradictions of Exclusive Debate', Paper presented at the On the Margins: Social Exclusion and Social Work conference, Stirling, September 1997.

Beresford, P. *et al.* (1999), *Poverty First Hand: Poor People Speak for Themselves*, Child Poverty Action Group, London.

British Social Attitudes Survey, Dartmouth, Aldershot.

Coates, M. (1994), *Women's Education*, SRHE, Buckingham.

Cohen, R., Coxall, J., Craig, G., Sadiq-Sangster, A. (1992), *Hardship Britain: Being Poor in the 1990s*, Child Poverty Action Group, London.

Coole, D. (1996), 'Is Class a Difference That Makes a Difference?', *Radical Philosophy*, no. 77, pp.17-25.

Corden, A. (1996), 'Writing About Poverty: Ethical Dilemmas' in H. Dean (ed), *Ethics and Social Policy Research*, University of Luton Press & Social Policy Association, Luton.

Croft, S. and Beresford, P. (1997), 'User Views', *Changes*, vol. 15, no. 3, pp. 232-33.

Dean, H. (1992), 'Poverty Discourse and the Disempowerment of the Poor', *Critical Social Policy*, no. 35, pp. 79-88.

Dean, H. (ed) (1996), *Ethics and Social Policy Research*, University of Luton Press & Social Policy Association, Luton.

Desai, M. (1986), 'Drawing the Line: On Defining the Poverty Threshold' in P.Golding (ed), *Excluding the Poor*, Child Poverty Action Group, London.

Evans, C. and Fisher, M. (1998, forthcoming), 'User Controlled Research and Empowerment' in W. Shera and L. Wells (eds), *Empowerment Practice: Developing Richer Conceptual*

Foundations, Columbia University Press, New York.

Fraser, N. (1995), 'From Redistribution to Recognition? Dilemmas of Justice in a "Post-Socialist" Age', *New Left Review*, no. 212, pp. 68-93.

Fraser, N. (1997a), *Justice Interruptus*, Routledge, New York & London.

Fraser, N. (1997b), 'A Rejoinder to Iris Young', *New Left Review*, no. 223, pp.126-29.

Glaser, B.G. and Strauss, A.L. (1967), *The Discovery of Grounded Theory: Strategies for Qualitative Research*, Aldine, Chicago.

Golding, P. (ed) (1986), *Excluding the Poor*, Child Poverty Action Group, London.

Golding, P. (1996), 'A Response to Beresford & Croft's "It's Our Problem Too"', *Critical Social Policy*, vol. 16, no. 2, pp. 121-3.

Green, R. (1997), *Community Action against Poverty*, The Kingsmead Kabin, London.

Harding, S. (1987), *Feminism and Methodology*, Open University Press, Milton Keynes.

Honneth, A. (1995),*The Struggle for Recognition*, Polity Press, Cambridge.

Jordan, B. (1996), *A Theory of Poverty and Social Exclusion*, Polity Press, Cambridge.

Kelly, L., Burton, S. and Regan, L. (1994), 'Researching Women's Lives or Studying Women's Oppression?' Reflections on what Constitutes Feminist Research' in M. Maynard and J. Purvis (eds), *Researching Women's Lives from a Feminist Perspective*, Taylor and Francis, London.

Kempson, E. (1996), *Life on a Low Income*, Joseph Rowntree Foundation, York.

Lawson, M. (1988), 'A Survivor's View', Presentation at Involvement of Users in Research Seminar, Mental Health Researchers' Network, London, February.

Levitas, R. (1996), 'The Concept of Social Exclusion and the New Durkheimian Hegemony', *Critical Social Policy*, vol. 16, no. 1, pp. 5-20.

Levitas, R. (1998), *The Inclusive Society? Social Exclusion and New Labour*, Macmillan, Basingstoke.

Lister, R. (1990), *The Exclusive Society: Citizenship and the Poor*, Child Poverty Action Group, London.

Lister, R. (1996), 'In Search of the "Underclass"' in R. Lister (ed), *Charles Murray and the Underclass Debate*, IEA Health and Welfare Unit, London.

Lister, R. and Beresford, P. (1991), *Working Together against Poverty: Involving Poor People in Action Against Poverty*, Open Services Project/Department of Applied Social Studies, University of Bradford, London.

Mann, K. (1996), '"Who are you looking at?": Voyeurs, Narks and Do-gooders', in H. Dean, (ed), *Ethics and Social Policy Research*, University of Luton Press & Social Policy Association, Luton.

Maynard, M. and Purvis, J. (eds) (1994), *Researching Women's Lives from a Feminist Perspective*, Taylor and Francis, London.

Middleton, S., Ashworth, K. and Walker, R. (1994), *Family Fortunes: Pressures on Parents and Children in the 1990s*, Child Poverty Action Group, London.

Millen, D. (1997), 'Some Methodological and Epistemological Issues Raised by Doing Feminist Research on Non-Feminist Women', *Sociological Research Online*, vol. 2, no. 3.

Novak, T. (1995), 'Rethinking Poverty', *Critical Social Policy*, no. 44/45, pp. 58-74.

Oliver, M. (1990), *The Politics of Disablement*, Macmillan, Basingstoke.

Oliver, M. (1996), *Understanding Disability: From Theory to Practice*, Macmillan, Basingstoke.

Phillips, A. (1997), 'From Inequality to Difference: A Severe Case of Displacement?', *New Left Review*, no. 224, pp. 143-53.

Piachaud, D. (1987), 'Problems in the Definition and Measurement of Poverty', *Journal of Social Policy*, vol. 16, no. 2, pp. 147-64.

Pixley, J. (1997), 'Employment and Social Identity. Theoretical Issues', in M. Roche, R. van Berkel (eds), *European Citizenship and Social Exclusion*, Ashgate, Aldershot.

Reason, P. (1994), *Participation into Human Inquiry*, Sage, London.

Robinson, V. (1997), 'Introducing Women's Studies', in V. Robinson and D. Richardson (eds), *Introducing Women's Studies*, Macmillan, Basingstoke.

Roll, J. (1992), *Understanding Poverty*, Family Policy Studies Centre, London.

Room, G. (ed) (1995), *Beyond the Threshold*, The Policy Press, Bristol.

Runciman, W.G. (1996), *Relative Deprivation and Social Justice*, Penguin, Harmondsworth.

Russell, H. (1996), *Speaking from Experience: Voices at the National Poverty Hearing*, Church Action on Poverty, Manchester.

Scott, J. (1994), *Poverty and Wealth: Citizenship, Deprivation and Privilege*, Longman, Harlow.

Shaw, A., Kellard, K. and Walker, R. (1996), *Barriers, Bridges and Behaviour: Learning from Income Support Recipients*, Department of Social Security/The Stationery Office, London.

Stanton, A. (1989), *Invitation to Self Management*, Dab Hand Press, Ruislip.

UK Coalition against Poverty (1997), *Poverty and Participation*, UK Coalition against Poverty, London.

UNDP (1997), *Human Development Report*, Oxford University Press, New York/Oxford.

UPIAS and Disability Alliance (1976), *Fundamental Principles of Disability*, The Union of the Physically Impaired Against Segregation and The Disability Alliance, London.

Wilkinson, S. and Kitzinger, C. (eds) (1996), *Representing the Other*, Sage, London.

Williams, F. with Pillinger, J. (1996), 'New Thinking on Social Policy Research into Inequality, Social Exclusion and Poverty', in J. Millar and J. Bradshaw (eds), *Social Welfare Systems: Towards a Research Agenda*, University of Bath/ESRC, Bath.

Williams, S. (1986), 'Exclusion: The Hidden Face of Poverty', in P. Golding (ed), *Excluding the Poor*, Child Poverty Action Group, London.

Young, I.M. (1997), 'Unruly Categories: A Critique of Nancy Fraser's Dual Systems Theory', *New Left Review*, no. 222, pp. 147-60.